THE WEEPING

THE WINDOW

THE WAY

JOHN O. DOZIER, JR.

THE WEEPING

THE WINDOW

THE WAY

WILL
SUFFERING
MAKE YOU
BITTER OR
BETTER?

TATE PUBLISHING & Enterprises

The opinions expressed by the author are not necessarily those of Tate Publishing, LLC.

Published by Tate Publishing & Enterprises, LLC
127 E. Trade Center Terrace | Mustang, Oklahoma 73064 USA
1.888.361.9473 | www.tatepublishing.com

Tate Publishing is committed to excellence in the publishing industry. The company reflects the philosophy established by the founders, based on Psalm 68:11,
"The Lord gave the word and great was the company of those who published it."

Book design copyright © 2009 by Tate Publishing, LLC. All rights reserved.
Cover design by Kandi Evans
Illustration design by Steve Edwards, SteveEdwardsStudio.com
Interior design by Stefanie Rooney

Published in the United States of America

ISBN: 978-1-60799-794-8
1. Religion, Christianity, General
2. Religion, Christian Life, Spiritual Growth
09.09.17

ACKNOWLEDGMENT

This book is dedicated first and foremost to the awesome Triune God of the universe—Father, Son and Holy Spirit with whom I have had the unmerited gift and unspeakable honor and pleasure of getting to know more and more during the course of my story and spiritual journey. Since before the time I did not know God—when he relentlessly pursued me—to the present time, when I know little else, what can I first acknowledge? "Our God is an awesome God!"

Second, to my wife Peggy and children, Polly and Teddy. My dearest Peggy has been amazingly patient with me as I have run up so many mountain tops and tumbled down into so many valleys. Most would have given up on this "'ole runner" long ago. My family has been an anchor and lighthouse. Even as I have been shipwrecked by my own poor compass settings, they have never abandoned ship.

Third, to the legions of angels, saints, and messengers God has placed into my life—in the form of myriad colors, creeds, and credentials and from places around the world. I have been immeasurably blessed by so many people God's providence has supplied me over the years. There are a handful of particularly stalwart encouragers who, at every turn, have pressed me to push onwards and upwards towards the goal.

Fourth, to my dad and mom—both gone now—who have meant so much to me in great and good ways and, at times, not so great ways. I now see how embracing *all of them*—in my own great and gruesome heart—I harbor no regrets that cannot be easily swallowed up in God's everlasting arms by his absolute truth and everlasting love. I am what I am, by *biological* birth and *spiritual* rebirth, it's *all* to the glory of God. The spiritual will triumph for all eternity while biological will mark my personal story—mightily redeemed by God.

Finally, to all of my extended family who have been along on so many parts of my amazing journey. What a family they have been! As God continues to ordain our earthly journeys, we grow closer together as the God of the infinite reveals his intimate plan to each of us separate, yet bound together as we travel forth in faith.

As the centerpiece of this book has to do with things so personal and yet so universal, the first circle of *family* is where the ripples of any declaration from me—dropped into the apparent calm of life—will have an impact. I pray that the disruption be all to God's glory and other's blessing. Amen.

"Don't you mind him," said Puddleglum. "There are no accidents. Our guide is Aslan."

CS Lewis, *The Silver Chair*

FROM A PASTOR TO
THE READER-FLOCK

Dear co-Laborer in Christ,

"How could a good God allow pain and suffering in the world?" is an age-old question that many Christians continue to hear from thoughtful unbelievers as well as disillusioned believers. My friend, John Dozier offers deeply personal and biblically reliable answers for such seekers in his new book.

In a letter written in 1949, C.S. Lewis said, "God, who foresaw your tribulation, has specially armed you to go through it, not without pain but without stain." John Dozier is a living illustration of Lewis' words. Though John has endured the indescribably painful trials of a difficult childhood, the loss of his mother early in life, numerous broken relationships, and the suicide of his father on Christmas night 2002, they have not "stained" him. To describe the same truth in Tim Keller's words, suffering has made John "better not bitter."

Guided by the tender hands of Christ the Great Physician, John performs open heart surgery on himself in front of all of us. In response to his Savior's grace, John reveals his heart for the glory of God and the blessing of his people. Not only is this a timely message, John's writing it down for us is itself an example of the Gospel message of service, "Not for ourselves..." (Romans 15:1; Psalm 115:1).

John urges Christians to live through their present suffering with purpose and without self-pity in order to experience and express the beautiful blessing God is creating.

Many years ago George MacDonald gave the same testimony: "It has been well said that no man ever sank under the burden of the day. It is when tomorrow's burden is added to the burden of today that the weight is more than a man can bear. Never load yourselves so, my friends. If you find yourselves so loaded, at least remember this: it is your own doing, not God's. He begs you to leave the future to Him and mind the present."

This book will be a blessing both for you and for those your life touches.

Sincerely in Christ,

George Robertson
Senior Pastor
First Presbyterian Church
Augusta, Georgia

TABLE OF CONTENTS

Wall". How an example of the Prophet Ezekiel as one of the Bible's "Watchmen" provides an example for all Christians.

B. "God's Redemptive Plan: Have Peace: There's a Person, a Promise, and Perfect Plan in Place." A boiled-down synopsis of God's plan of redemption that provides God's unbreakable promise for your assurance, peace, and purpose. Union with Jesus Christ: The Context for all God's Work.

C. "Go Deep!": Appendix of additional resources

There are only two kinds of people in the world. Both are sufferers. There are the people who build their trust on things beside God so that when suffering comes it takes away the sources of their joy so they become sadder and sadder, and madder and madder, and worse. And then there are the people who suffer, but who seek to build their trust on God, on the basis of his infinite suffering for us on the cross, so that God becomes the source of their joy. When suffering comes in their lives, it drives them into deeper joy. It drives them more into God. And so suffering makes them better and better, and more like Jesus.

There are only two kinds of people in the world! They're both going to suffer. There's the kind of person that suffering makes worse, because the source of their joy being taken away. And there's the kind of person who suffering makes better because the suffering is pushing them towards the one source of joy that is not subject to circumstances. Jesus Christ suffered not so that we might not suffer, but rather when we suffer, we could become more like him!

The Sufferer, Sermon by Pastor Tim Keller,
Redeemer Presbyterian Church, NY, March 7, 2004

THE STORY OF THE STONE: THE PERSONAL DYNAMIC

I am "two kinds of people." Both have suffered. I am the sort of person who has grown increasingly angrier, been made worse, become more bitter, and harder of heart—so hard of heart and embittered in spirit that I was hardly recognizable to myself. I am also the sort of person who has been made better by suffering. Even now, my trials continue to push me toward "the one source of joy that is not subject to circumstances"— Jesus Christ, his infinite love, and his suffering upon the cross for me. The "story of the stone" is my story. But at the same time it is a story focused on Jesus Christ, "the rock of my salvation." This book, the story of my stony heart and the ways in which God transformed it, is not just my story, but the story of God's purposes for every human being.

> The LORD is my rock, my fortress and my deliverer; my God is my rock, in whom I take refuge. He is my shield and the horn of my salvation, my stronghold.
>
> Psalm 18:2 (ESV)

As I tell my story, I am painfully aware that in doing so, I risk breaking a conscious and/or unconscious pact with my family and others close to me, a pact of secrecy, silence, and even shame. I grew up in an addictive and emotionally damaging family and, as all the literature on co-dependency will tell you, addictive families keep secrets. No one has a perfect childhood. All families are flawed in one way or another. "Hurting people hurt people," as the saying goes. This becomes truer the further we get from the fall in the Garden of Eden. It doesn't do anyone any good to deny this. It only avoids or postpones the hope of healing or lasting happiness.

The greatest challenge in facing the increasingly pervasive spiritual-emotional wounds that are passed down from generation to generation is that we now have a tendency to *harden* and *hide* our hearts. We avoid the vulnerability to further pain and discomfort. So much so that we have created a multitude of "alternative pains" to avoid the primary "joy-filled pain" involved in revealing the heart of our hearts—to be spiritually and emotionally naked and unashamed.

THE PUBLIC DILEMMA

Ever since Adam and Eve broke the one command God had given them, every person in every family has grown up with heart trouble, or "heart disease." Parents and children alike suffer from hardened, wounded, and broken hearts. We keep secrets from ourselves, from one another, and most of all, from God, which is impossible to do. It should come as no surprise that sowing the seeds of pain produces a crop of its own kind—every time.

Today, the very dynamic God has designed to providentially, paradoxically, and mercifully *use* suffering to transform our heart is being *avoided like the plague*. The dilemma is that we are, at least in "Westernized Christianity", "Christians living in a culture of comfort". More than anything, we hate all things uncomfortable, especially the heart-transformation offered by God. As we stay put in our times of suffering, the Holy Spirit can work to sanctify, purify, and make us holy. And more wholly devoted to God as our hearts most desire we be. In many ways, we are plagued by our comforts. Our conscious and unconscious pervasiveness towards avoiding all things discomforting is akin to picturing a beautiful fruit tree trying to avoid being pruned: it will quickly become unfruitful. As we will see later in the book, this truth has dire consequences of all sorts.

What I hope with all my heart to get across in this book, though, is that God has not left us to lick our wounds in isolation. Our best isn't good enough. Our parents did their best, but even in the most healthy and functional of homes, this wasn't enough to protect us from the reality of sin and the brokenness in the world. Someone once described this broken state as, "the accelerating impact of accumulating evil." No human being or system of thought could effectively address such an impact.

And so, in unimaginable mercy, God himself has provided the solution. He has promised to use our *weeping* to open a *window* into our hearts through which he joins with us to begin the healing process. As we heal, he also promises to send us on our *way,* transformed as agents of healing in the lives of others who hurt. In love almost beyond belief, God has redeemed us in the cross of his Son, Jesus Christ. Not content with that, he has also made us "co-redeemers" with Christ, bearers of the Revealing Light and stinging salt in a dark and dying and decaying world (Matthew 5:13).

I cannot tell the personal story of God's redemption in my life without describing the pit of despair out of which he rescued me. As I do that, it's necessary to open the doors to rooms that have been sealed up for decades—in my own heart, and probably in the hearts of others. A part of me wishes to apologize for "going there". My goal is certainly not to trash my parents or belittle them. Nor is it to disrespectfully intrude through doors I have not been invited to open. Instead, I hope, in love and truth, to let the light and warmth of Jesus' love flow into those "rooms of the heart," God has made ready. In turn, I pray this helps to enlighten, free, and potentially *redeem* the experiences of those who have suffered from living in a horribly fallen world, regardless of the specific circumstances.

Many of you will likely recognize parts of your own stories as I tell mine. Your story may be more dramatic and distressing than mine; it may be less so, but don't let that encourage you to avoid knowing your own story, it's good *and* bad side, better. What matters most is that God has provided a protocol for dealing with all hurts, no matter what their origin or intensity. I pray that God will use my words to put more sufferers on the road to healing, wholeness, and zealous and happy service to others.

THE PERFECT STORM

As you might guess from the introduction you read thus far, as a young child I endured some very painful wounds to the heart. *Criticism, shame,* and a dreadful sense of *anonymity* in my own home deeply damaged my heart, spirit, and life. A "perfect storm" of circumstances set up my heart to experience darkness and despair from an early age. It's clear that my parents did not set out deliberately to pummel my heart and spirit, but having been raised in similar, yet unique, environments, they were incapable of making different choices in raising my two sisters and me.

Mom grew up in an abusive, legalistic family and church. When finally freed from this repressive and oppressive environment by marriage, she set out to live—*to really live*—for the first time in her young life. Mom's insatiable appetite for life, created in part by a childhood that had not allowed her to express it, made it almost inevitable that she would approach almost every circumstance, every relationship, and every opportunity with questions like, "What does this have to do with me, with my dreams, with my agenda, and with my unfilled needs?"[1]

Mom's freedom came at a price. The double-guilt created in her heart by her childhood experiences *and* by her attempts to throw off the restraints had to somehow be mollified. So she brokered an agreement with God and her own conscience, forcing my sisters and I to participate in the same abusive and legalistic church she had endured in childhood. Church provided no more solace than I had experienced at home. Week by week, my heart experienced criticism, shame, and anonymity. But in church, God himself seemed to be the one pummeling my heart and spirit. These experiences simply reinforced—*on a theological level*—the damaging beliefs my life at home was teaching me. I hardened and compartmentalized my heart still more.

Looking back, I can see God's compassion at work for my good even then. I remember the church building itself as a refuge of quiet, colorful wonder, and calm. I could hide in the corners, even from God. I could gaze at the images and listen to the music. Somehow through these small comforts, the Holy Spirit planted a seed of hope in my heart. I didn't know where, and I didn't know how, but I knew my heart would not be entirely destroyed. Perhaps one day it could even be made new.

What I wanted most of all was to free myself from the emotional, spiritual, and existential pain of everyday life. As I grew older, I began to see some of the reasons Mom mothered the way she did. This understanding began to set me free from placing the blame on her shoulders. I tried as best I knew how to love her, befriend her, and laugh with her. Then, very suddenly, mom died of a brain tumor; I was nineteen. We hadn't "made our peace," as the saying goes. That part saddened me so much, and I could scarcely bear the pain—even though at the time I didn't identify it as such. Perhaps that's why I didn't mourn. My heart was too wounded, too hard, and too accustomed to keeping secrets. I stuffed the pain of it all into a deep, dark, and already-well-appointed compartment in my heart. I locked the door hoping against hope it would never again see the light of day. I consciously and unconsciously avoided any uncontrolled emotions that might remotely force me to have to "nose around in there".

Dad was a survivor. He grew up in not one, but two addictive and abusive homes. Dad's first home was more or less "normal for the day," as his parents cared little for their children. Instead, they focused on their social responsibilities, on their drinking, and on providing the material comforts of life. After a difficult divorce, Dad's mother re-married into an even more socially-focused, alcoholic, and abusive relationship. Dad and his two siblings were relegated to an area in the third floor attic so as to be out of sight and out of mind for the home's patriarch.

The cruelty and violence of the family eventually sent Dad's sister to an insane asylum and drove his brother to commit suicide after four failed marriages. Dad survived, and even flourished in many ways. Yet, wounded and tattered, his heart actively avoided every emotionally charged issue. As a child, I never experienced "Dad as Defender," even when Mom's pathological treatment of me hurt me deeply. Dad cared for us in the only way he knew how—financially, and with any of the benefits that accrued from that. He brought into our lives a great sense of humor, likely honed in the hope of hiding his pain. My dad was great, yet greatly guarded in many ways. This blessed us, of course, but a child's heart needs more.

I now know that my parents did the best they could, given the suffering of their own hearts and the limitations their wounds created. My parents had wonderful traits that endeared them to me and many other people. I'm blessed to love them both very much. I have spent so many years sorting through the memories, teasing out the truths and falsehoods of my experiences, and their extremely complicated impact on my heart, spirit, and life.

KNOW WHAT YOU KNOW

I go into these details about my background because my story is so unique to me and yet common to so many. More and more children today grow up in homes that are emotionally and spiritually abusive. Many children live in homes infected with rampant narcissism. Many are forced to live out a parent's dream of often-unattainable athletic success or career achievement. Other children find themselves ignored, emotionally abandoned, or treated as an inconvenience. Still, others live out a whirlwind of unending activities, making them ever distracted and always anonymous—devoid of being known except by their activities—in their own homes. They are never able to grow comfortable with their personal and miraculously unique identity created by God to transcend all worldly measures of fleeting fame or fortune.

Anonymity is to the heart of a child what weed killer is to weeds. It brings about systematic death. Anonymity kills the heart, the spirit, the psychological self, and if left unchecked, the physical body.

I believe there has never been a greater need for human beings to understand the "anatomy of the heart" as God so personally and carefully created it, to consider the ways in which human hearts have been impacted by sin, and to use the unique, ingenious, and specific plan God has provided for putting the heart back together again.

THE MIRACLE OF CHRISTMAS NIGHT

I believe I experienced a miracle of grand proportions in my father's garden on Christmas night 2002, as I knelt over his dying body lying in snow. He eventually died after having shot himself. God called me there and then created a timeless time and space for me as I cried out to him, asking him to help me as I moved through what I now call God's three-fold "protocol" for dealing with suffering—"the weeping, the window, the way."

As we will soon see, I believe that God may well have saved my father for a relationship with himself while he lay alive and unconscious in the snow. God spoke the Bible to me (and my dad, I believe) in response to three specific struggles I went through that Christmas night. I will not know for sure if God saved my Dad on Christmas night until I get to heaven, but I do know that God imparted to me a miraculous series of events that were not for me alone. On the contrary: that is why I've written this book.

> Blessed be the God and Father of our Lord Jesus Christ, the Father of mercies and God of all comfort, who comforts us in all our affliction, *so that* we may be able to comfort those

who are in any affliction, with the comfort with which we ourselves are comforted by God. For as we share abundantly in Christ's sufferings, so through Christ we share abundantly in comfort too.

2 Corinthians 1:3–5 *emphasis mine,*
see also Philippians 2:1–11

I have been freed to tell this story for God's glory and the potential blessings of others. I'm writing this book, at least in part, to encourage parents and their children to take a closer look at the story of their heart and then to believe that there is no heart's story, no matter how nightmarish, that cannot be redeemed and radically transformed by the truth and love of God. What's more, I write to assure readers that God intends to use *you* as a unique, powerful, and revitalizing force in a broken and desperate world.

THE GREAT ESCAPES

As a child, I adopted two main tactics to protect my heart and spirit. I would *hide* from the source of pain—either under the basement steps or in the dense woods surrounding the creek that ran in front of our home. And I would *harden* myself against the pain being deeply angry, short-tempered, compartmentalized, and being the clown of the party in order to hide my tears. Hiding and hardening, these were my survival techniques, and I was very good at both of them!

In hiding and hardening my heart, I was able to display to those around me a sort of "hideous strength," as C.S. Lewis calls it in his book by the same name. The forces of the fall, especially the fallen heart in me, resulted in all sorts of writhing about. I, too, became narcissistic. Like my mother, I did whatever I could to make it possible for me to squeeze from life the things my misguided, hungry heart and wounded spirit needed, things I felt the world owed me. The hiding and hardening created in me a *hideous strength* that blinded me to the pain it inflicted on many people.

For the most part, the ways I responded served me well, at least in childhood. My techniques protected me from certain psychological, emotional, and spiritual death. For example, most kids are afraid of the dark; I preferred it. Knowing and seeing the truth in the clear light of day was much harder than seeing only darkness and feeling nothing. I lied constantly to project an image of myself that would be most pleasing to whoever happened to be in my presence at the time. I was deathly afraid of failure lest I disappoint.

In an attempt to gain my parents' attention, I became accident prone and spent a great deal of time being stitched up, encased in casts, and injected with needles to prevent tetanus. I misused my sexuality in the search for pleasure and in the hope that someone might actually take an interest in me. I escaped for a while into drugs with my peers, joining the "magical mystery tour" of the 60's. I had a temper that was nearly murderous. I worked out and did various sports compulsively. I was outwardly praised for all sorts of things and yet inwardly a maelstrom of turmoil continued to ravage, harden, and hide my heart.

The void in my heart created an insatiable hunger for affirmation for a sense of self-worth that extended beyond my circumstances. I desired to be seen as unique, valuable, and valued for the person I was, rather than a *means* of fulfilling another's dreams or as a potential embarrassment when I faltered. I yearned to find an alternative to the lifestyle I was living, a lifestyle of ferocious acting out, of exploiting power, of using others, and manipulating reality.

Hiding under the dark, quiet basement steps protected me from many assaults on my heart and spirit. In adulthood, my continuing tendency to hide in response to challenges in silence or seek refuge in isolation destroyed many relationships. Adam hid from God after he had sinned. I had to hide as well, because I couldn't bear to come out from behind the bushes to the "wounded and wounding parent," *yet alone to God.* I was too ashamed, even though I couldn't name it as shame, or trace it back to its source within my heart for many years.

Hiding in the creek was much more fun and distracting than hiding in the basement or within my hardened heart. A dense woods and thick undergrowth framed the creek that ran in front of my childhood home. There, I found many places to play, alone, unseen, and protected from the prying eyes, the sharp words, and the silence of others. It was my own private world, or so I thought.

As a ten year-old boy, I saw the shape in the stone
that broke perfectly in half as a window. One day,
God would transform the window into a cross.

As I played, I talked to my imaginary friends, built dams, and broke rocks. In fact, I grew very adept at breaking all sorts and shapes of rocks. Like an apprentice jeweler, I would try to keep the pieces as large as possible as I looked for the cool shapes, colors, and sparkles inside the broken pieces. One day when I was about ten years old, I carefully positioned a very hard, maroon-colored rock on top of a larger "anvil rock". Using another hammer rock, I carefully applied increasingly harder taps on the smaller rock until it broke it perfectly in half. To my amazement, one half had opened to reveal the three-dimensional shape seen here in the Introduction and "Heart Application" section of this book. The image and metaphor of the stone offer the perfectly personal yet universally applicable doorway to heart transformation!

I ran home immediately to show it to my family. We all agreed that the shape inside the perfectly rectangular cavern was a "window." Today I see that stone as a visual metaphor, a picture of what was happening not only inside of me, but inside the heart of every person on the planet. The image represents how only God (By means of the Holy Spirit) can transform the heart—at conversion and in sanctification as we become more and more like Jesus Christ.

THE ROCK OF MY SALVATION

God himself ended "all" (not instantaneously, but gradually) the hiding and hardening. He began the process of draining away the hideous strength. The journey began quite abruptly. I was thirty-one and had arranged to meet my girlfriend in Paris after completing a solo bike tour around most of Scotland's coastline. We traveled together for a while until we reached a tiny town in the Dordogne Valley. There, she had finally had enough of my neediness and decided to take the rest of the trip with a friend. I was alone. God had me exactly where he wanted me. I couldn't speak the language. I couldn't go home—my scheduled flight was three days away. I had nowhere to go and no one with whom to be. My relationship with my girlfriend had been yanked so quickly out of its place of ascendancy within my heart, you could almost hear the sucking sound as the void was replaced with a vacuum of darkness and nothingness.

As I looked inside my heart, I was utterly terrified of the void and darkness I saw there. I sat near a fountain in the center of the village square, weeping and rocking back and forth. I felt paralyzed with fear and unable to see how I might ever move from this place. At that moment, someone tapped me on the shoulder and said something in French.

I looked up into the eyes of a comforter sent by God: a Roman Catholic priest. Father Steven, a total stranger, spoke only fragmented English. But I understood his invitation to come with him to morning Mass and then to breakfast. My brokenness, coupled with this simple invitation of hospitality and the opportunity to worship, began God's softening process within my heart. How ironic that he chose to use a representative from the church of my childhood pain to begin a process that eventually climaxed in the unashamed confession of all my sins and the experience of a deep and lasting fellowship with Jesus Christ, the Rock of My Salvation. Though I am no longer a Roman Catholic, I will always thank "the God of greatest irony" for sending Father Steven to me at the exact right time, to befriend me, to ease my despair in that moment and to set me on the path of hope and eventual healing.

A DRAMATIC CHANGE OF HEART

Back in Aspen where I was living at the time, after I had become a Christian, I took the stone I had found twenty years earlier out of its storage place. Immediately I saw the shape inside as a cross. Later, as I spoke to my sisters on separate occasions, each of them reminded me we had called the shape in the stone a "window." I had completely forgotten that fact. It dumbfounded me at first. How could something be so obvious at one point in my life and so completely different at another?

I believe there is only one answer: I was different. I had

changed in a very fundamental way. God had a very special plan for my story. The cross that as a child I had never seen in my heart of stone had been revealed to me.

What do *you* see in the stone—and the story of its origins? Your answers might well depend on how well you know God's redemptive plan, the details of your unique life story, and the true nature of your own heart right now[2].

God deeply desires to have his people know their own hearts and to trust him to transform them—with our cooperation. He has personally put in place a process for doing so that is not hidden, mysterious, or meritorious (do it well and *then* God will love you). He wants to remove our hearts of stone, and give us hearts of flesh[3]. *Not just once at conversion, but again and again as we become more Christ-like over time.*

At the core of my being, I now believe that God accompanied me at every moment throughout my childhood. He was my loving companion at the creek, under the steps, and in my darkest places, even though I was never consciously aware of his presence. I believe the stone I found and cracked open was a miraculous gift from my heavenly Father. God gave me the gift of a window into my heart which revealed something very special inside: a lovable, unspeakably valuable, and treasured little boy of inestimable worth.

As God might have it, my heart would be so miraculously re-created that it would result in my "having a heart for the heart of the heart" that exists within the heart of everyone—but especially those God has placed within the reach of my concern or influence. Today my story continues to unfold as a key part of God's own story, the story of his glory and blessings to mankind. I have a unique place in it. And so do you!

At an early place in my life's journey, God gave me the unmerited and grace-filled gift of the cross. He showed me how my heart would look after he had watered the seeds of hope he had planted there. It would take twenty years and more before that image would become reality for the fifth grader who found that rock and cracked it open. During those twenty years, my heart would be hardened, broken apart, redeemed, and born again. The plan of God the Father, the sacrificial love of Jesus Christ on the cross, and the person and power of the Holy Spirit would make this all possible. God would send friends to me, some of his faithful followers, to love me out of the pit of darkness and deep despair, and rescue me from difficult and life-changing times. Just like the Psalmist said: *He lifted me out of the slimy pit, out of the mud and mire; he set my feet on a rock and gave me a firm place to stand (Psalm 40:2)*. By God's grace and divine design, John, Carl and Father Tom rescued me by showing the unconditional love of Jesus that I had never experienced before.

SEEING SUFFERING FOR
WHAT IT COULD BE

Today, as God's irony, redeeming plan, and power would have it, I see more clearly than ever the truth of the Tim Keller quote offered at the start of this book:

> And then there are the people who suffer who seek to build their trust on God, on the basis of Christ's infinite suffering for us on the cross, so that God becomes the source of their joy. And when suffering comes into their lives, it drives them into deeper joy. It drives them more into God. And so suffering makes them better, and better, and more like Jesus.

This book is devoted to helping people of faith see, understand, and mightily embrace this truth for all it's worth—*in time and eternity, for it will be evidenced in both*. I want readers to comprehend more deeply the truth and merit of handling suffering in the ways in which the Bible calls God's people to do, and I want the Church to show this, wide open, to the world!

AMIDST THE SUFFERING, GOD'S MERCY OFFERS OPULENT OPPORTUNITIES

Fire is the test of gold; adversity, of strong men.
Seneca, *On Providence,* 5.9

As we will see in more detail later on, trials of any kind offer us an array of benefits that, if shunned, condemn each one of us to a living hell. Counterintuitive, right? How could suffering of any kind reflect anything *but* hell? This is truly a legitimate question that should never be placed under the shroud of "one of God's great and unknowable mysteries," as is often the case.

The stewardship of the answers the Bible holds to this question is in the hands of a church which, in many cases, stands just as wounded and silent as the world. This is indeed a crime that I do not stand in judgment of, but rather in tears about. I weep for the unnecessary confusion of the church created by a God who is not the author of the same: "For God is not a God of confusion but of peace" (2 Corinthians 14:33).

Suffering, well-used and redeemed by the Father, Son, and Holy Spirit, thplan and power of the Triune God of the Bible in a Christian community which reflects the community of God, offers the following sorts of benefits—that we risk passing over when we might try and escape from every form of discomfort. A Biblical response to suffering or trials of any kind will:

- motivate us to prayer (Psalm 30)

- increase our trust in the person, providence, and power of God (Psalm 119:71; 2 Corinthians 12:5, 9, 10)

- train us up in obedience, patience, and hope (Romans 5; Hebrews 1)

- promote the sanctification (moving closer to holiness, purity, growth) of our faith (Proverbs 3:11–12; John 17;17; Romans 8:28; 1 Corinthians 11:32; Hebrews 12:8; 13:12)

- conform us into the likeness of Jesus Christ (Proverbs 66:10; Romans 8:29; 12:2; Hebrews 2:10)

- increase joy, wisdom, temporal, and eternal meaning within our heart (Romans 11:33–34; James 1; Colossians 1:24).

- teach us to pity others who suffer (Psalm 72:12; 2 Corinthians 1:3–7; James 1:27).

- increase the depth and breadth of the fruit of the spirit (Matthew 3:8; John 12:24; Galatians 5).

- offer manifold opportunities of seeing God's glory and people's blessing—as we move *through* the trial, and not *around* it (Ezekiel 11:18–21; Luke 24:26; 2 Corinthians 1:5; Philippians 3:8; 1 Peter 5).

- humble us while prying our fingers off the perishable things of this passing world (Psalm 39:6; John 2:12; 1 Corinthians 7:31; 2 Corinthians 12:7; 1 Peter 1:24).

- teach us to bear one another's burdens and live in community (Genesis 48:4; Hebrews 13; Romans 1:12; Colossians 2:2; Galatians 6:2).

- set our heart on the hope and assurance of eternal glory.

For this light momentary affliction is preparing for us an eternal weight of glory beyond all comparison, as we look not to the things that are seen but to the things that are unseen. For the things that are seen are transient, but the things that are unseen are eternal.

2 Corinthians 4:17–18

BETTER OR BITTER: "CHOOSE THIS DAY..." (DEUTERONOMY 30:11–30)

Please take a moment to reflect back upon these amazing promises and benefits for treating our times of trials and suffering in a Biblical fashion. Then do the very same thing again; *except this time,* place the words *"Will not ... "* in front of each benefit. This, beloved of God, is what is at risk when we avoid trials of any kind or rush by them so quickly as to not take advantage of the difficult times in our life that God allows for his glory, our blessing, and the redemption of the world.

As we will see, God so deeply desires to use his people's suffering in universal yet personally redemptive ways. He wants to use life's many painful circumstances we sinful human beings have brought upon ourselves through the sin of Adam within each of our own hearts—to shatter the compartments of our hearts in which we daily scheme to hide our idols, the un-confessed sins and many unredeemed experiences of living in a tragically marred world far from God.

From this rubble, God intends to rearrange the ecosystem of our hearts in such a way that we become more like Jesus. This *is the life-long journey of faith to which God of the Bible calls us.* As the title of this book implies, the divine protocol by which God redemptively uses our heartbreaks to draw us ever closer to him—*the weeping, the window, and the way.*

The miraculous time that I spent with my dad as he died of a self-inflicted gunshot wound radically changed many things for me. But among the most precious and magnificent changes was an inexplicable peace in the one true God of the Bible *and* a nearly-fanatic sense of urgency to communicate his plan of salvation to the world. My own experiences with the *weeping,* the *window,* and the *way* before that night and after it was over, stripped away so much of my pride and pretense. I still seek more radical change of heart, spirit, and life even now.

The process that night revealed the authentic truths and terrible falsehoods of my heart. Repeated many times in the years since Dad's death, the process has given me a deeper sense of passion and peace about God's person and plan than ever before. As I have moved back into the "real world" to be God's agent *in* the culture, yet not *of* it, I have seen how shallow and comfortable that world is by contrast. This is not to lift me up in any way. It's to lift God up even higher, and to ask his blessing on my words in the pages of this book, that through them, I might help to redeem others as I have been redeemed.

FOREWARNED IS FOREARMED: I HAVE A HEART FOR THE HEART OF THE HEART

Following is a quote from Harold Simonson about Jonathan Edwards that we will see again later in the book. It's worth using here in the Introduction as well.

> No secrets of the heart and mind remained hidden when Jonathan Edwards called for self-scrutiny, this meant the relentless need to distinguish between the true and false affections; between those affections having to do with a redeemed heart, and those darkened by sin. To clarify these distinctions was Edwards' purpose in his life and in seeing the Great Awakening come to pass.
>
> Harold Simonson[4]

To one degree or another, "To help clarify these distinctions..." should be part and parcel of the calling of *all* Christians for the life of others God places in our midst: Each one of us should desire "a great awakening by a change of heart" each and every day for those who love God and one another as themselves.

The enlightening moments I spent with God during my father's death revolutionized my heart (E.g., my core beliefs and non-negotiables of my faith), spirit (E.g., my emotions or affections), and my life (E.g., the living out my faith in word and deed). This transformed me to the extent that I hope to devote my life to the ministry of helping others grow in Christian maturity in word and deed.

AVOID THE SHALLOW LIFE AND "GO DEEP"... IT'S GREAT FOR THE HEART!

This is an interactive book. Read it with a pen. Share it with a friend whose heart and life you care about. Make time for it.

Mark it. Fold it. Own it. But please, do not let it sit on your bedside table collecting dust. Do not put it off until a "tomorrow" that you may never have.

As you read through this book, I want to encourage you to "do the work" and "go deep" within your faith. *Please do not* be satisfied with a shallow and lukewarm faith that results from an insistence on living "the comfy, untested, and moderately effective Christian life." It will *harden* your heart...you will *hide* your light...as it has in my life as well!

1. Allow yourself to stay put and absorb any content that's worth considering at a deeper level (John 4:11; 15:4).

2. Use the many Bible passages referenced along this journey. The word of God can change the heart (Isaiah 55:11; 2 Timothy 3:16–17).

3. Use the interactive "Heart Application" section of this book to go deeper by being as truthful and vulnerable as possible, sharing it with a trusted Christian friend, and commit to being held accountable to Christ-centered sanctification, effectiveness, and service.

4. Make sure you check out and use the very rich Appendix A, B, and C portions of this book. They contain resources of truth, growth, and effectiveness that should not be passed up.

5. Engage a community of faith by telling someone when any content hurts, heals, or hampers your usual way of relating to life. You were born out of the community of the Trinity; and you will ultimately grow in *community* (Genesis 1:26–27; Hebrews 12:28–13:9).

6. Remember, if you are in Christ, you are Beloved of God. If you are reminded of this fact often enough, then you will be more and more open to his protocol for redeeming every trial this broken world might throw your way!

[God and] self-rejection is the greatest enemy of the spiritual life because it contradicts the sacred voice that calls us the "Beloved". Being the Beloved expresses the core truth of our existence.

Henri Nouwen, "Life of the Beloved"[5]—parenthesis added

PART ONE:

"LIFE CONFRONTED ... AT TERMINAL VELOCITY"

THE GARDEN: A MIRACULOUS ENCOUNTER WITH HEARTBREAK AND HEAVEN

The first three chapters of *The Weeping, the Window, the Way* detail the heartbreak I experienced on a snowy Christmas night in 2002 when my Dad took his own life after struggling for a time with operable cancer of the jaw. I arrived on the scene, fell to my knees, "alone" with my father as he lay mortally wounded and unconscious in the snow. While I waited for the EMTs and the police, God blessed me with a truly miraculous experience of himself.

God provided a sacred time and space in which he protected both my dad and me from the outside world and responded to my desperate outcries with a very specific sequence of passages from the Bible. The Word to which the Holy Spirit pointed me that night offers *everyone* in any kind of trial God's own protocol for using suffering in a redemptive way to transform the heart.

Chapter Four then moves to the days and months after the tragedy and describes four miraculous interventions God used to help me (and many others since) understand how he intended to use Dad's calamitous death to bring about the grandest triumph imaginable—over and over again!

CHAPTER ONE

FREEFALL AND A FIRM FOUNDATION

The LORD is near to those who have a broken heart; and saves such as have a contrite spirit.

Psalm 34:18

I am feeble and utterly crushed; I groan in anguish of heart. All my longings lie open before you, O LORD; my sighing is not hidden from you. My heart pounds, my strength fails me; even the light has gone from my eyes.

Psalm 38:8

Our deepest pain insists upon being attended to. God whispers to us in our pleasures, speaks to us in our conscience, but shouts in our pain: it is God's megaphone to rouse a deaf world.

C.S. Lewis, *The Problem of Pain*[6]

Christmas night, 2002. The phone rang just as my family finished dinner. It brought with it the news that would change my life forever. "Johnny?" moaned my step-mother, Marge, on the other end of the line.

"Johnny, I found a note from your dad. I think he's killed himself. Please come right away ... Oh, God ... "

"Oh, God ... " I stammered my reply in a half-whisper to contain the shock that just rifled through me. "Uhhh ... yes, yes, I'll be right there."

Stunned, I put down the phone, choking back the flood of emotions that rushed into my throat from a place deep within my chest. My wife Peggy walked toward me, drawn by the pallid look on my face. "Is everything okay?" she asked.

"That was Marge," I responded. "She thinks Dad killed himself." As I said it, I shuddered, sucked in my breath, and then whimpered involuntarily. Tears began to pool in my eyes.

"Oh, John!" Peggy cried. She wrapped her arms around me. "Oh, John. I don't believe it!"

By now our kids, Polly and Teddy, and Peggy's parents, Ted and Margaret, had left the dinner table and found seats in the living room. "I have to go over there," I said as I drew Peggy even closer, my voice cracking. "You had better tell your folks about dad's cancer now. And tell the kids something ... I'm not sure what for now ... has happened to Doz. I'll call as soon as I know more. I'm sorry. I have to go ... "

THE WALLS OF MY HEART BEGIN TO CRUMBLE

Standing there, clinging to Peggy, I felt as though I had already left the house. I yearned to drop to my knees in a heap of emotion. Avalanches of pain had begun to cascade through my body, threatening to blow open a window into my heart. I struggled to keep it closed. I pictured Marge alone in the house with Dad. Was he dead? I presumed so, but how could I be sure? Then something powerful began to pull me. Everything else could wait. I had to find dad, to be with him. The pull consumed my heart. Now. I had to go ... *now!*

After an eternal moment, I released Peggy and snapped into "mission mode." Heading out into the cold and snow, I could feel my instincts taking over. Like a well-trained soldier, I moved forward on autopilot ... and in God's presence and mercy. Like so many other times when an emergency had called me to "head out, hurry up, or help along," the rescuer-adventurer in me clicked through procedural steps, just as I had been taught. I began to talk it through, attempting to hold myself together while believing that each moment "might make all the difference."

Hang in there, John. Breathe. Oh God ... Oh God ... hold it together. Find the keys to the car, you've got to get over to Dad's, don't drive off the road in the snow, it's going to be okay ... You can do this. Focus ... Oh God, help me through this ...

The snowy night evoked dim, but familiar feelings. I had taken part in many rescue efforts while living in the mountains of Colorado. But this was different. Very different. I felt like several people all in one, each now vying for recognition and a voice. Before Marge's phone call, each of them lived in its own compartment inside my heart. I had separated them from one another, some with walls thin enough to be veils, some with walls thick and nearly impenetrable. Now, the walls were coming down, the separations pulling apart. The carefully arranged, well-managed cubicles crumbled and crashed. Desperate to control it, I snatched at the shards that fell all around me attempting to catch every piece and put it back where it belonged. If not, I feared the blow would convulse, paralyze, and render me useless.

I had no time. No time to feel, no time to snatch up the pieces and repair the damage. I had to hang on and get to Dad. "Breathe, John," I repeated the words to myself. I had good training for helping others cope with this type of situation. But nothing could have prepared me to face it for myself. How could I help Dad? How could I help Marge, with something so enormous, so unspeakably painful and sudden? And yet, from within a place deep inside, the assurance grew. I could move forward into the darkness. One step. It would be all right. I would not be alone.

SECRETS THAT HAUNT AND HURT

Suicide never happens in a vacuum, but outside observers often think so. The horror of Dad's probable death weighed more heavily on my heart because of the secrets. For all but a few close family members, the news would not, could not, be set in a meaningful context. A few weeks earlier to this moment, Dad had been diagnosed with bone cancer—cancer of the jaw to be precise. They had scheduled surgery, but Dad had wanted no one to know. He had sworn us to secrecy. Like many families, we had grown accustomed to keeping secrets. And now, the suddenness and sadness of what Dad had done would unload both of its barrels into the hearts of all who knew him, but who had not had the benefit of background and time to prepare those hearts to understand and fit the tragedy into context.

Dad's work and his active social life had drawn his self-effacing focus on others—his warm smile, his jokes, his stories, across the paths of many and varied people from many walks of life. He had made many friends over the years. We had a large extended biological and social family. Yet, that family had created a wide and deep culture of "secret-keeping" over time. Our unspoken rules about secrets only exacerbated our own shock and pain—and that of Dad's friends. As I drove through the Christmas night, I clenched my fist and pounded the steering wheel. Hard. Grimacing in pain and anger, I thought of all this. "Damn, damn, damn the secrets!" I wept and whispered fiercely.

Dad had endeared himself to so many people, in part because of his own deep fears of being endeared or beloved by others. I pictured my dad's pain, his loneliness and fear. It hurt deeply. I knew his plan that evening had been forthright, logical and simple. How many times had he said it? "I don't want to be a burden to anyone." But was the burden really too much for us, Dad? Or for you? I asked the question, but no answer came. I could envision my dad masking his heart-of-the-heart fear as he, unconsciously perhaps, considered the possibility of being more deeply loved and more deeply vulnerable than ever before in his life. Was this love, this vulnerability, the overwhelming burden he had not been able to face? "Oh God, have I missed the chance to love Dad in a state of vulnerability, mine and his, which I have never experienced before … and never will again?" The question crushed my spirit.

The choice Dad had made fit perfectly within his belief system: Pragmatism. We had talked about it many times over. I knew his decision to die the way he did had actually made a sort of twisted sense, at least to him. "Damn it!" I repeated, as something deep inside my heart told me I should have anticipated his defective, yet "logical," reasoning before it had come to this. "Damn it!" I swore again. I should have listened to my instincts. I should have been more thoughtful, more insistent. I should somehow have done more, because I knew more! But I had stuffed my knowledge and my instincts somewhere down deep inside, somewhere inaccessible. "Damn!"

Dad held the hurt and hopelessness inside of him. And I was doing the same, just like him. This flash of insight stabbed at my heart. Then, just as quickly as it had come, the pain eased as I felt rage and dark anger rising in my gut, anger that focused on Dad's well-honed ability to control events and avoid emotion. How could it be that all my neatly devised plans to console and counsel Dad through his fight with bone cancer had been circumvented by his choice to end the story earlier than I had planned? "Damn it! How could Dad have short-circuited my plans to help him get through this?" I asked myself. Then, ten seconds and a half-block later, guilt seized my heart again. "What shamefully selfish and stupid thoughts, John," I scolded myself. My thoughts and emotions ran wildly free from the containment of my own previously hardened, compartmentalized, but now shattered heart.

A FATHER, A BROTHER, A HUSBAND

The trip to my dad's house was only a short distance away, but it seemed to take forever as, block-by-block, an array of ideas and emotions wrestled for supremacy inside my heart and spirit. I felt an overwhelming urgency to be with my children, to console them and to explain all I could about why and how these sorts of things happen in life.

Thirty-one years earlier, my mom had died suddenly of a brain tumor. I had seen our family struggle through the crisis, not handling it well at all. I knew what Polly and Teddy would soon be hearing from friends, neighbors, and family members. I wanted to be there for them, to help them frame the events through the window of their faith, rather than through competing worldviews forged in the fires of pain processed apart from the cross and open tomb of the Savior.

"With them and not with them," I wrestled back and forth. Back when Mom died, I had repressed much of the shock, sweeping it under a large and very bumpy family rug. The sudden memory of that death now set ajar several carefully locked compartments in my heart and emotions. Peggy and others would have to be there for Teddy and Polly right now since I couldn't. I prayed for them, "Oh, Holy Spirit, hold them close and give them the understanding, trust, and peace only you can offer."

Then my sisters and their families flashed across my mind. Were they all together in Seattle tonight? The step-side of my family had come to town for the holidays. I wondered if they knew yet. I considered the pain they would soon feel. I imagined the shock, the flood of tears, the desperate hugs, the initial denial, and then the inability to find words big enough to fill the gaping hole in one another's hearts. No doubt, the same scenario would repeat itself again and again before this was over. "Oh, God!" I said to myself. Of course, it would never really be over would it? Everything would just be radically different from this moment on. *Hold it together, John. One step at a time, man. One step. Just another step.*

Then, finally, I thought of Peggy. She had keenly felt Dad's pain and fear as he revealed the news of his cancer diagnosis. Peggy had given Dad a special gift in the form of a small angel that he treasured earlier this Christmas night. I knew Peggy would want to be there for the many who would be rocked by the news of his death. I knew I had to call her as soon as possible, to tell her what was going on and to talk about a way for her to help. I knew dad's choice would hurt her deeply. Most of all, I needed to hear her soothing voice.

As all the separations of the walls of my heart—the names, various timeframes, images of the past, present and potential future—and as the faces of loved ones crossed my mind, I felt myself wanting to be with *each and every person* as they heard the news about Dad. For most of my life, I had spent a great deal of energy learning how to recognize my emotions and how to grow emotionally mature. In my newfound self-awareness, I felt myself desperately hoping to influence everything and console everyone, and yet, I clearly could not. I would have to trust God in the hellish chaos—trust him more than ever before. I would have to trust that the Holy Spirit would be there for everyone, all at the same time, to do all the right things. In the grand scheme of the universe, it was not my job to influence and console *everything*. I could be in only one place at a time, offering comfort and being comforted myself by whomever God might place with me at the time. God must do the rest.

ENCOUNTERING ANOTHER HEART

Almost without realizing it, I had pulled into Dad's driveway. I stepped out of the car and let myself into the house. Marge limply sat, near the kitchen phone. "Oh, Johnny, you're here. I just can't believe it. I just can't ... I'm just trying to find their number. I have to call ... Sonny (Dad's internist) is on his way. The police, too ... I can't remember the phone number ... Oh, if I had only ... Maybe I could have ... If only ... I should have ... Oh, Johnny ... Oh, God!"

She stood up, and I gave her a long hug. Then she told me where Dad was and sat down again to pick up the phone.

I walked through the living room where just a few hours earlier I had celebrated Christmas with Dad and the rest of the family. As I walked out onto the glassed-in back porch, my eyes began to adjust to the darkness. Then I saw it: A spotlight atop the roof of the house lit a small area under a tree in the snow below. Dad's body lay there, in the tiny pool of light that appeared almost to caress him. Ross, dad's faithful Portuguese Waterdog, stood facing the big glass door that led out into the yard. He pressed his nose against the glass, whining as if his heart would break.

"Hey, Rossie! Is your dad out there? It's okay, Rossie boy. Good boy," I said as I patted and nudged past him to get to the door. As I took hold of the doorknob and stepped out into the cold of night, my stomach jumped directly into my throat.

STEPPING INTO GOD'S TIME, THE ONLY TIME

The moment I stepped outside—*at that very moment in time*—everything changed. Time and space took on a sense of "otherness." Events slowed and seemed to stop, or nearly so. My need to be with dad dissolved every other concern. I felt as though I had entered some kind of protective bubble. Maybe it was shock. Maybe I was momentarily deluded or hallucinogenic. Or maybe God had simply blessed me with the space and the time to be with my dad and with him, my heavenly Father. I didn't know. But as I approached my dad's body, I had a clear sense I had stepped into a place reserved specifically and especially for Dad, myself, and for one "other"—one who had not yet fully revealed himself to my senses.

The spotlight in the garden seemed to be the only light in the entire world. The cold disappeared. Noises from the street, even the approaching sirens, sounded oddly muffled. As if in slow motion, I fell to my knees, sobbing: "Oh, Dad ... Oh, Dad ... Oh, Dad ... "

With each successive cry, I felt myself plummeting deeper and deeper. I was falling ... and falling ... and falling. Downward I fell with an ever-increasing sense of panic, a sense my free-fall might never stop. I rocked, fell and wept. Nearly nauseous, I looked around me, desperate to find something solid, something on which to steady myself. I looked down—and saw Dad's favorite nine-millimeter pistol lying next to him, under his right hip in the snow where he had fallen. Then I saw the blood pooled under his head.

That's when I noticed Dad was still alive. He was shivering occasionally, barely breathing, and I had the distinct sense that he was both "here, yet not here" anymore. Although the first aid and rescue experience I had gained over the years of living in the Colorado Rockies told me to try to stabilize him, I knew there was nothing I could do to help or bring him back. I simply and absolutely wanted only to be there.

I knew I was meant to be exactly where I was, to kneel next to my dad in the snow. The sense of urgency I felt upon first hearing of Dad's probable suicide was now reinforced by the "near fanatic conviction" that I needed to be here at Dad's side: I was here to pray to God, to weep, to seek the Holy Spirit's help, to cry out to God and plead for help. To speak, and to listen, until that moment when I knew deep within the rest of the world would come crashing in upon the disastrous and dark, yet sacred, bubble of timelessness and space I had entered.

Somewhere in the deepest recesses of my heart I knew that I would never have this time with Dad and God ever again. I knew then why I felt such a sense of urgency to leave my home and be exactly where I was: *I was called here.* The reality of this divine appointment was clearly evident in all the details of this moment.

A WEEPING HEART... IN FREEFALL... CRIES OUT

I rocked and wept uncontrollably, grasping to maintain some connection to "the real world," whatever that was. As I wept, I fell and fell ever deeper into my own personal and yet very public abyss of pain. It was personal because I sensed my own father's fear, loneliness, and determination. I also saw my own emotions stripped bare, the loss of my dad, the guilt, the regret of the things I could have or should have done or said but had not. It was public because I saw in stark relief all of humankind's desolation, self-isolation, and shattered hearts. The shame of vulnerability and the dread of being seen for what we truly are. Self, self, self... The word epitomizes and embodies sin.

Part of my own heart often said, "I do not need God. I do not need God's or any other's bleeding charity!" I could imagine how the backed-into-a-corner "necessity of suicide" had overtaken my dad, as I considered how it had captured parts of my own heart at times. The darkness grew more real to me than I could ever have imagined. It was a darkness of my deepest fears and loneliness, and added sadness for my Dad flung into an entirely new realm of desperation. Nothing would come to my rescue! Then, just as I felt I would completely lose myself in despair, I squeezed out a small cry from the very center of my heart: "Lord Jesus, please help me in this. Please help, Lord. Please."

It was then I noticed that each barely audible cry—"Oh Dad... Oh, God... Please..."—received a unique and specific "response." Yes. That's what I would call it: a response. It came from within me and yet from outside of me as well. At first I tried to push the words away. It was too scary. I had to stand up to silence the words. I walked back to the porch to gather whatever blankets I could find. Then I knelt again next to Dad. I covered him, protecting him as best I could against the winter's night. Pitifully, it felt like too little, too late.

"Oh, Dad... Oh, God..." As I repeated the tearful refrain, the responses began again; this time, I heard the words more clearly—a series of verses from Scripture, verses that the Bible and the Holy Spirit had specially given to me over the past fifteen years of my faith journey:

In the beginning... God said, ... (Genesis 1:1)

In the beginning was the Word... (John 1:1)

Be strong and courageous. Do not fear or be in dread ... for it is the LORD *your God who goes with you. He will never leave you or forsake you* (Deuteronomy 31:6).

Commanding, yet quiet. Scary, yet soothing. Distinct, yet elusive. The words began to tie me to an entirely new reality in the present moment. They formed the perfect answer for my pain. *Truth.* I shuddered deeply and sucked in my breath, wiping my tears and the phlegm that had pooled on my lips and chin.

The words of each passage began distinctly overlapping, and then melting away into the night. The "circle of sounds and words" then repeated itself, distinct yet still, quiet and overlapping. Oh, how I had loved these passages, these truths, and these promises. Nevertheless, I could not have imagined how tightly I would hold onto them in this moment of deep weeping as I peered into the window of my own heart. I could never have anticipated the context into which God now placed them and the deeper meaning of sweet solace they would bring both to me and eventually to the many others who would be crushed by dad's suicide.

A FIRM FOUNDATION

Suddenly, I realized my rocking had slowed. I painfully straightened my back and glanced around. I checked my dad's condition. It was the same. The sirens still wailed in the distance, still strangely muffled yet timelessly imminent, but my free-fall had stopped.

Without knowing when exactly, I had somehow "landed" on something as firm, more rock-solid than I could ever imagine. Hundreds of attempts with thousands of words to describe what had happened would never fully explain the experience.

I had landed. I *knew* it. I knew I could never go lower or sink deeper. This foundation I was now on would not allow it. I was resting fully on God, on "The Rock." I knew somehow my family and I would make it. The one and only true God who had in the beginning spoken creation into existence would never leave me. The Word who was there "in the beginning," the Savior of the world, the God of those magnificent "beginnings," held even Dad's choice this Christmas night within his perfect and providential purpose. I knew, at the core of my being, yet without being able to explain it, that God's plan was perfect and rooted in something solid, deep, and abiding.

I had no idea what would happen after this moment, nor did I need to know. I could trust God for the future, whatever might come, because I was kneeling, resting on something as solid, immovable, and reassuring as the eternal Rock himself that consisted of his mighty acts of *creation*, incarnating *Christ*, and the promise of never-ending *covenant* love.

It was particularly important that this first group of three responses from God ended with his promise to intimately comfort and encourage me, to keep on caring for me, with his promise never to leave me nor to forsake me ... ever. His love *just for me* buoyed me up, brought confidence and hope in a way nothing else could have. I didn't realize it at the time that God was perhaps perfectly and especially there for my dad as well. This Christmas night I grasped afresh how unspeakably vast God is, and yet, how so very personally he cares for me. I saw for the first time the full glory and greatness of God who was there just for me, who is always there so *infinitely* and yet so *intimately* for each and every heart that turns to him in times of weeping or a freefall of any kind.

CLUTCHING ... AND LETTING GO

Admittedly, I am one who pays a great deal of attention to the grandness *and* granular stuff of life. It is indeed a mixed blessing.

But now in this most sacred place where I felt a sure foundation beneath me, I sensed a deep need to move on and yet, *at the same time*, a need to circle back into the passages offered by God and dig into more detail. I couldn't do both.

It was as though the world's time was about to come rushing in and overwhelm me with the chaos of the world's response. I wanted and needed to consider for a time a level much wider and deeper concerning the passages I received from God. I wanted to trace back and tightly hang onto them. At the same time I felt an urge to move forward, somehow knowing this timeless place that God created would not last forever. As I knelt over Dad, these ideas rushed through my mind. The enormous tension of "time-bound timelessness" threatened to rip me in two, but God had blessed me with just enough wisdom and trust to stay put a bit longer still.

I choked back my tears and uncontrollable groans and shaking just enough to trace back to how God by reminded me of *creation* first, and found I could begin to breathe more easily and calm myself. I could remember how God had started and sustained *everything,* from the very core of my own heart and the atoms that made it up, to the furthest reaches of the infinite universe. *God thought,* and all creation leapt into existence. He had sustained every detail and grand design until this very evening, which God had planned so perfectly.

All creation "thought, uttered, and fluttered" into existence by God the Father, Son, and Holy Spirit? Oh yes, I was reminded that this is so true. What an awesome creating and sustaining God he is! Could God then be trusted to remember my dad and me in the garden, right now in this place? Absolutely. God always has a specific reason for the things he does, and reminded me that he began the whole of creation of the universe. He sustains all of it to this day, and, if I can trust in anything, I can trust that he hasn't left out even the smallest details within it. In God's mercy, akin to addressing Job in his greatest distress (Job 38:4), he reminded me of the beginning of all beginnings, and his tender care of me this very night. Within this first verse that God mercifully gave me was an implicit and actual assurance that he most carefully *sustains* it all as well, in every detail providentially and humanly imaginable.

It was as if God reminded me, "John, I hear your pain. I feel your deepest despair. I know you're intense fear of freefalling into the shock and darkness of this tragedy. I didn't form you for this sort of freefall. It's not in your true nature as it was 'in the beginning'... And it's completely the *opposite* of the security and safety I intended for you, beloved. But remember, I began it *all* and I am in and through it *all* today... until I bring it *all* to consummation."

CHRIST IN ME... THE HOPE AND GLORY

Then, just as the first moment God answered my cry for help, the second verse and truth began to overlap and ascend into and through my heart for attention, *"In the beginning was the Word..."*

While kneeling in this sacred moment in time, this incredibly rich and jam-packed "second beginning", referring to none other than Jesus Christ himself, carried with it an even greater measure of remembrance, meaning, intimacy, and gratitude than I could ever fully describe. Moving from the words of remembrance in God forming creation from nothing (Genesis 1), to the Word incarnate in Jesus Christ (John 1), no more appropriate gift could have followed the first reminder of God's created order. The Word incarnate in Christ... *born, died, and resurrected for me.* These realities were utterly incompatible with any thought that Jesus would leave me alone this Christmas night.

It was as though the perfect next step from creation as a "reflection of God's nature in himself" to the remembrance of the intimate word manifest in Jesus Christ "dwelling among us" was offered to me so intimately and in ways that I had never dreamt possible.

"NEVER, EVER... NO NEVER..."

This remembrance of "Christ's beginnings" that echoed back from my outcry—still intertwining the first with the second beginning—could not have been a more perfect way for God to reach down into my heart and stop my freefall. These were the next truth-full words God responded to my cries with: *the words from God to not be afraid and to have courage. To know that he would never ever leave me or forsake me* with a promise of the love of the Trinity-God that reached into the center of my being.

Again it was as though God had said, "John, dear one, remember I spoke it all in the beginning for my pleasure and your blessing; I sent my son to redeem it when it all went wrong. Surely, beloved son of mine, you can trust in the fact that I am not only aware of your deep hurts and needs, but I am right with you now and will never ever leave or forsake you in any way, as we move through this *together*. I began it *all*. I am sustaining and redeeming it *all*. Remember, I'm with you for time and eternity.

The remembrance of these foundational promises and facts of the Godhead himself moved down to the final level of promise in, "I will never leave you ... never ever, no way, no how, no matter what sort of freefall, of any kind, I will always be with you, John.

Get out your faith. Use it now. Do you trust me in this? That you can be so blessed by me? I can and will bless you and others by faith that I will always be with you. I will never leave you or forsake you no matter what may come? Yes, and lots more will come. Many trials, many joys, many changes and challenges are to come. But in it all I am always with you, John."

I now knelt upon this unshakable foundation. I was now resting on this unfathomably unique and blessed assurance of God's answer to my pain and outcry. This blessing from God himself cannot be compared to any gift except, of course, the gift of God's final glory and seeing his face when all things are made new at the end.

TREASURING UP REMEMBRANCES

While in this place of sanctuary, there were fleeting treasures I was reminded of as God had used the same approach to coming to the aid of his beloved freefalling and wandering ones in the Bible. Examples like I mentioned briefly above such as God finally sitting Job down near the end of his trials to remind him of exactly where Job was when God *created* everything, Paul and other inspired writers' predictable approach to the suffering first century church by reminding them of who they were *in Christ,* and finally the Old and New Testament writers referring multiple times to God's unswerving love of his beloved based upon his *covenant* promises to them. Remembrances of the Bible's *creation, Christ,* and *covenant* assurances flew through my mind as I struggled to stay connected to the time with Dad in the garden as well as the things of God beyond this moment.

In retrospect, the experience of that Christmas night and the ways in which it began to change me had yet to be fully revealed. Even so, the abstract faith that I had held, about certain things, and on certain levels, became the real thing. The change was huge. My powerful Creator-God and his son, Jesus Christ, were the rock-solid foundation of the universe and I was resting on them.

For the time being, I knew better than I ever had known that "God's beginnings" and his promise to never forsake me would make it possible for me to take my next step. As I regained my composure for just that moment, I saw that in my deep and painful *weeping, a window* within my heart had been opened. Through that open window, I would soon see important connections between the past, the present, and the future. Through that window, I would see how God would use even this horror for his glory and for the good of many people. Through that window, I would eventually see *the way* closer to him and to those around me.

I wanted to pause, to stay in this bubble of God's protective care forever. Yet, I knew I could not. The crush of the world's response to my Dad's suicide as well as the crush of another sort lay just around the corner. This "crush of another sort" was creeping into my mind as I began to look back on my relationship with my Dad. As much as parts of my heart didn't want to go there, it was clear the choice at this point was not mine to make.

GOING DEEPER...

For further reading, see:

Buechner, F. Telling Secrets. New York: HarperOne. 1991

Nouwen, H. Turn My Mourning Into Dancing. Nashville, TN: Thomas Nelson, Inc. 2001.

CHAPTER TWO

FALLEN, FORGIVEN AND FREE

I am feeble and utterly crushed; I groan in anguish of heart.

Psalm 38:8

You hurled me into the deep, into the very heart of the seas, and the currents swirled about me; all your waves and breakers swept over me.

Jonah 2:3

God's sanctuary of protective care held me. The promises of his creative power and personal presence had placed this firm bedrock beneath me. I had landed. I would fall no further. Sirens wailed in the distance, still muffled and seemingly a long way off.

Slowly, I straightened my back to breathe, clear my head, and check my surroundings. My body ached from immobility, the stress of the emotions coursing through me. It felt as if I had been straining and ripping apart every muscle in my body. Tears still welled in my eyes as I leaned back, then forward, to place my hands on Dad's side and shoulder.

By now the pain of everything that had happened— the *weeping*—had flung the *window* of my heart open wide. Through that window I could now see previously hidden parts of myself far more clearly than ever before, especially as I considered my relationship with my dad. Certainly in such a time feelings of false guilt would likely arise, and they did. Far more troubling, though, were the blotches of real self-centeredness and sin I saw within my heart.

How many times, how many places, and how many opportunities had God given me to be with Dad over the years? How many times could I have spoken with him from my heart about so many things? Yet I had held myself back in ways that revealed my loyalty to self and man rather than to God. To say I felt some deep regrets would be a huge understatement. I had often guarded my words for fear of revealing too much. I had not wanted to offend him, causing emotional discomfort of any kind or crossing the boundary lines that our family had set in place so long ago. I had not wanted to break the "secret-keeping" pact that had regulated family interactions for so many years— and not just interactions within our family, but also those of families of the wider culture in which I had grown up and, for that matter, most of the rest of the world.

Unspoken family taboos had ruled my own words and actions long after I had become a new creation in Christ. I had let it happen. Seeing that now hurt me deeply. I had parceled out too sparingly the rich fare of the Gospel—thinking tomorrow would afford me another chance. How much I was like my Dad! And now it was too late.

I could no longer hide behind the pretense and self-righteousness of the pride, control, and anger that separated Dad and me. I had too many times reserved saying something important for "tomorrow". For Dad and me, there were no tomorrows left. I had said some safe things, but could have said so much more.

Many years earlier I had toured the Orkney Islands of Scotland on my bicycle. The unrelenting roll, crash, and crush of the waves had made an indelible impression on my mind. As I knelt next to my dad's body on this dark night, the "would-a, could-a, should-a's" began to roll in upon me as inexorably as the waves upon those rocks, though now the waves pounded against the walls of my own heart, threatening to crush it. Wave after wave of regret and guilt, both true and false, pounded down upon me and against the foundation upon which I knelt. Quietly, *remorse* transformed into genuine *repentance* which began to seep out from the deepest part of me. I wept in anguish and in hope—the certain hope of forgiveness that forever pours from the heart of Christ Jesus, broken on Calvary's cross.

THE WAVES ROLL IN

Perhaps I could have ... been forceful, loving, insistent, or intrusive in offering Dad my help during the past few weeks. He must have experienced the deepest fear, and yet the determination to manage things in his own way. Perhaps much earlier when I had moved back to St. Louis from Aspen, I could have worked harder to create a new or different relationship with Dad. Then, even though the cancer would have come just the same, perhaps Dad might have found it easier to reach out to others. Or to me. Like all of us to some degree, his deep desire to have people really and truly close to him frightened him. He was like me. And I was like him. Dad's heart had been deeply wounded at various points in his early life, and he was naturally inclined to avoid more vulnerability and potential wounding.

Perhaps if I had ... sent him another article, a different book. Perhaps if I had told a different story about someone who had faced a similar situation and had found hope in a relationship with the Savior ... Perhaps then suicide would not have seemed so irresistible a choice.

Maybe that would have ... allowed him to reach out in a different way. If I had not hesitated to interrupt his well-honed routine, if I had asked him to play golf with me or eat lunch with me more often, if I had joined him and Ross on their daily walks, maybe then I wouldn't be kneeling here in the snow now.

Perhaps if I had ... managed to overcome the secret-keeping that had become such a deeply entrenched expectation in our family, perhaps if I had overcome my fear of offending Dad's "sense and sensibilities," perhaps if I would have shared my own volatile emotions, my own stories, the experiences that prevented me from breaking through, then I could have made meaningful, more authentic connections with him.

Maybe I should have... taken better advantage of the times when Dad and I visited Mom's gravesite to place the holiday holly boughs. Maybe I should have used those opportunities to just be with him. Maybe I should have had more patience, through those all-too-brief-moments of awkward silence that inevitably occurred. What deeper, more meaningful things might we have said to one another in that setting? *Maybe... Perhaps... If only... The painful regrets, remorse, and repentance rolled in...*

My heart felt as if it might collapse under the weight of it all—especially in light of the fact it was now too late to retrace my steps, too late to do or say what I could have said or done.

I knew I could never lose the firm foundation of my Lord's love for me. And yet, at the same time, I felt the weight of condemnation for the (even small or retrospective) part I may have played in this tragedy. The window of my heart had opened wide to reveal the truth.

I would certainly have many other chances to tell my story and, much more importantly, to share Christ's story, the story of redemption—God's and mine within it. I might be more bold in the future after living through this tragedy. But not with my Dad. If only I had allowed God's love to surmount my shame! "Oh, God, forgive me! If only... If only..."

THE ULTIMATE FUTILITY

No one can change the past. No one can live there in peace. Even so, Satan tempts us to think we can. If we believe his lie, he uses it to torment us and harden our hearts into a flinty-hard bitterness and near-indelible sense of inferiority. Clinging to our regrets and guilt, we create a miserable present and a future devoid of hope. I had known this for a long time. And yet, here

I knelt, tormented by what *might* have been ... what *could* have been ... what *should* have been.

Adding to the torment I saw, more starkly than ever before, my motives for not doing more to grow beyond the boundaries that kept me from "speaking the truth in love" (Ephesians 4:15) on a more frequent basis, the motives that kept me from loving those around me enough to speak and act more genuinely, more authentically, with them:

- The family-secrets stigma
- The "you-just-don't-go-there" boundary
- The emotionally uncomfortable issues taboo
- The respect-your-parents' invisible-sensitivities door
- The we-don't-talk-about-private-issues-like-religion gate
- The that-would-set-someone-off no-no
- The that-would-sound-like-some-liberal/communist idea bomb
- The fear of opening-some-floodgate-of-emotion and responsibility that would require more love than I could offer door
- The you-outta-be-ashamed-of-yourself threat that, even though it was healed, had festered in my heart for so many years; and the deepest motivation of all:
- Favoring the world, the flesh (sinful behavior) and/or the devil over God.

Wave upon wave, *the regrets that revealed the real merit of my faith* relentlessly rolled in. How I now hated all of it so much more than before! The pressure of that hatred multiplied inside me until I feared I might explode like some long-over-crusted volcano. I wanted to scream in rage. I wanted to beat the ground, now covered with *Christmas* snow of all things.

RAGE AGAINST THE DARKNESS

Christmas night, of all nights! The night God's people celebrate their Savior's birth. That Savior had come to rescue me from the very same selfish and isolating behaviors that were crowding in on me from the outside and, at the same time, perpetually welling up within me.

Generations upon generations had continued the pain, the fear, the isolation and self-protection. Some time before this night, I had begun to release the self-loathing my brokenness and sin had evoked in me. On some level, I had grasped for some time the need to "hate the sin and love the sinner" in myself. But my heart had not yet completely committed to that truth.

How many people—even Christian people—might have offered some supposedly soothing line, had they knelt with me there in the snow! How many times even God's people grasp at palliatives, at well-intentioned "comfort" like "You can only be who you are at the time...," "You can't blame yourself...," "This too will pass...," "I'm sure you did all you could..."

Well..."yes." Sometimes. Maybe. Sort of... as we squirm about considering the innumerable things we might have done and didn't. I mean, what about all those annoying "NO's"? What about all "the good intentions" that make up the well-worn pavement to hell? What repository are we supposed to place those in—if it's not the choice between the place of locked compartments and rotting corpses within our own hearts *or* at the foot of the cross where every "good-intention-gone-bad," past, present, and future, was put to death with Jesus Christ?

Instead, as the Holy Spirit held me close to himself, he helped me weep hot tears—tears of authentic repentance that he himself had worked in my heart. Tears for my dad's pain and aloneness. I whispered down to Dad and up to God as I owned what I knew and sought to see what I didn't know before the window was blown open. I had seen my sin for what it was. How well I knew well the passage about "being ashamed of Christ" and he of me as a result (Luke 9:26; Romans 1:18–39).

That was the real sin that lay beneath and behind all the regrets, the false guilt, and the "if-onlies."

In this most sacred place, I had the great blessing and the great sadness of seeing the sin beneath the sin: how easily I could make something *other than Christ* my sufficiency, my identity, my worth. The pounding had taken me to a necessary level of self-awareness while I rested on the foundation of God's love for me:

It was not punishment, but rather the potential for purification that had to reveal my deepest motivations in order to have its way with my heart. I saw what I had done so many times to satisfy the sinful urges to be accepted by other people. I saw how many times I had denied my Savior and Lord. I could see so clearly now the high cost I had paid for favoring peace at any price.

Kneeling there in the snow, I knew.

Oh God, how I knew.

THE PAIN AND BLESSING OF LOOKING IN

Human hearts so reluctantly embrace the truth of our guilt and our need for forgiveness. The Spirit used this time to reveal my sin in such an overpowering way I could no longer deny it or paper over its seriousness. It ripped my heart into pieces … but for the goal of peace. I now understood the depth of David's pain as he pleaded, "Hear my prayer, O LORD, listen to my cry for help; be not deaf to my weeping" (Psalm 39:12). God had brought me to a second, blessed cry of the heart.

"Father God," I prayed, "Please forgive me. Please forgive my silence. Forgive my pride, my will for control, my neediness, and my slavery to the opinions of others. Forgive me for presuming upon your mercies, for just assuming you would always give me another day to muster up my courage, to tell *all* my story—the story of sin and of your Son's cross, the full story I never shared with the consistency and courage I could have with Dad. Forgive me for living, not out of your power, but my own. Please forgive my sins of omission and commission. Forgive me especially for the hypocrisy which you abhor, Lord. Please forgive it all. Please, Lord. Before I'm utterly crushed, please."

As I fell suddenly silent, a response to my cries began to form. Just as before, the words came from within me and yet from outside of me as well. In this place, however, my heart embraced them, grasping the truth as never before. The *way* was opening before me, as I revisited again and again the sweetest, most delicious words possible at that moment:

> *The wrath of God is being revealed from heaven against all the godlessness and wickedness of men who suppress the truth* (Romans 1:18).

> *Therefore, there is now no condemnation for those who are in Christ Jesus* (Romans 8:1).

A shivering chill ran throughout my entire body as I took in the truth of my sinful condition *and* the promise of God's incredible, forgiving, and unending love. "Suppressing the truth ... in wickedness"—I had done that! These words pierced my heart to reveal the dark truth that my fears, shame, control, and pride had prevented me from "speaking the truth in love." These things had kept me from sharing with my own dad, and with many others too, my own spiritual journey!

As that truth cut through me, threatening to separate sinew from bone, another truth flowed over me as well: *"There is now no condemnation!"* Now, nothing—no thing—could separate me from the love of God! By means of the sacrificial death of Jesus Christ, God has taken away all of my sin!

These words, perhaps the most powerful and reassuring promises in the entire Bible, exploded across my mind and heart, blessing me with peace beyond my comprehension. I could almost taste the truth of the Gospel message as it had been summarized by the words of Jack Miller, "You are more sinful than you could ever imagine; and yet you are more loved than you ever dared hope for!" There it was, the "bookends of the Gospel" so starkly laid out before me.

THE PERFECT ANSWER, YET AGAIN

"It's true," I thought! But now I knew it to be true on an *entirely* different level than ever before. If it weren't for this bloody-awful occasion, I would never have imagined how the truth and love of God would unfold for me from within these two pivotal passages. My heart had melted as I, though in a fresh, renewed way, thought about my sin *and* about the promise, in Christ, of no condemnation. I would never have asked that God's character and promises be made so real and personal to me—especially in this way. Not in *this* way!

But perhaps I had. Hadn't I asked the Holy Spirit to help me to know Christ more intimately? Hadn't I asked to grow closer to him? To move further and further away from my besetting sins? Could this be the all-time, ultimate situation to illustrate the over-used quip, "Ya gotta watch what you pray for"? God had not caused the tragedy, but he was so obviously using it. And in the garden was just the beginning...

I had spoken, written, warned, counseled, and consoled others many times about how God will providentially and powerfully use the circumstances of this broken world to bring people *back* to himself. First, if they do not already believe and have a faith in Jesus Christ his son; or, second, *closer* to him if they already did have a relationship with him—and were being conformed to the image of God's son.

I had meditated often on his promise to reveal and remove idols and other gods hidden in our heart in order to "break and remove our heart of stone and, purely by his mercy, give us a heart of flesh" first in *conversion* (e.g., Ezekiel 11; 36; John 3:3; 2 Corinthians 5:17) and then in *sanctification* (e.g., John 17; Romans 6:5–6; 2 Corinthians 4:7–18; James 1:1).

I had considered ways in which the Holy Spirit uses difficult circumstances to draw his people toward increasing holiness (Romans 8:13; Philippians 3:10), to make us more wholly devoted to God, and then, ultimately to shape our hearts so that he might use us in ever more powerful ways to achieve his redemptive purposes in a broken world.

But this? On Christmas night? To my dad? To me? And to so many others who would be blasted and possibly broken—*but maybe blessed*—by the shock and the loss? I did, and yet I did not, fully know how to answer the questions flying through my heart and spirit. But I did know one thing with more confidence than I could ever have imagined knowing anything: *It's true!* What was that *it?* Simply and beautifully this:

> For God so loved the world [*he so loves me*] that he gave his one and only Son, that whoever believes in him shall not perish but have eternal life.
>
> John 3:16-parenthesis/emphasis mine

Again, "the tug-a-war between going deeper and getting on with it" pulled at me from both sides. The test of the foundation laid beneath me not moments before would now be used in the function and form for which it was designed. The crush of the "would-a, could-a, should-a's," and the unshakable foundation where I knelt, offered a time to peer into the open window of my heart with the Holy Spirit close by my side.

THE PARACLETE* AND PEERING IN
one who consoles, one who intercedes on our behalf, a comforter or an advocate

The assurance of being on a firm foundation of God's creation, Christ and his covenant love for me, all while being at a window peering through and into my heart, was extremely real. The beginning of this next part of the journey had emotions associated with it that were, on the one hand, extremely scary and threatening, but on the other hand extremely reassuring.

JOHN O. DOZIER, JR.

I felt the very real presence of the Holy Spirit offering a place alongside him as we peered through the window of my heart. This window was created—*actually blown open*—by the circumstances of a broken world, and by God to move into the next step in the answer to my outcries: "Please stop the waves, the crush of my sinful, misplaced or misconstrued involvement in my dad's life ... as well as in his death!"

Mine, in fact, everyone's "would-a, could-a, should-a's" can and should be viewed in the light of God's love and truth—in relationship to Christ. Viewed from *God's* perspective of our faith in him, whether it be true or false faith can only be seen from this perspective.

Being with the Holy Spirit of the Trinity looking into my heart is no small matter and it is an unspeakable gift offered to me and all who would, by faith, stay put for a time. I could have stayed in this scary yet secure and safe place, but for the time being there was a sense of urgency to move forward.

Seeing the two sides of my true nature through the window into my heart (being more sinful and yet more loved) was a view of reality that would have been impossible to fully accept if it weren't for two main facts: first, I was on the foundation of creation, Christ, and covenant promise; and second, being very close to the person of the Holy Spirit placed me in a sacred place. I felt a strong sense that I should take full advantage of this rare and rich time to be with the loving guide, counselor, and pointer to Jesus Christ: The Holy Spirit. To see my heart more and more as God sees it.

It's important to note again that no other circumstance of life would avail me to this "foreboding fact-finding" yet blessed and sacred experience of seeing truth and embracing it so that I could (with the help of The Helper, the Bible and my Christian community) eradicate the lie and live more according to who I really, truly am in Jesus Christ.

The idea and temptation to *avoid* this scary and sacred time at the window of my heart was real as well. I'm certain the sins encompassed by the world—the flesh and the devil that hates me as a new creation in Christ—hoped I would simply fly right by!

And yet I was overwhelmed by an opportunity to see my heart as God sees it and accept the fact that he was not doing this for any blessing he would receive (other than being glorified … which is huge) but rather purely out of love for *me* … for *my* purification and the eventual holiness my heart would benefit from.

Like Paul, I had the rare chance to really distinguish between the *"I as sinner"* and the *"I as saved"* (Romans 7) as I peered into the recesses of my heart. Time spent at the window blown open by life's many travails is a trial and a treasure. The treasure *far* exceeded the trial, but the trial had to occur for the power of catharsis to promote the kind of change offered as my heart was crushed and re-created by the Holy Spirit. This is, in fact, the "sanctified suffering" God desires. The truths and falsehoods that had become more obvious in this time and as they are seen by God were now *both* available to be claimed as true, or cleansed as being false, by applying God's Holy Word, the merits and/or mediocrity of my faith in Christ, and loving counsel to my *heart,* my *emotions,* and my *life.*

The theology of being at the window and seeing "the two sides of the Gospel" more clearly gave me glimpses of how important and necessary this time really and truly was. It is ultimately is the most wonderfully freeing time one could ever spend. It's a time that now appeared as such an obvious benefit while also I could tell that moving by it and taking no notice at all, "merely" because the difficulty of doing so would be a disastrous mistake.

Utterly surrounded by God the Father, Son, and Holy Spirit's mercy, I was compelled to stay in this place where Jesus' words faintly echoed, "I did not come to bring peace, but a sword … to divide … truth from falsehood … beginning in the heart … " (Matthew 10:34—paraphrased). Don't waste the *cut-*

ting in the curse of suffering, by avoiding the power and process of the *cure* offered at the window.

The humble confidence I felt as the Holy Spirit assured me that my specific outcries tied to the true and false guilt would be answered was palpable. The specific outcries related to this time and my relationship with my father was applied in *practice* to my heart in a most blessed way, imparting a *principle* that shot through every particle of my being: times of great trial and suffering allow us a chance to see our heart more and more as God sees it—*so that* we can take part in choosing life or death, darkness or light, self or Christ, idols or the living God of the Bible, wisdom or foolishness, freedom or bondage, and guilt-ridden servitude or service to The King!

In this place with God and Dad, I had seen the monumental gulf between "the wrath of God being revealed against all who suppress the truth" and the blessed, gracious promise that now there is "no condemnation for those who are in Christ Jesus." The nearly unbelievable assurance of "no condemnation" had swept away every one of my *would-a, could-a, should-a's*.

Will the blessing ever overcome the curse in total victory? No, not completely, not until Christ comes again in glory to drive away every last shadow of sin from our hearts. Still, no promise from the throne of God has ever taken a higher hill in life's battle than had this promise. "It's true!" I wept, even as I knelt over my dad's body in the Christmas snow, bitter-sweet tears squeezed from the True Truth of the Gospel—or Good News—that I was a sinner saved by Grace himself.

As I straightened my back again, I was suddenly more aware of what was going on around me. The now-imminent sounds of the rest of the world responding to an emergency began to break into my protective bubble. Once again, I checked Dad's condition. Once again, it was unchanged. His body continued to shiver occasionally, and his breathing was more shallow and erratic now.

GOING DEEPER...

For further reading, see:

Simonson, A. Jonathan Edwards: Theologian of the Heart. Grand Rapids, MI: Eerdmans. 1974.

Allender, D.B., Longman, T. III. Breaking the Idols of Your Heart: How to Navigate the Temptations of Life. Wheaton, IL: Tyndale House Publishers. 2007.

CHAPTER THREE

REDEEMED TO REDEEM

I had no idea how much time had passed; it had lost all meaning. "Oh, Dad,..." I said for the last time as I rested my hands on his left side and shoulder. How thankful I was for the answers God had provided to my outcries, though I did not yet comprehend the extent of his blessings.

I tried to ease my stiff body as I continued to kneel next to Dad. Moving in a slow, surreal motion, I turned my head and shoulders to glance behind me. My head pounded. My eyes burned. My upper body ached. As I turned, I noticed a new sensation. It seemed as though I had somehow re-entered worldly time, and though the "bubble of protection" still existed, it had changed as the outside world drew closer and began to intrude.

As the first of nearly a dozen emergency medical personnel and law enforcement officers approached the garden gate, I could see lights flashing on the snow all around the neighborhood. Black rubber boots. Red, blue, and orange flashing lights swarmed around me. Chaos threatened to encroach into the place of calm, turmoil, peace, and horror I had experienced with Dad and God. I tried to refocus on what was happening, but it was no use. I wasn't ready to leave this place, to leave my dad. Not yet.

I turned back to him for what seemed like a last good-bye. The anticipation of entering a whole new hell of consequences and shattered hearts made me feel sick to my stomach. "Breathe, John," I kept reminding myself.

It was inevitable that I would be the one to take charge of the many details concerning my dad's death. I was the only blood relative who lived here in town. Somewhere deep within my mind and heart I accepted that charge. I knew I would be ready, and in the recesses of my heart, now shored up by God's comfort, I felt honored and deeply blessed by it. I knew people would come rushing in to help. I also knew that God had been preparing me in so many ways for this exact time, for this exact moment and set of circumstances.

Still, I didn't want to leave the garden. "Oh God, oh God,..." my heart cried out. I felt as if I had just finished a double marathon—and now I had to stand up just as the starting gun exploded again, sending me off on the next one. My heart and emotions lay in shambles, and yet I was not lost by any means. Oh no ... I was resting on a rock-solid foundation. I was reconciled to being fallen and forgiven. Then, gradually, I began to realize that I could breathe a lot better—physically, to be sure, but also emotionally, intellectually, and spiritually. Though I could not have articulated the impact of the "conversations" I'd just had with God, I felt a deep sense of purpose, of promise, and of peace. The Holy Spirit was very close by, and he would bring many others along side to help me and those I loved get through this horrific tragedy. God would use even this senseless tragedy for his glory. He would use it to bless other people—somehow, some day. I knew this to be true.

Then, as I faced Dad and waited for the EMTs to cross the front lawn and take charge of the scene on this holy and most dreadful Christmas night, I heard new words circling my heart, words of prayer, and total dependence:

Oh God. I'm so blessed to have been here in this place, but what now, Lord? Please tell me, what now? I need your help to get through this, Lord. I cannot do it alone. Please, Lord, please give me the strength, the love, and the heart to move forward from here. Please hold me up, Lord. Please give me the hope and show me the way to make it through this next horrible, yet hopeful, part.

As I prayed, God's blessed responses to my heart's cry enfolded me. Passages from the Bible came to me. These verses were clear yet faint, bold yet quiet, overlapping yet discrete:

I will give them one heart, and a new spirit I will put within them. I will remove the heart of stone from their flesh and give them a heart of flesh (Ezekiel 11:19).

We know that for those who love God all things work together for good, for those who are called according to his purpose (Romans 8:28).

Do not be conformed to this world, but be transformed by the renewal of your mind, that by testing you may discern what is the will of God, what is good and acceptable and perfect (Romans 12:2).

For I know that my Redeemer lives, and at the last he will stand upon the earth (Job 19:25).

COMFORTED TO COMFORT

These verses? These words? These truths? These treasures? Amazing! I felt a deep shiver course through my body. It was as though God were giving me an extra-measure—a second and third helping—of his mercy. I took deep solace in each of these rich and redemptive passages.

Then, two contrasting emotions flooded my heart and began to overwhelm me: an inexplicably deep sense of peace and a sickening foreboding. The Scripture passages quietly, yet unequivocally coursed through me, deepening my peace with each breath and remembrance of the Truth. I had soaked in these God-inspired words, promises, declarations, and commands many times before that night, but they lifted my heart and spirit as though I were hearing them for the first time. They felt brand new, yet somehow familiar, like the many pre-dawn mornings I had spent with the Lord in the Bible and with my fellow Christians.

The peace washed over me as did the sickening foreboding of what would happen next as people heard the shocking news of Dad's suicide. How would they respond? Very likely, not well at all. Yet how might God use this tragedy in all sorts of different ways? How might he invite me to become intimately involved in that? How might I witness about the redeeming reality of God's plan, turning sin's tragedy to God's triumph and his people's blessing?

Many times before that night I had seen God fulfill his magnificent promises to use pain redemptively. I had experienced in my own life his "redemptive protocol," had watched him use my *weeping* to open a *window* into my heart and then through it set me on the *way* closer to him.

Even given all that, Dad's decision to take his own life and my experience with him and God this night would become for me a transformational experience of grand proportions! Much would happen as a result, more than I could take in as I knelt there in the garden. God was using even this experience as yet another answer to my many prayers. When suffering or crisis of any kind happened to people God had placed in my sphere of influence I would boldly and lovingly step into the gap for them, providing the hugs, help, and comfort that come from God's love and his truth.

Firmly resting on the rock-solid foundation, being comforted by the counselor in the Holy Spirit, seeing the truths and falsehoods of my heart in a brand-new way... was the perfect set-up for *the way* to move forward from here.

DWELL FOR A TIMELESS MOMENT
EZEKIEL: MARK THE CHANGE OF HEART

The first verses of Ezekiel were offered by God to remind me of *the fact of my conversion*. This was a doubly-powerful verse to give me because of two awesome things: A) it described how my sinful heart of stone was supernaturally removed when I first saw it for what it really was and cried out to God to save me twenty years ago. The *fact of my conversion* was the basis upon which God was preparing me to stand up, turn from my Dad, and humbly yet boldly move into the chaos of the world.

B) Within this specific verse, there are two "before and after verses":

> And when they come there, they will remove from it all its detestable things and all its abominations.
>
> Ezekiel 11:18

> And I will give them one heart, and a new spirit I will put within them. I will remove the heart of stone from their flesh and give them a heart of flesh,
>
> Ezekiel 11:19

> ... that they may walk in my statutes and keep my rules and obey them. And they shall be my people, and I will be their God.
>
> Ezekiel 11:20

A new heart and new spirit occurred within me when I became a Christian twenty years before being with my Dad in the garden on Christmas night. But, in the garden, God reminded me once again, a change of heart is not a one-time event. Being *saved* and being *sanctified* are two different things. And, second to being born-again when first coming to faith in Jesus, a life continuously being transformed more into the likeness of Jesus "over and over, again and again," is a central benefit offered one who will use trials and suffering in the way prescribed by God for *sanctification:* a real, live, you-can-bet-your-transformation-into-holiness-and-Christlikensss "change of heart"!

Just as Jesus said to his Father immediately prior to his resurrection:

> [Jesus speaking to his Father] They [Jesus' disciples / Christians] are not of the world, just as I am not of the world. Sanctify them in the truth; your word is truth. As you sent me into the world, so I have sent them into the world. And for their

sake I consecrate [set apart, dedicate, declare sacred through suffering] myself, that they also may be sanctified in truth.

John 17:16–19—parentheses added

In the garden that night, God reminded me that real change begins supernaturally, and in the heart. Changing a heart of stone into a heart of flesh. I was not *saved* again; but rather "saved from more and more worldliness" and *sanctified for service*.

God was saying, in the first part of these final verses before I had to turn and leave Dad, *"John, do not ever discount what a change of heart only I can impart to you can do—in you, and in the world! Doing so would be as detrimental as denying the change to the universe I had when I spoke it into existence in the beginning. Please have faith in me to re-create a change of heart in you that is promised, real, life-transforming, and set apart—to help change the world with me as we move forward from here."*

"A real change of heart is a vitally important thing, John. In fact, it's at the very center of my redemptive plan. A supernaturally and cathartically (emotional purged) changed heart is what my creative power in this broken world does to use trials to transform my people ... and, in due time, the universe as well. Do not suppress the change; for if you do all of this will be wasted and your heart will be left needlessly hardened, deeply wanting, and further from me, beloved."

PAUL: ALL THINGS WORK TOGETHER FOR GOD ... AND GOOD

Having been reminded of God's plan to continuously strengthen and transform from the inside-out, God then reminded me: *"We know that for those who love God, all things work together for good, for those who are called according to his purpose"* (Romans 8:28).

That's me. That's you if you have placed your faith in Jesus Christ as your Savior *and* Lord, *"All* things work together for good!" God generously reminded me that I was one who, albeit highly imperfectly, loved God and was called according to his purpose. I would experience again and again how God would use this tragedy for his triumph and the blessing of many, many people.

This was such a blessed promise for me as I was faced with turning and leaving my Dad cold and dying in the snow: Dad was safely in God's providence as he always had been. But those of us left behind, new life in other hearts would bloom out of his death! And it was time to turn and see how God would fulfill his promise of redemptive blessings over and over again...

PAUL: TRANSFORMATION OVER CONFORMATION... BEGETS GODLY DISCERNMENT

I knew deep in my heart the world would try to "conform and mold me to its image"—and in this case, how I should respond to my Dad's death: to suicide, death, grief, adjusting, moving on, forgiving, and forgetting.

Not to elevate myself above anyone else's heartfelt response to Dad's tragic death, but I knew instinctively it would be a battle of worldviews that would be akin to several rounds with a spiritual-emotional boxer in the ring each day. I was deeply anxious and fearful to enter the ring, and yet, at the same time, somehow trained and readied by my faith to "fight it out" by representing, in the best way I could, the truth and love of God.

And God knew just what I needed to be reminded of and encouraged about. He was saying, "Stay close to me, John, and be renewed each day so that you will know my will, know what is good and perfect, know what is acceptable and what is not, in response to this terrible trial in your life, be wise, John. Walking with me in wisdom and trust is what we'll do each day. You will hear many well-intended, true, and flat-out-falsehoods along the way. Be continuously transformed by staying close to me; and others who love me. You are mine, not this world's. Your power to help many be conformed to me and into my likeness is rooted in surrendering to my transforming power in your life first. There will be daily, moment-by-moment opportunities for you to be a force of transformation in others by this tragedy and in the time we've spent together here on Christmas night!"

When any heart breaks, there is a choice for change. A choice to move towards the *good* or the *ungood*. I knew I would see many occasions that this would be used for the good of those who love God and have been called according to his purpose as co-redeemers: sent to bring the Good News to others. I also knew it would provide an opportunity for those who do not yet have a relationship with Jesus as their Lord and Savior too. In God's design, *heartbreak* is always a potential for God's *breakthroughs* as well. "So we do not lose heart!" Check out this awesome passage from St. Paul that reflects this truth:

> So we do not lose heart. Though our outer self is wasting away, our inner self is being renewed day by day. For this light momentary affliction is preparing for us an eternal weight of glory beyond all comparison, as we look not to the things that are seen but to the things that are unseen. For the things that are seen are transient, but the things that are unseen are eternal.
>
> 2 Corinthians 4:16–18

JOB: ON THE OTHER SIDE OF SUFFERING ... MY REDEEMER KING REIGNS!

God graciously reminded me: "I created and now sustain this world. I sent my son to be sacrificed for the freedom from the bondage of sin. For no reason other than my independent love for mankind, I chose never to leave or forsake you ... ever! I offer saved sinners a window to see into their hearts. I do this so that one can choose more clearly to be a redeeming force for my love and truth. In suffering, I mercifully offer a change of heart and life which empowers my disciples to not be worldly but rather transformed, co-redeemers with me."

In the last verse, God reminded me: "I am your Redeemer King and you are a co-redeemer, John. My Spirit Counselor, my disciples, and the church will be with you as you have been powerfully present in a wretched yet redeeming time so that you will be more able to help redeem this sad, sickened, and suffering world. You have been redeemed much in this time of heart-shattering pain and woe so that I may be glorified and you might be a more committed servant of me. Yes, you have been 'redeemed to redeem'..."

I STOOD AND TURNED...

Much, much more than I can ever express, these promises, remembrances, and realities enabled me to say goodbye to Dad, to stand up and breathe, and to face the sudden rush of medical and law enforcement personnel. I said to myself and to God: "It's going to be okay. It's going to be really hard, but it's solidly in your hands, and I will get through this with your help. I will miss my Dad so much! But this will be redeemed. I know that, over time, all this will be redeemed in manifold ways, Lord! First in my own heart, and then as I reach out to minister to people whose hearts are crushed by the news. I will reach out to receive ministry and comfort myself when I need it. And I will sit as a friend near open windows of the heart when those around me most need it. I will offer *the way* closer to you, God in Christ, through the Holy Spirit when I am honored enough to be a witness to how tragedy can be transformed into triumph!"

The days and months ahead would be really rough. But God had a plan. His purposes were good and his promises were sure. I could trust completely and utterly in him.

A DOWN PAYMENT ON GOD'S PROMISE

I stood up, shaking and weak. In the next few moments I answered many questions for the police and EMTs. I haggled with the paramedics about where to take Dad. I told Marge I would see her at the ER, and then stepped into a police car. It was warm, blessedly so. I sat there silent and stunned for quite some time.

I don't know how long the silence lasted before I broke it.

Without turning my head, still staring into the flashing lights in the lane, I asked the officer, "Do you have a faith in Jesus Christ?"

Almost without hesitation he answered, "Yes. Yes, I do."

I responded just as quickly, "Awesome." Then, I followed up with a second question, "Are you sure your folks do, too?"

He thought a moment. "I'm pretty sure they do," he said finally, "But I should make sure. Sometimes a person can just assume these things. We sometimes just don't talk about the most important things in life with those we love until it's too late. I'll make sure … " his voice trailed off.

At those words, I released a quiet whimper and shuddered in amazement and tearful joy. I couldn't help myself. Somehow the officer knew my heart's deep hurt. Somehow God was at work. Perhaps the tragedy had opened a window in the officer's heart, a window into some unchallenged assumptions and dark corners, corners that had remained unexplored or even closed to the weeping of others. That thought triggered an incredible rush.

A chill ran up and down my spine. A rush of hope flooded my heart as tears overflowed my eyes and ran down my face. I was overwhelmed at the sudden realization that the redemptive *promise* God had given me was already being fulfilled. New shoots of God's redeeming love had *already* begun to poke through the white, cold snow and the dark ashes of this awful night of the soul. Silently, I thanked God that even if nothing else positive came out of it, one heart, perhaps even more, had potentially changed for time and for eternity.

My Redeemer really does live, and he was alive right now, right in the midst of this mess. A hellish game of "Consequence Dominoes" had begun. But so had the blessed promises of God. As the police car in which I was sitting left the lane and headed toward the hospital, God's peace flooded my heart. The Lord would attend me on the journey of the next moments and months in all sorts of amazing ways. I could count on it.

COULD IT REALLY BE TRUE?

I stared out the window as we drove the twenty-five minutes to the ER Many things flew through my mind and heart during the drive. But three facts quickly rose to top the list.

First, of all the people who had looked up to Dad and loved him, hearing about his suicide. Second, Dad's own pain, his loneliness, his eternal destiny, and the loss of the opportunity God had offered Dad to be more vulnerable and yet more loved than ever before in his time of greatest need. Third, how the story being written this night reflected the entire story of God's redemptive plan. The time in the garden epitomized the story and personalized it as well.

As the police cruiser drove to the hospital, I prayed to God:

Is it possible that a God so vast, so unspeakably wide and deep, so far beyond our wildest imaginings ... Is it possible that a God like that is calling all of humankind back to himself? Calling me personally back to him?

With all that God has done, his deepest desire is that all people know him, trust him, love and serve him. Each the passages from Scripture that have been given to me tonight were given to me before this night, just for this night, and, what's more, carefully planned before "nights" even existed?

God does so love the world, each and every tender and unique heart in it, and he gave his only Son just so that he could be with the brokenhearted ones he loves? Could a God so perfect and powerful be so intimately involved in the hearts of each and every person?

Was all this possible?

I asked myself this question multiple times. Iterations of them encircled my heart and spirit as we glided over the snow-packed road. Suddenly I shuddered ... deep ... and held back a groan as I said to myself, "It's true! It's not just *possible*. It's unequivocally true!" I shook myself out of this dream-like reverie as we neared the hospital.

We pulled up to the ER door, and I took a deep breath. The ambulance crew was moving Dad through another door. Just like that, the next part of the journey began.

FLAT LINE

Once inside the hospital, it didn't take long before a flurry of information began to fly at me and my stepmother Marge. Status reports from nurses. Opinions from the emergency room physicians. Conclusions and suggestions from the staff. The decision about what to do with Dad had landed in my lap, because I was the only blood-relative on the scene. Within a few minutes, it became obvious that the best thing to do was just to let Dad's heart stop on its own. I was told it had already stopped twice in the ambulance on the way to the hospital. Evidently, though there was no medical reason Dad should be alive, God was graciously giving both him and the family and friends who had begun to gather at the hospital some precious last moments to be with Dad, a time to say goodbye.

It took only about thirty quiet and mournful minutes as the family members who were in town gathered and waited. The heart monitor gave irrefutable evidence of Dad's slowly-dimming life. As each beat grew weaker and came more and more slowly, all of us realized the end was near. We stood around the bedside in stunned and exhausted disbelief at what had happened. Then quietly, Dad was gone. The heart monitor buzzer sounded, and all the lines went flat.

Only hours earlier, each of us had kissed Dad goodbye after a typical Christmas family celebration. Now he lay dead in a sterile hospital bed. The words *shock* and *disbelief* barely began to capture the feelings. One by one, the family members wandered back into the small waiting room area. We all thought the same thing: "My God, has this really happened? It's simply unbelievable! Now what?" We sat in a tight little clutch, holding onto each other.

As we struggled to take it all in, my thoughts began slowly to focus on who needed to know and how I would tell them. My two sisters in Seattle, Lynn and Lisa, came first to mind. I had to phone them. I wanted to be close to my sisters as they learned the news, yet at the same time, I did not want to make that call. Not ever.

Lisa's husband, Ron, answered on the first ring. In shaky words, I told Ron what had happened. He dropped the volume of his voice until it became almost a whisper. "Oh God," he said, "Oh, Johnny..."

"I'm so sorry to have to tell you this, Ron," I responded.

"Oh God," he repeated. "I'm so sorry, Johnny. Uh, well, let's see. Oh, God... The kids are in the other room with Lisa. Uh... Let me see what I should do. Let me get Lisa. Uh, I'll take the kids..." He didn't finish his sentence, but simply continued, "Lynn just left our place headed for her home. Please hang on, Johnny. Oh God..."

Lisa came to the phone. "Johnny? How are you? Is everything okay?" Hearing her sweet, voice, I immediately lost the ability to speak in sentences longer than a couple of words.

LISA'S SCREAM ... MANKIND'S SCREAM

"Lisa, Dad killed himself tonight," I stammered through my tears. With that, Lisa released a blood-curdling scream, a scream so forceful that it pushed me against the wall in the waiting room. In pain so deep and intense it threatened to shatter my heart, I pulled the phone away from my ear. As Lisa screamed, my heart melted for her. I felt so helpless and so very far away. Whenever I could, I interjected, "Oh, Lisa. I'm so sorry, Lisa."

Within the next few moments, I slowly disengaged from the situation. I realize this sounds very bizarre. As I pictured my dear sister's beautiful face, now contorted with grief, I could see all of her deep pain, her dark regrets, and the anguish she felt for Dad. But along with that, I could also sense the fearsome darkness of *the scream* itself.

As eerie and improbable as it sounds, the scream took on a life of its own. Like a vehicle sent by hell, it swept me up and carried me, careening back over decades of family life: the tip-toeing and denial, the cocktail hours, my shame as I hid under the steps in childhood, the dinners with grandparents, laughing hysterically at "the old chestnuts"—family jokes told again and again, the many times of laughing and being together as a family, the "unmentionables" no one ever dared bring up, secrets layered upon secrets, the deepest regrets and darkest guilt. All of it run together to form a fast-forward of our lives together.

In the garden with Dad, the window of my heart had been flung wide open. Now, Lisa's scream, her free fall, and everything it invoked had torn the window off its hinges.

Over and over I repeated Lisa's name. I did my best to console her, to tame the scream. But all my efforts proved pitiable and insignificant. She had to reach the bottom of her freefall on her own. I prayed that God would be with her, just as he had been with me.

Eventually, Lisa was able to calm herself. We then took the next baby step together, strategizing about how to tell our sister Lynn and talking about how to console all the grandchildren. We decided that Lisa, Ron, and their girls would drive the thirty minutes to Lynn's home so that she would not be alone when she heard the news. Once more my heart sank as I imagined what it would be like. How I wished we all could have been together. Lisa and I arranged to talk after her family had spoken to Lynn. "We'll take it a step at a time," we both agreed.

The next step for me would be filled with an amazing series of miracles that God, once again, placed into my life.

CHAPTER FOUR

THE FOUR MIRACULOUS MESSENGERS FROM GOD

"I almost wish … no I don't, though," said Jill.

"What were you going to say?" said Eustace.

"I was going to say I wished we'd never come. But I don't, I don't, I don't. Even if we are killed, I'd rather be killed fighting for Narnia than grow old and stupid at home and perhaps go about in a bath chair and then die in the end just the same."

C.S. Lewis, *The Last Battle*[7]

We've come a long way on a miraculous yet arduous journey. Let's press on …

Soren Kierkegaard once observed, "What is the most personal is the most universal." This chapter recounts four personal encounters—encounters I see as being miraculous. In each, a messenger from God shared with me truths that have personal and universal application. Through each encounter, God used truth and suffering to create tremendous opportunities for knowing, sowing, and growing forward! God used these messengers to help me overcome the temptation to close the window of my heart too soon. Through them, he helped me see the need to fully capture the lessons he had offered me by embracing the *weeping*, the *window*, and the *way*.

MESSENGER 1—THE MESSENGER OF TRUE TRUTH

On the Sunday after Dad's suicide, my family had our first opportunity to attend worship at our church home, Greentree Community Church. I so greatly looked forward to it. Still, I also found myself frightened at the prospect of being with people, both those who did know what had happened, as well as those who didn't. I had become attached to this faith community at a heart level. Yet, as my heart was so tender, I didn't know how I would respond emotionally to the worship or the preaching and teaching of God's Word. I didn't know what it would be like simply to be in that place.

My family and I made our way to "our row" near the front. I stepped in and then glanced down the row. There, at the opposite end, stood a close friend, Laurie Davis. You need to know that for months running on into years, Laurie waged war with a deadly form of cancer. Despite the medical predictions that she would lose this battle, despite the opinions of medical professionals that she should have died long ago, Laurie had struggled on—still victorious, still alive. She had seen God's mercy at work deep within her own heart and spirit. Laurie had suffered much. Wept much. Trusted much. And walked in The Way a great distance. At the most basic level, Laurie "knew it was true," the Bible, the whole of the Gospel claim.

Laurie moved toward me, and as we stepped within a foot of hugging one another, we both said the exact same thing to each other at the exact same time: "It's True!"

That's it. Just like that. Two words. Unrehearsed and unprompted, the words came as overflow from the cup of sanctified suffering. The Holy Spirit had been at work in our common experience. The message—so compact, yet bursting with meaning and assurance. We said no more. We didn't need to. God gives the triumph of the truth in times of trial!

"It's True!"

Through Laurie God delivered that message at the perfect point in time! In only two simple words, God had given me the gift of knowing in a new and even deeper way, *It's True!* The personhood of the Triune God, his redeeming purpose and plan from beginning to end, all of it is absolutely true. I could rely on it, both at the moment and eternally

God used his messenger to reassure me, fill me, and set me solidly on the next part of my journey. God also used it to open wide many issues for me. Here is a handful:

- *The Church:* The first messenger came to me in my church. God commissioned his church as the repository of the Truth. The church stewards the Truth and administers it. By definition, the church is responsible for battling Christ's enemy—the Deceiver. Those who want to avoid wasting their suffering need to remember that the message of the church, Christ's community, is true. God wants to use that message in the lives of all who suffer.

- *The Community of the Saints:* Laurie had allowed God to use her suffering to refine and purify the core truths held deep in her heart. Guided by the Word, she had sifted out the falsehoods, and could in unshakable faith utter those two words of quiet affirmation.

- *The Importance of Truth to the Heart:* By allowing the Truth to reshape our hearts, we allow the Holy Spirit to work in us. Our words and deeds become more fully and vitally aligned with those of Jesus. In suffering rightly redeemed, we become more like the Redeemer.

- *The Deadliness of the World's Comfort:* On the other side of the coin, we can choose to avoid letting God transform our hearts. We can welcome the world's false remedies, and in them find our pain begin to deaden. But that deadening is the sensation of our hearts slowly hardening and dying. This is a deadly formula for guaranteeing we never come out of the freefall of following falsehoods.

May the truth that is in Jesus eliminate in me all that is dark; establish in me all that is wavering; comfort in me all that is wretched; accomplish in me all that is of thy goodness; and glorify in me the name of Jesus. I pass through a veil of tears ... but bless Thee for the opening gate of glory at its end.

Puritan Prayer, Excerpted from *Truth in Jesus*

THE TRUE TRUTH—MAKING IT REAL FOR ME

Consider questions like these. Please try and be as specific as you can.

- Where do I come from?

- Where am I going?

- Why?

- Death is inevitable. In the face of death, what brings me peace?

- What causes me anxiety?

- What is the meaning of my life? Of my death?

- Have I told anyone else about what my Truths consist of? Why or why not?

- For what Truths would I die?

- How might my Truths tie into a vision, purpose, mission, or core values for my life?

- Ask yourself, "Who among my family members, friends, co-workers, neighbors, and acquaintances needs to hear me share my Truths? What are the top things in my life that tend to distract me or dissuade me from sharing it?"

- Do I need to repent in any way for not pursuing or suppressing God or my Truths?

MESSENGER 2—THE MESSENGER
OF MIRACULOUS MERCY

Within the next week, our family decided to go skiing at a local ski area. I had just mounted the ski lift chair when my cell phone rang. It was my dear friend and brother in Christ, John Russell, calling from Hawaii. "Doz," John said, "I just got your message about your dad. I'm so sorry."

I thanked him for his support and for getting back to me so quickly. Then, my voice cracking, I continued, "You know something, John, the worst part of this whole thing is the idea that Dad likely died without knowing Jesus as his Savior and Lord, without being saved. It's just so painful to think about him all alone, lost, and in such a dark place."

"Well, Doz," John responded in his own off-handed way, "all I can tell you is thank God that he has more mercy than we do, eh?"

"Uh ... ," I paused, then stuttered. "Yeah, John. Yes. Thank God for that." Then came a few moments of silence. Finally, I said, "You know, John, you're so right. How in the hell would I know? God *is* merciful, awesomely merciful. I just don't know how he might have been working in Dad's life and heart."

As the call ended, I sat quietly, stunned by John's words. Wow! Some might dismiss his message as an unimportant or pietistic quip. But I had not considered my fears about Dad's eternal destiny in light of how wide and deep God's mercy really is. John's reminder touched my heart and spirit in a powerful way. I had presumed Dad's lack of faith, and therefore his hellish destiny in the afterlife. But, I had left no room for God's mercy on Dad's soul. I had not considered the many things that may have been going on between God and Dad on that very night—just as they had been going on between God and me!

Was it probable that someone who had committed suicide—self-murder—could be saved? That in the Judgment, God could count such a person as among the faithful followers of Jesus

Christ? I didn't think so. But I didn't know the whole story.[8] I did know that God had used Dad's death as a catalyst to rend my heart. I did know that I had been radically changed in certain ways. I did know I was wiser about God and about life, and that I'm still growing in wisdom. And I do know that what is most important about Christian growth is not so much *wisdom* as an end in itself, but rather the careful *stewardship* of wisdom in relationships. But now God was teaching me something new, deeper about himself.

I sat staring into the sky for many moments. Thinking back, I now know my friend John's words changed me forever. That brief, God-ordained conversation began an amazing journey for me, a journey of exploration focused on what might *really* have been going on during my time with God on Christmas night. I began to ask myself these questions:

- What things had I missed that night?

- How might the exchange of Bible passages between God and me have involved my dad?

- If I could see the extent of God's mercy, and comprehend its width and depth, would I even be able to stand in its presence?

- Could God have been displaying his incredible mercy toward my dad that night, even while I dismissed it as improbable?

Over time it has become more obvious to me that God always shows more mercy than meets the eye as he works in our lives. Through John Russell, I received a heart-enlarging gift that was huge. That message of the magnitude of God's mercy has helped to drive away many of my fool-hearty notions about when, whether, and how God may choose to show mercy to us. As Job, the Bible's consummate sufferer wrote, *"God thunders wondrously with his voice; He does great things that we cannot comprehend"* (Job 37:5).

GOD'S MERCY—MAKING IT REAL FOR ME

Think about God's mercy and the limitations you may have put on it in the past. To guide your thoughts, answer these questions:

- How would you best describe what God's *mercy* means to you?

  _____

  _____

  _____

  _____

  _____

- What do you consider God's ultimate display of mercy? What is your response to that display?

  _____

  _____

  _____

  _____

- What does God's mercy say about *him*, especially as you compare the Christian faith with other world religions which are based on a perfect performance to merit God's favor?

  _____

  _____

  _____

  _____

  _____

- What difference do you see between the *mercy* and the *grace* of God? (Example: "mercy" is defined by God's withholding his justifiable and immediate destruction of everything evil; "grace" is defined as not only not destroying all things impure or unholy—like you and me—but blessing those he is pleased to bless with an abundant life.)

  _____

  _____

  _____

  _____

  _____

- In what ways has God most clearly displayed his mercy, first in your own life, then in the lives of others? (Examples might be how God answered my prayers for me and my Dad as I witnessed them on Christmas night; how he offered me salvation and purpose even after all the destruction I had caused in my life and others; how he promised to use the most horrific suffering *that man initiated at the fall* to bring about our joy, wisdom, and peace; or how God is withholding his hand of justifiable judgment on a nation like ours which has abandoned him in so many ways.)

  _____

  _____

  _____

  _____

  _____

JOHN O. DOZIER, JR.

- In what specific ways have you shared the message of God's mercy with the people in your life?

  _____

  _____

  _____

  _____

- What do the words, "God's mercy is new every morning" (Lamentations 3:22–24) mean to you?

  _____

  _____

  _____

  _____

- Suppose you could go back in your life and do one or two key things with an extra added measure of mercy. What differences would you hope to create? What is keeping you from implementing those differences now—*even today* (Psalm 95:7–8)?

  _____

  _____

  _____

  _____

MESSENGER 3—THE MESSENGER OF THE SUPERNATURAL REALM

About two months later, the third messenger arrived. I was telling the story of Dad's suicide to Charlie Fay, who I had never met before that time. After hearing it, Charlie said to me, "Your story reminds me of something miraculous that happened to me. Several years ago someone asked me to pray with a lady I didn't know. She was a friend of a friend of mine. She was in a coma, John. I prayed beside her bed for some time. I ended my prayer asking that God would lead her to repent of her sins and believe in her heart that Jesus Christ was her Lord and Savior. I asked that God would forgive her and that Jesus would live in her heart forever."

Charlie continued, "Well, incredibly enough, three months later my friend told me that the lady had come out of her coma. Her physical recovery was a miracle, in and of itself. But as she emerged from the coma, practically the first thing she did was to announce that she had become a Christian and that Christ was her Savior and Lord. Wow! How remarkable was that? Praise be to God!" Charlie said, shaking his head as though he still hadn't gotten over it.

Again, I sat completely silent, stunned by Charlie's story. Why had God put *this* person into my life at this particular time? Why had he shared this particular story with me? What was God trying to tell me? I knew beyond doubt that not even the smallest thing happens without God's providential knowledge and permission. But what work might he do in hearts and spirits? Could God work "behind the scenes," so to speak? The answer seems obvious. God can do *anything* that will bring glory to himself and blessing to his people.

Had my own self-centeredness and ego inserted itself into the explanation? Could I instead have been merely a bystander in the garden? Could I have been eavesdropping on a holy conversation between my dad and the Holy Spirit? Could the Spirit have brought my dad to faith that very night—and then taken him into Jesus' presence? Could this unfathomably bitter story have been so incredibly sweet at the same time?

I won't know for sure until we all reach the other side, until all believers gather around the throne of our Savior in heaven. But as I thought about the three messengers and their words thus far, my perspective began to radically change, to grow, to expand my heart until it nearly exploded. Their words made an epiphany-like, scales-falling-off-the-eyes difference in my relationship with God. As I began to consider how merciful God truly is, and how unnecessarily I had been limiting his ability to work in supernatural ways, I saw more and more clearly that the *least* likely answer was *most* likely true!

As a tsunami of questions, answers, and emotions swept over me, I wept there with Charlie. This was an entirely new and stunning dimension of what God might have been doing *before, during,* and *after* the miraculous Christmas night in the garden with my dad. The pieces of the puzzle were coming together in a strange, yet magnificently beautiful and God-sized ways.

Since my conversation with Charlie, I have prayed for people who are physically unconscious. On a particular occasion, I prayed with a young lady who had attempted suicide. After a few days in a coma, her brain waves went flat. Prayers spoken at her bedside were answered by God as this beautiful girl's brain waves came back to life! The Intensive Care chart read, in so many words, "Brought back to life by a miracle." Today, this very same young lady has a relationship with Jesus and counsels women on a suicide hotline. God be praised!

I absolutely believe a supernatural God can and does work on the heart and spirit, despite the limitations on their natural senses. God's mercy extends much further than our hardened hearts or limited sense and sensibilities are willing to believe. God will pursue us until the end.

GOD'S SUPERNATURAL POWER—
MAKING IT REAL FOR ME

Think about any limitations you may have put on God's power in the past. Use these questions help guide your thoughts:

- What is the first thing that comes to your mind when you hear the word "supernatural"? Is it being above or beyond what is observable to the naked eye? Characteristic of, or attributed to a deity? Ghosts, goblins, or other un-human beings?

_____

_____

_____

_____

- What do you believe about the realms of "the supernatural"? What about that reality shapes your beliefs?

_____

_____

_____

_____

- Are there ways in which your understanding of science has impacted your ideas concerning the supernatural?

_____

_____

_____

_____

- What clear evidence have you seen that God does sometimes work in supernatural ways?

- Do you sometimes attribute events to "coincidence"? Could these instead be acts of God? Or "Godcidences"? How do you know?

- In the big picture, do these distinctions matter? Is it worth the time it takes to dig any deeper into your own beliefs concerning these things? Why or why not?

MESSENGER 4—THE MESSENGER
OF PRAYER AND TRUST

The fourth message came from another stranger, Ned Durham. Our first conversation had gone on for only ten minutes before we began to share our spiritual journeys. As we shared, we discovered that we had a lot of things in common.

As I talked about God bringing me back to St. Louis after many years away, the details of my dad's suicide began to unfold. My point was to illustrate how, as we look back on things, we can so often "connect the dots," seeing God's obvious involvement in our circumstances.

After Ned had heard my story, he said, "John, in my own life, I have seen over and over again my need to trust the promises God has connected specifically to prayer in Scripture. Among other things, I've seen that God takes special note of our prayers for friends and family members. In Romans, for instance, Paul talks about his prayers for his loved ones, people God had placed upon his broken and grieving, yet faithful heart:

> I am telling the truth in Christ; I am not lying, my conscience bearing me witness in the Holy Spirit, that I have great sorrow and unceasing grief in my heart. For I could wish that I myself were accursed, separated from Christ for the sake of my brethren, my kinsmen according to the flesh ... Brethren, my heart's desire and my prayer to God for them is for their salvation.
>
> Romans 9:1–3; 10:1

"So many times," Ned continued, "I need to be reminded that God hears and answers our prayers. Sometimes we see the effects, and sometimes we don't. But either way, we trust the living God, the God of the Bible. Over the years, as I've grown older and more mature in the faith, I've begun to trust more and more that God hears me and that he will take care of my requests in his own time and in his own way. But he *will* take

97

care of them, and I can fully trust in that! I've seen this trust result in peace. I don't need to be anxious. I don't need to worry that God has somehow fallen asleep at the wheel. Every once in a while, he will answer my prayers in immediate, obvious, and awesome ways. It seems to me when he does that, he just wants to affirm and encourage my often very weak faith. Something will happen that shows me he's listening and working, glorifying himself as he answers my prayers. I believe you should trust that, too."

He paused, then asked, "You had prayed for your dad in the years before his suicide, hadn't you, John? Prayed for his salvation, I mean?"

"Yes, of course, Ned. Many times. In fact, all the time for all my family ... *unceasingly,* as Paul said," I replied. I knew many Bible verses about prayer and God's promises to answer our prayers. I had learned many passages of Scripture—some of them by heart. Yet I had not applied many of these truths to my life, to my spirit. I asked Ned somewhat facetiously and feeling sort of ashamed by the weakness of my faith, "Ned, do you mean that all those passages in the Bible about prayer and God's promises to hear and answer are true? You mean I can trust them?" The meagerness of faith about such a fundamental issue as prayer embarrassed me, yet there it lay, in the clear light of day.

COULD IT BE TRUE?

Once more, questions began to cascade through my mind. Another of the four "miraculous messengers" was telling me something I needed to know about the night dad had died.

Could it be true? Had God taken me by the hand and brought me into the garden on that blessed Christmas night just so I could be there to see my own father's conversion? Just so that I would realize in it God's answer to two decades of my prayers for his salvation? Just so I could stand astonished at God's incredibly vast mercies and miraculous reach into the hearts of those who cry out to him? Once again, the dots were being connected right before my eyes. I recalled the intensity of the feeling I had upon first hearing of Dad's suicide on Christmas night and how urgently I needed to be right at his side. I felt as if my heart might explode.

Right there at the lunch table with my new friend, Ned, I began to weep. I shook my head as if trying to make sure I wasn't dreaming. Was I attributing too much miraculous power and too deep a desire for intimacy to God? What silliness! Obviously, the Holy Spirit wanted to use this conversation in a significant way. He intended to expand and deepen my heartfelt beliefs about who God is and who I am in relation to him.

I am quite sure that when the time comes for me to stand before God face-to-face, I will be speechless as I see how little faith I've really had. I felt myself reeling yet again. How complete! How perfect! How incredibly well-planned these events had been. They were almost like ... providence!

There at the lunch table, I wept. I wept in wonder at the ways in which God so perfectly oversees every detail of this vast universe, while also carefully guiding every detail of my own existence. And the lives of each of his people who, even in broken and highly imperfect ways, attempt to live in ways that honor him.

> God honored the Biblical men's prayers for the souls of the lost; He'll honor yours too. Whether friend or foe; whether moral or immoral; whether you know them or not—pray for the lost. For those God brings your way, open your mouth in love and compassion to tell them the truth. Warn them of God's judgment for their personal offenses against his holiness, but then tell them the good news. There is salvation in Jesus Christ from God's eternal wrath, if they will only repent and believe. Once you've told them the truth, keep praying for them and trust God for the results. You will rejoice as you see God use you in his plan to save people from their sins and grant them new life in his Son.
>
> John McArthur, "Alone with God"[9]

PRAYER AND TRUST—MAKING IT REAL FOR ME

Think about your prayer life and how God might want to challenge, then renovate it. To guide your thoughts, answer these questions:

- How do you define *prayer?* Is it generally a last-ditch effort to change something you think needs changing? Is it a continuous state of the heart which the Bible calls "unceasing prayer" (Luke 18:1; Romans 12:12; 1 Thessalonians 5:17)? Or perhaps something in between?

  _____

  _____

  _____

  _____

- In prayer, do you sometimes try to conjure up a Divine Genie to help you accomplish the *agenda* you have envisioned for your life? And then get agitated when "the genie" disappoints you and your visions of how life is supposed to be?

  _____

  _____

  _____

  _____

- How was prayer modeled in the home in which you grew up?

  _____

  _____

_____

_____

_____

- Would "The Lord's Prayer" ("Our Father whom art in heaven...") possibly come to mind as a prayer that's more *rote* than *real* for you? How might you make it real for your life?

_____

_____

_____

_____

- Do you believe prayer changes God? Does it change you? Or both?

_____

_____

_____

_____

- Scripture seems to create four basic categories of prayer for us—*adoration, confession, thanksgiving,* and *supplication* (making requests). Which of these comes easiest for you? Which is hardest? Do you regularly engage in all four? Do you accent one more than the others?

_____

_____

_____

_____

- What answers to your prayers have you seen?

  _____

  _____

  _____

  _____

  _____

- What motivates your prayers? Is it answers you have experienced, God's command, or a desire to honor and please him?

  _____

  _____

  _____

  _____

- Where do you believe you stand on the spectrum between these two extremes:

  - "I have greatly underestimated and under-utilized prayer and the powerful promises God has connected to it."

  - "I have greatly overestimated and over-utilized prayer and the powerful promises God has connected to it. (By praying much, and yet possibly maintaining a distance from the difficult relationships I pray about.)"

  _____

  _____

  _____

  _____

WHAT'S MOST PERSONAL...
IS MOST UNIVERSAL

After my dad's suicide, God blessed me by sending four distinct messages through four distinct messengers. But he did not intend these messengers solely for me. I hope their messages have blessed you also. I pray that anyone who is, by God's grace, even remotely interested in cultivating a heart that is soft, repentant, wise, and Christ-like will hear and heed the messages the Holy Spirit has begun to teach me:

- *It's True!* The Bible is God's Truth. Truth is a feast for the heart. We need to know the smallest details of Truth. Then, once we know it, we need to model it for others. We have to establish our own God-given realities of what's True because we have uniquely true stories and transformations of how God has led us to them! Sin exchanges God's glory for falsehoods; suffering offers you the chance to reverse the curse by recognizing and exchanging falsehoods for the Truth.

- *God's Mercy Is (Immeasurably) Wide and Deep.* The blessing of God's mercy will always be in direct proportion to our awareness of sin in the world, and the sin in our own lives. We need to consider everything God has taught us about his grace and mercy, and meditate on the impact these blessings have had on our lives. In whatever form you believe in God's mercy, please be open to its width and breadth as you seek each day to know and live it more!

- *The Realm of the Supernatural.* Our faith tends to hold tightly to what can be seen, felt, heard, or pragmatically experienced. These things are only a tiny sliver of the reality God has created. We need to avoid limiting God to our secular and materialistic ways of thinking. As we have seen, God can influence things mightily even when WE think all is lost. *Never, ever give up on God's supernatural ability to change the course of things!*

- *Prayer and Trust in God's Promise.* It's quite likely, especially in the Westernized church, that prayer is one of the most under-valued gifts God has given. This ties in closely to the point above, because we can't always "see" the many outcomes of our prayers. So, we simply don't use prayer very much. But God invites us to bring all our needs, thanksgiving, and praise to him. He promises to hear and to help us. We need to trust those promises and act on them. *Prayer changes things, beginning with our own hearts!*

HEART APPLICATION: CHOOSING BETTER OVER BITTER!

As a reminder, *The Weeping, the Window, and the Way* is about the change in heart God the Father, God the Son, and God the Holy Spirit can bring about as we embrace his protocol for redeeming inevitable suffering. Part Two of the journey now begins. It's all about applying what we have examined thus far to our hearts, spirits, and faith walks in concrete, personal, yet universal ways. Heart Application will free us to be made *better* by our trials, and not *bitter*.

Remember, if we choose to deny or delay this challenging part of the journey, we have made the choice for living the bitter, angry, and resentful life; the life fraught with the challenges of a hardened heart; the way of incessant *repressing*, and not much *expressing*, the love and truth of God within us.

Please have patience and empower this process to have the greatest impact on your heart and faith by including some form of Christian community along this arduous yet extremely rewarding journey—for time and eternity.

"And I will give them one heart, and a new spirit I will put within them. I will remove the heart of stone from their flesh and give them a heart of flesh, that they may walk in my statutes and keep my rules and obey them. And they shall be my people, and I will be their God" (Ezekiel 11:19).

A REMINDER OF THE HEART
APPLICATION JOURNEY AHEAD

REMEMBER. RECONCILE!
RECOIL?

Chapters Five, Six, and Seven of *The Weeping, the Window, and the Way* remind us of God's repeated and urgent invitation to remember "... that in all things God works for the good of those who love him, who have been called according to his purpose." (Romans 8:28—NIV).

We humans are a forgetful lot, tending to grow too attached to the things of this world. We become too enamored with our own selfish agendas and continually fall prey to Satan's wiles. To circumvent the remnant of sin within us, the Holy Spirit gathers his people around the process of *remembering* the foundations of our faith as he revitalizes our faith and continues his transforming work in our hearts.

When we as individuals remember, it opens the opportunity for *"re-membering in community"*. We "re-member" by coming together in a fresh way as the people of God, his community of faith, encouraging one another toward deeper commitment to God, and his Church.

In these chapters, I invite you to join me in remembering the distinctions the Bible draws between the human heart and the human spirit, as well as how they work together to *reconcile* and revitalize the human will.

Recoiling has to do with the vitally important answer to the question, "Why is it so hard to embrace the real God of the Bible and his desire to transform our hearts, spirit and lives, even—and especially—through suffering?"

CHAPTER FIVE

REMEMBERING: THE HEART OF THE BIBLE

No secrets of the heart and mind remained hidden when Jonathan Edwards called for self-scrutiny... This meant the relentless need to distinguish between the true and false affections; between those affections having to do with a redeemed heart, and those darkened by sin. To clarify these distinctions was Edwards' purpose in his life and in seeing the Great Awakening come to pass.

Harold Simonson[10]

As the Introduction suggests, God was at work in my heart and spirit on that life-changing Christmas night as I knelt in the snow beside my dad. But before I describe in detail the miraculous occurrence and offerings of truth of my time in the garden on that night, I must place all of the transformations of my heart and spirit into their proper context. Come back to the beginning, as I lay the best foundation possible for fully seeing all that God has to offer in his miraculous and merciful interventions in our lives and hearts.

HEART STORY

"In the beginning..." (Genesis 1:1), God spoke creation into existence. He culminated his work by creating man:

> Then God said, "Let us make man in our image, after our likeness. And let them have dominion over the fish of the sea and over the birds of the heavens and over the livestock and

over all the earth and over every creeping thing that creeps on the earth." So God created man in his own image, in the image of God he created him; male and female he created them.

Genesis 1:26–27

Then the LORD God formed the man of dust from the ground and breathed into his nostrils the breath of life, and the man became a living creature.

Genesis 2:7

In the beginning, Adam's heart bore the image of God's heart and the Garden of Eden's as well.

Even though there is no explicit Biblical evidence for my musings, I have long imagined God reaching down into the clay and forming Adam. He breathed life into his creation's nostrils, and with great delight, noticed Adam's heart, instantly animated, begin to beat. I imagine Adam's beautiful heart as the dominant feature of God's creative work, which initiated the creation of mankind. God made Adam's heart in his own image, albeit a "spirit image" (Genesis 5:1). Then I imagine the Triune God smiling and with deep satisfaction, celebrating with joy the "culmination and accumulation" of his now completed work: the culmination in the form of Adam and the accumulation in the amassing of all of the previous days' work. All taken together, this is something akin to the crescendo in God's marvelous creative symphony—the joy of this creative work within the Godhead:

> God saw everything that he had made, and behold, *it was very good.* And there was evening and there was morning, the sixth day.
>
> Genesis 1:37—emphasis mine

For me, the heart of Adam, as yet unblemished by sin, surpasses in beauty any of the amazing array of wonders God had spoken into existence *before* Adam's creation. When God had finished creating all these other things, he pronounced his creation "good;" after he formed and animated Adam, God declared his creation "*very* good." The emphasis in the Hebrew is intentional: God the Father, Son, and Holy Spirit, could not have been more pleased!

A MOST DREADFUL CHANGE OF HEART

Adam's heart, though finite, nevertheless mirrored the unblemished ecosystem of the infinite Creator's own heart, mirrored it in goodness, truth, wisdom, justice, holiness, mercy, patience, compassion, righteousness, and sacrificial love. Adam shared—though in a finite, limited way—God's own limitless beauty, his creativity, and his delight in him. Such was the heart of Adam in the beginning.

Adam's heart was perfectly created by God's love and truth. But, within the context of the definition of love, Adam was given a *choice* to love and obey God, or not. Adam chose poorly. Sin entered into Adam's heart, and the hearts of all of mankind ever since (Genesis 3; Psalm 51:5).

Our planet lives under the shroud that Adam's sin drew over humankind. Even Sunday school children know the story of Adam's rebellion and exile from Eden, but I invite you to look with me in a fresh way at the account, considering the "change of heart" that resulted from the first sin:

> The LORD God took the man and put him in the garden of Eden to work it and keep it. And the LORD God commanded the man, saying, "You may surely eat of every tree of the garden, but of the tree of the knowledge of good and evil you shall not eat, for in the day that you eat of it you shall surely die."
>
> Genesis 2:15–17

> So when the woman saw that the tree was good for food, and that it was a delight to the eyes, and that the tree was to be desired to make one wise, she took of its fruit and ate, and she also gave some to her husband who was with her, and he ate. Then the eyes of both were opened, and they knew that they were naked. And they sewed fig leaves together and made themselves loincloths.
>
> Genesis 3:6–7

Adam's heart, the glorious culmination of God's creative act, changed immediately. A moment earlier, it had mirrored God's own character and many of his most wonderful attributes, but now it was filled with self-trust and idolatry, shame, and fear. Gone were Eden's sweetest smells, its most glorious light, its freshest streams, and most beautiful glades. Gone was the shameless nakedness, and the joy of intimacy with God. Gone was the ability to worship God perfectly, freely, and within the realms of his own majestic love and truth.

The heart that turned from God died (Genesis 2:17), and Adam and Eve began the decline toward death in every realm, incrementally turning into a hardened and decaying version of the clay from which God had formed them. Their hearts, now scarred and misshapen, no longer reflected the peace and joy the Creator had intended. Adam's heart moved from being "sacred-centered" to being self-centered, and we have all inherited that same hardness and damnable decay:

> The LORD saw that the wickedness of man was great in the earth, and that every intention of the thoughts of his heart was only evil continually.
>
> Genesis 6:5

> The heart is deceitful above all things, and desperately sick; who can understand it?
>
> Jeremiah 17:9

Scripture paints a bleak picture of the heart as:

- Bent, on suppressing the truth (Romans 1:18–32; Ephesians 4:19; 2 Peter 2:14; 2 Thessalonians 2:11)

- Idolatrous, worshiping lesser gods (Leviticus 26:30; Deuteronomy 30:17; Exodus 20:1–7; Psalm 24:12; Ezekiel 11:21; Luke 16:15; 2 Thessalonians 3:5)

- Uncircumcised (Jeremiah 9:26; Ezekiel 44:7; compare Acts 7:51)

- Hardened (Exodus 4:21)

- Wicked (Proverbs 26:23)

- Perverse (Proverbs 11:20)

- Godless (Job 36:13), and

- "Split Spiritual Personality" (Romans 7:15–20).[11]

The Westminster Confession so clearly and completely expresses the results of sin, particularly as it relates to human beings:

> By this in they [Adam and Eve] fell from their original righteousness and communion with God, and so became dead in sin, and wholly defiled in all the parts and faculties of soul and body. They, being the root of all mankind, the guilt of this sin was imputed, and the same death in sin, and corrupted nature, conveyed to all their posterity [all human beings] descending from them by ordinary generation. From this original corruption, whereby we are utterly indisposed, disabled, and made opposite to all good, and wholly inclined to all evil, do precede all actual transgressions.
>
> *The Westminster Confession*, Article 6:1–4

We are sinners not because we sin, but rather we sin because we are sinners. And therefore, as King David bemoans his state, "surely I was sinful at birth, sinful from the time my mother conceived me" (Psalm 51:5).

Adam's heart, and all of mankind's inherited heart since then, was horribly marred and selfishly compartmentalized by the choice of being God—rather than allowing God to be God.

Foreign or repugnant as it may seem to us, ever since the Fall all human beings have had to "fashion fig leaves" to cover our shame, to whitewash over the enmity we carry in our hearts toward the Creator and Sustainer, who with such grace and love breathed life into our being.

But once we have removed God as the centerpiece of our heart's origin, duty, and desire, lesser gods (idols) of all sorts rush into the vacuum created by the void. Idols destroy the heart. *"Therefore, my beloved, flee from idolatry"* (1 Corinthians 10:14; see also Exodus 20:1–7).

117

THE HEART AND ITS "PRECIOUS"

In J.R.R. Tolkien's masterful trilogy, *The Lord of the Rings*, the once-Hobbit Sméagol, accidentally finds the One Ring belonging to the Dark Lord Sauron. He takes it for his own, commits murder to keep it, and rapidly transforms into a monstrous version of himself—Gollum. Rejected by his community and his family, he follows a path up into the Misty Mountains and disappears into a cave, taking the One Ring with him.

The ring has the potential to make Gollum god-like in knowledge and control, and he spends 500 years underground consumed by thoughts of it. Helplessly isolated with his heart torn in pieces by his choices, Gollum flees further and further into the heart of darkness, away from anyone who would scheme to steal the ring, which he calls his "Precious." Again and again he repeats the mantra *"My Preccciousss ... "* He is helplessly held in bondage by his idolatrous fascination with power and control and tortured by an internal tug-of-war.

Tolkien saw the truth clearly: Idols will incrementally and utterly destroy human hearts. Gollum's "Precious" took up residence in a place meant only for God's residence and rule. It demanded as much as God did, but without bestowing any of God's mercy, forgiveness, or the joyous warmth a living relationship with him brings. Yet, despite the anguish they cause, the allure of pride, the mystery of power, and the illusion of control tugs at *every* human heart due to the inheritance of Adam's choice to turn *his* heart away from God.

As a result, our "split personality," our isolation and pain, lurk just below the veneer of everyone's behavior. For example, when people are asked how are they doing, most quickly respond with a simple "fine" or "really busy." Much of the time, however, this response masks the truth and silences a desperate voice inside that is really crying: "Help! My heart is breaking about something today, but I can't let it show. I'm too prideful, ashamed, wounded, alienated, or fearful of my emotions to let you know." No one is immune. To one degree or the other, all humanity shares the impossible task of living in two worlds! Impossible, that is, without the One who can take a schizophrenic heart and make it brand new: *"Therefore, if anyone is in Christ, he is a new creation. The old has passed away; behold, the new has come" (2 Corinthians 5:17).*

When weeping forces us to our knees by means of the Holy Spirit's work in us, it simultaneously holds out a mirror in which we can gain perspective on the true state of our hearts. During these times we have an opportunity to see into the window of our hearts and catch a glimpse of false gods we have held "Precious." Few of us will linger there long enough to scrutinize our heart's love affair with lesser gods. We choose instead to believe the lie: "What you don't know can't hurt you." In fact, though, what we don't know about our hearts can indeed hurt us.

GETTING TO THE HEART OF THE HEART

Scripture calls King David "a man after God's own heart" (1 Samuel 13:13–14), though he faced the same temptations you and I face each day. When confronted with his most grievous sin of adultery, he dropped to his knees and confessed, *"Against you [God], you only, have I sinned and done what is evil in your sight ... " (Psalm 51:4).* David's weeping and penitential prayer serves as a powerful example for us. He recognized the internal cause of his external sins, the "sin beneath the sins", that had dethroned God and had made adultery and murder first possible, then attractive, actionable, and finally consummated.

The word "heart" and its various synonyms show up in the Bible over 1,500 times. Does that tell you something about the high priority God places on your heart? Does it compel you to consider how high a priority you place on the true nature and condition of your own heart? When I first came to realize and understand this emphasis in Scripture and began to discern the distinction between the heart and the spirit, it radically transformed my perspective. How important it is that we give our hearts the kind of focused attention God gives them, the kind of scrutiny Jonathan Edwards recommended in the Harold Simonson quote above. (Jonathan Edwards (1703–1758), American puritan theologian and philosopher.)

The heart is the seat of the entire self. It includes our core commitments and our idealized image of how the world should be. What is your heart's default mode? What do you think about when you are experiencing no pressure to think about anything else? What sorts of ideas, hopes, and ambitions most regularly compete for ascendancy in your heart? What do you most hope to accomplish in life? For what would you practically die to achieve? Pause for a moment right now. Before you go on, think it through. In your heart of hearts, on what do you focus?

Though the actual words may vary, most answers may sound strikingly similar to yours. Again, as Soren Kierkegaard observed, in the realms of the heart, "What is most personal is most universal." The sweetest fruits of God's love and truth for us as well as our darkest secrets and marks of the fall... all humankind shares in this journey together.

When God is *not* seated squarely in the center of our hearts, then, just like a black hole in outer space, *all else besides God* will rush into the vacuum. Nature abhors a vacuum. Chaos, pain, guilt, fear, internal conflict, shame, anxiety, and all the other fruit of misplaced priorities result. Always.

St. Augustine, once defined sin as "making a *good* thing, the *only* thing." When we place good things at the center of our hearts, it feels almost natural and right. But be warned, for they are only a shadow of the heart's Maker, Sustainer, and King. No good things exist apart from God (James 1:17), yet "good things" that usurp God's place on the throne of our hearts quickly become deafening, deadening, and disastrous. Satan cleverly uses them to tempt us into worshiping the creation rather than The Creator. Since Satan the Deceiver has no original creative power in himself whatsoever, he must borrow God's good things to do what he does best: deceive, distract, delude, and eventually destroy any who might worship God! The heart is meant to be the throne room of God only. When "the lesser gods of good things" slip onto that throne, they do so intending to stay there! They will defend this place of honor to the death—the death of the heart, of a positive emotional life, and of all real, true, temporal, and eternal Life!

Such was *not* the destiny our Creator intended for us, beloved! Thus, he is passionate about revealing to us the true nature of our hearts so that we might know ourselves as well as God knows us, and, in knowing our need, we might throw ourselves on the salvation Jesus won for us on his cross.

ASPIRATIONS, AFFECTIONS, AND EXPONENTIAL COMPLICATIONS

Now we come to another word the Bible links to our hearts, the word *spirit*. This word refers to our *emotions* or *affections*. Our emotions are linked directly to those things we treasure as most important to our well-being; they link directly to the things of the *heart*—our hopes, dreams, core beliefs, values, and deepest desires.

The implications of the Bible's distinction between "heart" and "spirit" extend still further. Each and every person God has created clings to a different set of "essential things" within their heart. These, in turn, link directly to various sets of emotions or feelings that surround, guide, guard, and defend each truth or falsehood of the heart.

This creates individuality and uniqueness among all God's children. God, in his omniscience, knows the smallest of detail of each and every emotion, aspiration, and dream within his creation. But here is where it gets better: Not only does he know, but he cherishes our hearts and spirits to such a degree that he sent his one and only Son to redeem them from death.

Are you getting a sense that there is one apparently insignificant, and yet very big thing that you could say about the human heart and spirit that makes all the difference in the world? That's right, *it's complicated!* And not treating it as such can be as disastrous as not recognizing it at all.

Only God's wisdom, patience, compassion, and perseverance can assist us as we help one another work through the issues of the heart, spirit, and will.

HEARTS SET FREE

Scripture clearly describes Christ's deep and compassionate care for our hearts. His entire life was filled with the agony of anticipation of the price he would pay on the cross to redeem God's children from the fall.

In much of his teaching, our Lord confronted the chaos created by divided hearts. Jesus confronted the confusion that was created by religion—defined as man's designs for reaching out to God, not God's design to redeem mankind. Take care of this distinction. Consider, for example, his angry description of the divided heart: *"You hypocrites! Well did Isaiah prophesy of you, when he said: 'This people honors me with their lips, but their heart is far from me; in vain do they worship me, teaching as doctrines the commandments of men.'"*

In contrast, Jesus continually called attention to the purposes of the Godhead for human hearts. Consider these examples:

> One of the scribes came up and...asked him, "Which commandment is the most important of all?"
>
> Jesus answered, "The most important is, 'Hear, O Israel: The Lord our God, the Lord is one. And you shall love the Lord your God with all your heart and with all your soul and with all your mind and with all your strength.'
>
> "The second is this: 'You shall love your neighbor as yourself.' There is no other commandment greater than these."
>
> Mark 12:28–3

But Jesus' ministry went well beyond mere warnings and instruction. The Son of God willingly stepped out of the timeless, perfect relationship of the Trinity, came to earth as a vulnerable infant, lived as a man of sorrows, despised, rejected, and daily agonizing over his unavoidable crucifixion. Jesus sacrificed himself upon the cross, suffering the undeserved condemnation and silence of his own Father as he cried out to him from the cross—all to make it possible to fulfill God's promise to all who would by faith believe:

> I will give them one heart, and a new spirit I will put within them. I will remove the heart of stone from their flesh and give them a heart of flesh.
>
> Ezekiel 11:19

> For God so loved the world that he gave his only Son, that whoever believes in him should not perish but have eternal life.
>
> John 3:16

> Therefore, if anyone is in Christ, he is a new creation. The old has passed away; behold, the new has come.
>
> 2 Corinthians 5:17

> And he who was seated on the throne said, "Behold, I am making all things new." Also he said, "Write this down, for these words are trustworthy and true."
>
> Revelations 21:5

In further defining and explaining his ministry, our Lord identified himself as "the way, the truth, and the life" (John 4:16). Our hearts need him, and him alone, more than anything else in the universe. Only when we allow him to possess our hearts can those hearts be most joyous, free, and full of abundant life:

> [Jesus said,] "If you abide in my word, you are truly my disciples, and you will know the truth, and the truth will set you free."
>
> John 8:32

That which was from the beginning which we have heard, which we have seen with our eyes, which we looked upon and have touched with our hands, concerning the word of life— the life was made manifest, and we have seen it, and testify to it and proclaim to you the eternal life, which was with the Father and was made manifest to us—that which we have seen and heard we proclaim also to you, so that you too may have fellowship with us; and indeed our fellowship is with the Father and with his Son Jesus Christ. And we are writing these things so that our joy may be complete.

1 John 1:1–4

God's truth sets our hearts free for the authentic life that he intended, and for the complete joy that flows from that kind of life. On the other hand, Jesus warned his followers many times of the danger in harboring untruths, of the bondage to falsehoods of various sorts, and of the "dead-end discipleship" that would vanish when challenged by the slightest threat or temptation.

This is why the Psalmist so persistently and passionately implores God to help him *recapture* and *retain* the state of the heart as it was "in the beginning:"

Search me, O God, and know my heart; test me and know my anxious thoughts. See if there is any offensive way in me, and lead me in the way everlasting.

Psalm 139:23–24

As we will see in the upcoming section, this is the prayer of a person who understands the deep need to have our hearts radically restored. This prayer embraces "the weeping, window, and the way" as God's healing work in the human heart. (Exodus 20; Matthew 22:34–40; 2 Corinthians 1:3–7).

Please consider right now your own heart condition. Have you:

1. Considered the utter holiness of God?

2. Faced the impossibility of standing face-to-face with a holy God who cannot bear imperfections of any kind?

3. Understood the need that you have for covering the indelible stain of sin you can do nothing about?

4. Embraced the response of humbling yourself by repenting, from the depth of your heart, for Jesus Christ to save you from God's just condemnation and be the Lord of your life?

5. Tasted the sweet gratitude that comes, in faith, from trusting God's character and promise to love you as he does his one and only son?

6. Set a course for discipleship and being on Christ's mission of serving and giving your life as a ransom for many?

DECONSTRUCTING, RECONSTRUCTING

Most renovations begin with a process of tearing down the old so that the new can emerge. One can't happen without the other. God intends to use the deconstruction of our hearts caused by suffering as the first phase in his renovation of our hearts. The degree of deconstruction is usually proportional to the intensity of our suffering and the level of denial we might live in at the time. The daily woes of life may make only a slight impact on our hardened hearts, but events as sudden and shocking as the death of a family member can shatter a person's heart. Suffering like this can mark the first phase or the continuation of God's renovation process.

We cannot insist on maintaining the compartmentalization of our hearts if we want to mature in our faith relationship with God. It is impossible to keep the compartments of our hearts intact while, on the other hand, having a desire to become more like Jesus Christ. In times of deep fear and pain like the one I experienced with the death of my dad, the sensation of freefall marks our sudden heartbreak. We remain sinfully focused on two things: *pride* and *maintaining control*.

Why do I say *pride?* If we were to release our hearts completely to the saving lordship of Jesus Christ, we could no longer look down on other people in their differences and vulnerabilities. Pride keeps us from seeing our sin and depending on the one who saved us from it. Why do I say *maintaining control?* If we were to release our hearts completely to Jesus' saving lordship, it would also mean giving up the right to direct our own lives. Instead, we would relinquish it to Christ and thrive in the freedom of obedience to him. To hearts that are suspicious of God's motives and methods, this feels downright suicidal! But this is exactly what the Bible commands. We must die to self in order to fully live for Christ (Galatians 2:20; Philippians 1:21).

A BASIC NECESSITY OF WARFARE: KNOW YOUR ENEMY

Even for the born-again, supernaturally changed Christian, the devil seeks to tempt us into sin. Sin is the enemy of the heart.

There was a time about fifteen years ago when I prayed ardently that our Lord would grow me in his *way*, in his *truth*, and *life*. I prayed that he would give me the gift of his wisdom and obedience so that I could serve him more fully. Ironically enough, within one week I received the answer: an opportunity to participate in an in-depth study of sin and of my own heart. I spent nearly six months in the study of Romans 1:18–32, the text I now consider the grandest passage in all of Scripture dealing with sin and the consequences of our separation from God.

Two essential lessons from that study were a basic definition of what sin really is and the way it manifests itself in human hearts. Let me personalize that definition from verse 18: *My sin suppresses the truth of who God is. In pride, I demand the right to control my life in every way. At the end of the day, in the very heart of my heart, I hate God.* That truth was not easy to take, but it was the medicine for my heart for which I had prayed. That's what Adam did. That is what I do. That's what all of human-kind does as a direct result of our sinful hearts. That's the condition from which Christ came to redeem us.

We live in a culture of misguided self-centeredness. The world seeks to improve itself by intensifying the focus on education, improving social engineering, and emphasizing family values, all through conservative and liberal approaches alike. All these avoid getting to the heart of the matter and are, at best, half-measures. At worst, they bury the root cause of our problems until we become unrecognizable to ourselves.

Praise God... Praise God I saw both extremes of my true existence:

- I was far more sinful than I ever dared to imagine and yet,

- I was loved far more deeply than I could have dared to hope.

God did answer my prayer, but not at all in the way I could have or would have expected. The deeper understanding of sin's destructive power helped prepare me for that snowy night in my dad's garden. I had the amazing benefit of having a heart re-made by the Word of God. That night with Dad crushed my heart, but opened it still further to God.

The Holy Spirit has used all of this and more to give me "a heart for the heart of the heart" as God places me in the midst of other broken hearts to minister to. Like all surgery performed on the physical body, the work of the Spirit in our hearts hurts, but it also heals. Praise God, he is a heart surgeon beyond compare! You can trust him completely, with all your heart, mind, soul, and strength. Once dead in sin, now alive by the Holy Spirit you can choose to live as God intended, no longer harboring idols in your heart, mis-prioritizing your affections, and restrained by your heart's misplaced priorities.

JOHN O. DOZIER, JR.

You can be free to live in accordance with God's perfect and intimate love for you and his plan for your life.

> The answer must be some-*one*, not just something. For the problem suffering is about someone ("God—why does he … why doesn't he … ?) rather than just some-*thing*. To question God's goodness is not just an intellectual experiment. It is either rebellion or weeping. It is a little child with tears in its eyes looking up at Daddy and weeping, "Why?" This is not merely the philosophers' "why?" Not only does it add the emotion of tears but also it is asked in the context of relationship. It is a question put to the Father, not a question asked in a vacuum.
>
> The hurt child needs not so much explanations as reassurances. And that is what we get: the reassurance of the Father in the person of Jesus Christ, "He who has seen me has seen the Father".
>
> John 14:9
>
> The answer is not just a word … but The Word; not an idea but a person.
> Peter Kreeft, *What is God's Answer to Human Suffering?*[12]

Now let's take a closer look at another vital aspect of how God has designed you to glorify him and to bless others.

GOING DEEPER…

If you would like to go deeper in your study of the fallen human heart and the ways in which our emotions serve as a key indicator concerning the state of the heart, I recommend these five resources to help you along:

1. *The Book of Psalms.*

    At no other place in the Bible does God speak more clearly to the intensity and range of human emotions than here. Psalms expresses the gamut of our affections, thereby freeing our anger, sadness, surprise, perplexity, disillusionment, outrage, and delight by standing unashamed and adopted before God who loves us. Praying the Psalms opens our hearts to our heavenly Father for his help and healing. Further, the Psalms encourage us to work through our emotions with honesty and persistence. By doing this, the Holy Spirit will produce in us a whole-hearted allegiance to God, a deeper love for our neighbor, and a fuller submission to our Lord's good and gracious reign. The Book of Psalms denies no emotion from us, or from God himself. The psalmists open their hearts fully to God so that we might open our own hearts to God in the same way.

2. Allender, D.B., & Longman, T. The Cry Of The Soul: How Our Emotions Reveal Our Deepest Questions About God. Colorado Springs, CO: NavPress. 1994.

As the Forward to this book points out, "Rather than explaining our emotions in order to help us gain control over them, Drs. Allender and Longman take us into new country. Their central idea... is that our emotional life, including those emotions we shouldn't feel, forms a *window* that lets us see deep into the heart of God. Their rather surprising suggestion is that we explore our emotions not to get rid of the bad ones and replace them with good ones but rather to know God more fully" (p. 10; emphasis added). *The Cry of the Soul* explores in depth how our emotions must inescapably reflect God's true and rightful place within our hearts, because that's how we're designed to really LIVE!

3. Colbert, D. Deadly Emotions: Understand The Mind-Body-Spirit Connection That Can Heal Or Destroy You. Nashville, TN: Thomas Nelson, Inc. 2003.

Colbert, a medical doctor, shows the connection between the truths to which our hearts cling, and how our emotions, our spirituality, and our mental and physical selves are inex-

JOHN O. DOZIER, JR.

tricably intertwined. He outlines these connections in ways that are scientifically verifiable, deeply convicting, and also commonsensical.

Colbert asserts that we begin to heal only when we see, accept, and reconnect the dots in ways that lead to truth and hope. Like the Bible, Colbert proposes that only the love of God experienced through an authentic relationship with Jesus Christ can holistically heal deadly emotions, making it possible for us to replace the idols and falsehoods of our hearts.

4. Goleman, D. Emotional Intelligence: Why It Can Matter More Than IQ. New York: Bantum Books. 1995

Goleman writes, "If your emotional abilities aren't in hand, if you don't have self-awareness, if you are not able to manage your distressing emotions, if you can't have empathy and have effective relationships, then no matter how smart you are, you are not going to get very far. When I say manage emotions, I only mean the really distressing, incapacitating emotions. Knowing and feeling your emotions is what makes life rich. You need your passions" (Jennifer Fox, *Your Child's Strengths,* New York: Viking, 2008, Daniel Goleman is quoted, page 275)

"Emotional Intelligence" has gained increasing acceptance in the marketplace of ideas. It is becoming the standard by which great leadership is identified, measured, and modeled. Proverbs, the Wisdom Literature of the Bible, reiterates many of Goleman's assertions. Having the worldview and the concepts of the books of Psalms and Proverbs in mind makes reading Goleman's work fascinating, and highly practical as well.

Goleman has proposed that the four broad dimensions of Emotional Intelligence are *self-awareness, self-management, social awareness, and social skills.* These four categories are interdependent and, to some degree, hierarchical.

5. *The Book of Proverbs.*

In this book, Solomon expresses his own sense of "holistic self-awareness," while at the same time offering us amazing, multifaceted insights as well. This Bible book plumbs the depths of the human heart (those core truths that lie at the center of our lives and on which we base our life's agendas) and the human spirit (our emotions). The Bible claims again and again that true wisdom is the key to transforming life's tragedies into triumphs (See, for example, James 1:2–8).

The following verses from Proverbs offer some amazing examples of the mind-boggling complexity as well as the depth and breadth of emotions one can experience. Several of them also suggest keys for mitigating conditions that often beset and bewilder the human heart.

Anxiety and worry are heavy burdens to bear; love and encouragement can bear any burden. "An anxious heart weighs a man down, but a kind word cheers him up."

Proverbs 12:15 (NIV)

Hopelessness creates heart disease; the good news of the Gospel restores the heart to its Garden of Eden state. "Hope deferred makes the heart sick, but a dream fulfilled is a tree of life."

Proverbs 13:12 (NLT)

Every story, every heart, every emotion is unique; being ultimately alone is a shared experience. "Each heart knows its own bitterness, and no one else can share its joy."

Proverbs 14:10 (ESV)

Putting on a happy face works for a time, but the heart desires deeper healing. "Laughter can conceal a heavy heart, but when the laughter ends, the grief remains."

Proverbs 14:13 (NLT)

Truth at peace is powerful and pervasive, while discontented-ness is as deadly as a fast-spreading cancer. "A heart at peace gives life to the body, but envy rots the bones."

Proverbs 14:30 (NIV)

True words of Eden-like creativity heal; deception deals a deathblow to the emotions. "The tongue that brings healing is a tree of life, but a deceitful tongue crushes the spirit."

Proverbs 15:4 (NIV)

A happy heart makes for happy demeanor; wisdom and fool-ishness perpetually vie for control through the journey of faith. "A happy heart makes the face cheerful, but heartache crushes the spirit. The discerning heart seeks knowledge, but the mouth of a fool feeds on folly."

Proverbs 15:13–14 (NIV)

Subjectivity is never innocent. God is a God who knows all and intervenes to help us discern our true intentions. "All a man's ways seem innocent to him, but motives are weighed by the LORD."

Proverbs 16:2 (NIV)

A guilty conscience is all-consuming; being right with God creates a humbly confident heart the world will never under-stand. "The wicked are edgy with guilt, ready to run off even when no one's after them; Honest people are relaxed and con-fident, bold as lions."

Proverbs 28:1 (The Message)

CHAPTER SIX

RECONCILING: THE HEART AND THE BIBLE

When the fullness of time had come, God sent forth his Son, born of woman, born under the law, to redeem those who were under the law, so that we might receive adoption as sons. And because you are sons, God has sent the Spirit of his Son into our hearts, crying, "Abba! Father!" So you are no longer a slave, but a son, and if a son, then an heir through God.

Galatians 4:4–7

Chapter five painted a dismal picture of "True Truth" (*True Spirituality*, Francis Schaeffer) as it described the depth to which every human heart has sunk.

JOE'S WEEPING, WINDOW AND WAY

Along the long journey of writing this book, God has been incredibly generous in providing me with innumerable real-life situations in which his protocol for best responding to suffering has been demonstrated in many wonderful ways.

I went to visit my eighty-three year-old friend, "Dr. Mac," who recently had hip surgery. I had taken along several books because I thought he might enjoy them during the weeks he would spend in rehab. As Dr. Mac's wife and I looked through the books, we started to talk about the impact Dr. Mac's health challenges had placed on his faith. We found ourselves praising God that times of difficulty and trial can also be times in which God's people can garner rich rewards, if only we will slow down and pay closer attention to God.

Dr. Mac explained that even in the deepest pain he had ever experienced—the sudden loss of his eighteen-year-old grandson Charlie—he had seen God at work. Dr. Mac believed his beloved grandson Charlie was exactly where God wanted him to be. "I have a new peace in my heart today, John," Dr. Mac said. During a break in the conversation, a voice from the other side of the room chimed in. Dr. Mac's roommate, Joe, had been listening. Joe had landed in rehab after an auto accident that had damaged many bones in his body, from the neck down. His hip was fractured, and many bones in his arms, legs, and feet had been nearly annihilated. Joe's doctors had performed numerous surgeries. Other than God's clear intervention, there was no reason Joe should have lived through the extreme trauma.

Yet, there he lay. As Joe drew back the drape, I saw a kind, warm smile that revealed a heart of faith. Joe asked that I come over to his side of the room so he could introduce himself. "It sounds like you're a pastor or a man of faith of some kind. I've had a wonderful time eavesdropping on your conversation," he said.

"I am a minister," I replied. "All Christians are called to minister to one another, right? That's what I love to do." After a minute or two, we began talking about our mutual faith in Christ, and Joe began to share something of his faith journey.

"About six years ago I was in another car accident," he said, "and that was really my 'Saul time.' What I mean is that immediately afterward, and then while I recovered, God gave me a chance to see how much I needed a Savior. I couldn't have been in a place where my need was more obvious, and so I repented and asked Christ into my life. It was at that same time I also saw how God was using the accident.

To be honest, John, I thought *that* accident was God turning me around and bringing me to himself. But now I'm not sure ... "

THE WEEPING

Tears welled up in his eyes as he continued. "Now I'm lying in bed again in such a state of utter and literal brokenness. I have to be honest. I'm asking God, 'What is the purpose in this for me now? I mean, how much more can you ask of me? I already gave my life to you as my Savior and Lord. I thought I had committed my life to you ... What more do you want from me?'"

THE WINDOW

Joe looked up at me, heartbreak in his eyes. "Do I have to go through this again?" he asked me. "What lesson is God teaching me now? I've begun to search my heart for the answers but ... But I just don't know."

THE WAY

I gave him a smile of tearful compassion as I looked at my new friend's face, the only part of his body that hadn't been maimed. Until that moment, I hadn't thought about what to say. Compassion welled up from deep inside my heart: "The answer to your question, my friend, is incredibly simple but more rich than you could ever imagine. God wants you to glorify him and bless others. That's it."

Joe looked at me for a moment and then averted his eyes from my face and stared at the ceiling in silence. As he lay there, his eyes slowly began to close, and he began to weep almost uncontrollably.

"Are those tears of joy, Joe?" I asked.

"Yes. That's it, isn't it?" Joe said. "It's so simple! I can see that with every breath, heartbeat, word, and ounce of strength that I have, I can glorify him and bless others. That's the way! It's the only answer I need!"

Joe was now ready to take his next step on the journey toward holiness, toward being more wholly devoted to the truth and love of God. I had spoken with Joe for only a few minutes, yet I could see the truth so clearly. The Holy Spirit wanted to take Joe from the place he was before this accident and freefall, clearly a man of faith, a man who knew Jesus as his Lord and Savior, to the next level in that faith, to a place where God had been waiting for Joe to join him in renewed wisdom, compassion, and perseverance. His *weeping* during a time of doubt created the opportunity for the Holy Spirit to open a *window* into Joe's heart.

The Spirit used the fruit of suffering in my compassion and willingness so that I could pass it along to others. God gave me the blessing of being there to help Joe see *the way* forward. Additionally, to reinforce in my own heart the power of what I have been calling God's "protocol" for using our suffering for growth into the likeness of Christ. In this encounter I saw that protocol at work in Joe in a powerful and obvious way. Since this time, I have been continuing the journey with Joe to encourage him along the way. I cannot tell you how blessed I was to be with Dr. Mac, his wife, Joe, the Holy Spirit, and the host of saints who had stood there before us, at that precise spot on the journey heavenward.

KNOW THE "TRUE TRUTH"—HEARTS DEPRAVED AND REDEEMED

In the midst of his freefall of faith, the truth helped Joe affirm the foundations and take the next step on his journey of faith. Truth, active in hearts made humble and receptive by faith while living in a broken universe, always nurtures the maturing process. This is, in part, the process of sanctification[13], of growth and increased commitment to the concerns of Jesus and the Holy Spirit in us. God has created our hearts to be repositories and stewards of Truth.

Many in the church today have forgotten the True Truth and need to be reminded of it by fellow believers. Scripture calls Satan the Deceiver, and for good reason. He focuses on one thing—destroying the truth in the hearts of God's people so that they will worship the array of false gods (E.g., idols–Deuteronomy 5:6–11, 32:31). These false gods automatically rise up in the heart to take the place of God.

Yes, every age has had its "progressive thinkers," skeptics who have dashed their hearts against True Truth. But, no manner of misshapen logic, however modern, will deter God from his person and plan! Skeptics continue to claim to be True Skeptics, all the while refusing to be skeptical of their own skepticism— and therefore sounding foolish in every age (Romans 1:21–22).

The "True Truth" of God's heart is a matter of fact. We may try to soften the blows inflicted upon our hearts by life's daily circumstances, but hard-heartedness will not change reality. Never believe the lie: "Sticks and stones may break my bones, but words will never hurt me." Words can and do hurt, and they can heal as well (Proverbs 4, 12, 18, 119; John 1:1–5).

The fallen human heart is the factory in which all the harm is created. The stories we tell ourselves, stories that are not rooted deeply in sound theology are more than foolish sentimentality, irresponsible blather, or juicy gossip. These stories have real consequences. They create a state of reality that can take us in one direction or the other—toward utter chaos, isolation, and despair or, alternatively, toward redeeming the effects of the fall, toward reconstructing perfect order, and unassailable joy.

The redemption of the heart begins with God and God alone (Matthew 2:1; John 3:3; 1 John 5:1). The Holy Spirit effectually calls the sinner to faith, regenerating the heart, and bringing it to a new, eternal life.[14]

The heart born-again through the Holy Spirit, real
repentance, and in faith beseeching Christ to be our Savior
and Lord, begins a journey as a new creation in Christ.

As we saw in the last chapter, the regeneration of the heart
cannot begin in any other way. Fallen human beings are totally
incapable of regenerating themselves in any way, shape, or form
(Isaiah 57:11–13; John 1:13, 3:3–8; Ephesians 2:9;). Anyone who
seeks after God, can do so only because the Holy Spirit first
touched that person's heart with his regenerative, re-creative
power (Romans 3:9–18). Some in our society see those who
claim to be "born again" as a group of particularly needy Christians or as members of some over-zealous sect of the Christian

faith. Most born again Christians understand that re-birth is absolutely necessary for anyone's heart to be "turned from stone into flesh" (Deuteronomy 30: 6; 2 Corinthians 3:3). If we have not understood the depth of our sin, we will not likely see the need for a total heart regeneration and renovation. Not understanding our need does not change the fact that we need a Savior and a Sanctifier both. God loves us just the way we are, but he's just not nearly satisfied to leave us there!

THE CENTERPIECE OF YOUR STORY: GOD'S PATH TO GLORY

After the Holy Spirit's initial work of regeneration, he invites us to respond in the life-long process of *sanctification*. Through this process, the Spirit sets us apart, purifies us, makes us holy, consecrates us for service, and makes way for the growth of Christ within each re-born heart. Only after we have been born again do we have the ability to recognize the symptoms of our defective hearts. The "cutting of the heart" by the Holy Spirit produces faith, repentance, and the confession of sin (Acts 2:36–41). All these are given to us as God's gift, purely by his grace (Acts 15:6–11; Ephesians 2:1–10).

In this ongoing process of sanctification, God reshapes hearts that were once dead in sin, but now have been animated by the Holy Spirit and made alive in Christ (Romans 6:11; 1 Corinthians 15:22). The new life we receive from him represents not the end, but the *beginning*.

Once we belong to him through faith, and have become sons and daughters, he wants to engage us in glad service for Christ (Romans 15:1). He invites us, as I shared with Joe, to continually glorify him and bless others, not merely *regardless* of the circumstances in which we find ourselves, but rather in and through them (Psalm 126: 6; Romans 8:17)! Our greatest breakdowns are meant to be our greatest breakthroughs. Sanctification is not some sort of end unto itself. It is not God's remedy for the anxiety we feel because we live in tough times. It is not part of a self-help program either.

Rather, it is the means God has designed to magnify Christ both within our hearts and by its outworking in our lives. It is the engine by which day-by-day we grow into the likeness of Jesus Christ and more certain in the hope he has given us. In the same way, the persecuted and beleaguered believers of the first century church sought to live out their faith:

> Since we are surrounded by such a great cloud of witnesses, let us throw off everything that hinders and the sin that so easily entangles, and let us run with perseverance the race marked out for us. Let us fix our eyes on Jesus, the author and perfector of our faith, who for the joy set before him endured the cross, scorning its shame, and sat down at the right hand of the throne of God. Consider him who endured such opposition from sinful men, *so that* you will not grow weary and lose heart ...
>
> Hebrews 12:1–3, 13; emphasis added

We will at best serve begrudgingly and, at worst, serve expecting God to credit our "good works" to our account or reward us at every turn. Our "damnable good works," as John Gerstner has called them, works by which we hope to merit God's favor, will destroy the heart as well. By the process of sanctification, the Holy Spirit prepares the whole person—heart, spirit, and will—to serve with the proper motives.
Meditating on those True Truths, we "*will not grow weary and lose heart*" (Hebrews 12:3). We will not be so tired, anxious, worried, fearful, and emotionally disillusioned. As we allow God's protocol of "the weeping, window, and the way" to work in our lives, we are *sanctified for service* and given the power of Christ within to persevere!

OR NOT...

For thus said the Lord GOD, the Holy One of Israel, "In returning and rest you shall be saved; in quietness and in trust shall be your strength." But you were unwilling, and you said, "No! We will flee upon horses"...

Isaiah 30:15–16; see also: Matthew 7:13; Hebrews 3:15

We can, of course, choose to shun God's design for using suffering to glorify him and bless his people. The *unbeliever's* heart will become harder as they move away from God's love:

Keep on hearing, but do not understand; keep on seeing, but do not perceive. Make the heart of this people dull, and their ears heavy, and blind their eyes; lest they see with their eyes, and hear with their ears, and understand with their hearts, and turn and be healed.

Isaiah 6:9–10; see also Acts 28:26–28

God gave them up in the lusts of their hearts to impurity, to the dishonoring of their bodies among themselves, because they exchanged the truth about God for a lie and worshiped and served the creature rather than the Creator, who is blessed forever! Amen.

Romans 1:24–25

But, for the *believer*, our faith in word and deed for which we have been saved will become less and less effective for the purposes it was created by God: we are saved to serve; redeemed to redeem; comforted to comfort; paid for sacrificially to offer as a sacrifice. This is the difference between the Christian who is "on fire for Christ" as opposed to merely living a morally constrained life, or being "lukewarm":

And to the angel of the church in Laodicea write: "The words of the Amen, the faithful and true witness, the beginning of God's creation." I know your works: you are neither cold nor hot.(AM) Would that you were either cold or hot! *So, because*

141

you are lukewarm, and neither hot nor cold, I will spit you out of my mouth. For you say, I am rich, I have prospered, and I need nothing, not realizing that you are wretched, pitiable, poor, blind, and naked.

Revelation 3:14–17; emphasis added, see also
18–22; 2 Peter 2:21; Hebrews 6:4–6

Remember, beloved, God can forgive *every* sin, but God cannot forgive *any* sin if we do not avail ourselves of the salvation he has put in place. If people use their God-given freedom of choice to *refuse* the merciful offer of the Holy Spirit's intervention in their lives, then he will not force them to do his will. Similarly, he will not force us to let him renew and transform our hearts. Repeatedly rejecting the way by which God intends to change the heart is hardening one's heart against the Holy Spirit:

> [Jesus said,] "Truly, I say to you, all sins will be forgiven the children of man, and whatever blasphemies they utter, but whoever blasphemes against the Holy Spirit never has forgiveness, but is guilty of an eternal sin."

Mark 3:28–29; see also Matthew 12:31–32

As we will see, the Holy Spirit's role in "the weeping, the window, and the way" aligns closely with his primary work in *sanctification:* counseling, encouraging, convicting, and inspiring the Christian heart as we move ever-closer toward holiness, and in conformity to the likeness of Jesus Christ. What an awesome, unspeakably merciful, and *ingenious* plan of God's to redeem the heart and set it aflame for his purposes. Praise him!

THE SPIRIT'S WORK

As Chapter Six pointed out, the word *spirit* (vs. Spirit or Holy Spirit) directs us to the purpose of our *emotions* as a barometer for the condition of our hearts. This God-made connection helps us to see if we are living in alignment with the True

Truth of God, or if we are living the *lie,* which is the fruit of the fall into sin. All of God's redemptive plan is designed to help us be very clear about our choices. Will we live by the fruit of the Spirit or the fruit of the Fall? In Scripture the word *heart* refers to the repository of what we care most about: our hopes, dreams, core beliefs, and values. The heart is the seat of the entire self and it contains our core commitments and our idealized image of how the world "should be."

If the truth we hold in our heart aligns with the truth and the will of God for us, then our *emotions* and *spirit* will mirror the emotions and Spirit of God. We will live at peace, joyous and fully vital, finding meaning and purpose in our existence. We will be righteously angry at injustice and energized by our anger to act in ways that will productively address the injustice. (See Psalm 18 and Mark 11:15). Our lives will become perfectly balanced by love *and* truth (Ephesians 4:15), because God himself is the perfection of love and truth, and we are his image bearers.

On the other hand, when our hearts reflect the disease and death of *the lie,* our spirit will begin to work against the very purposes for which God created them. God's plan is perfect. It's not confusing or cruel, because God would never give his sons or daughters anything that would harm them in any way:

> For everyone who asks receives, and the one who seeks finds, and to the one who knocks it will be opened. What father among you, if his son asks for a fish, will instead of a fish give him a serpent; or if he asks for an egg, will give him a scorpion? If you then, who are evil, know how to give good gifts to your children, how much more will the heavenly Father give the Holy Spirit to those who ask him.
>
> Luke 11:10–13

In the Sermon on the Mount, Jesus addresses this True Truth in a magnificent way (Matthew 5:3–12). He begins the sermon with what have come to be called the Beatitudes. Each Beatitude begins with a statement of fact concerning the "blessed." Blessed are all those whose hearts are brought into the presence of God, who live face-to-face with him as sons and daughters in his eternal Kingdom. The Beatitudes describe the state of *heart* and *spirit* that make it possible to live in intimate relationship with the living God of the Bible.

- Blessed are the poor in spirit…

- Blessed are those who mourn…

- Blessed are the meek…

- Blessed are those who hunger and thirst after righteousness…

- Blessed are the merciful…

- Blessed are the pure in heart…

- Blessed are the peacemakers…

- Blessed are those who are persecuted for righteousness' sake…

- Blessed are you when others revile you and persecute you and utter all kinds of evil against you falsely on my account…

As the Sermon ends, Jesus repeats the promise of the rock-solid assurance offered to those who are blessed by an abiding faith in him:

Therefore everyone who hears these words of mine and puts them into practice is like a wise man, who built his house on the rock. The rain came down, the streams rose, and the winds blew and beat against that house; yet it did not fall, because it had its foundation on the rock. But everyone who hears these words of mine and does not put them into practice is like a foolish man who built his house on sand.

The rain came down, the streams rose, and the winds blew and beat against that house, and it fell with a great crash.

When Jesus had finished saying these things, the crowds were amazed at his teaching, because he taught as one who had authority...

Matthew 7:24–29

In these words, our Lord reminds us, "My truths are the home in which your heart and spirit will be truly blessed, happy, anchored, rock-solid, and fulfilled, even amidst the great storms of life. Don't harden your heart, and refuse the blessings I intend for you in your trials. Don't turn from me toward lesser gods that will destroy your heart! Choose to be blessed as you live for, by, and in My True Truth, beloved!"[15]

As you consider this and its applications, recall the section in Chapter One that briefly describes the first moments I spent with my dad as I knelt beside him in the snow. Consider the frightening freefall into utter darkness and fear. Remember how, in response to my cries, God graciously placed a rock-solid foundation beneath me, reminding me of his personal promise never to leave or forsake me. Later we will explore these vitally important truths, but for now I would like to use the events of that night to call attention to the way God used his Word to bless me with a "Beatitude heart change". I know from personal experience that the fruits of suffering can include an increasingly sweet sense of the Savior's peace within the heart!

EMOTIONS—THE BAROMETER OF THE SPIRIT... TO MEASURE THE HEART

At the risk of being repetitive, let me reinforce the interplay between each human being's heart and spirit is enormously important, extremely complicated, and exceedingly consequential! The degree of dissonance, of disunity between one's heart and spirit and the True Truth revealed by God in his Word creates its own ecosystem of natural cause and effect that will eventually heal or destroy a human being. Distractions, regardless of the form they take, can only encourage our hearts to serve other, lesser gods. They cannot change the truth about the means by which God has created and chooses to sustain the human heart and spirit.

Still, God's people often choose to ignore or deny our heart condition. Or we try to anesthetize our emotions—the barometer of our faith in God's True Truth—with alcohol, drugs, or by participating in trivial activities. We "make good things the only thing" as Augustine once defined sin. We concentrate on externals like hyper-athletics, higher education, or "success" on the job. Or we focus on our physical appearance. Or we create a rash of other "if-only" goals in an attempt to keep life pleasant or safe. Our efforts are like jumping off a skyscraper to catch a cab. Gravity works, and you will likely beat the elevator to the street, but in the end, the consequences could scarcely be more serious.

Yet decade by decade human beings go right on ignoring the marvelous realm of the heart-spirit alliance by which God has promised to transform us into the image of his Son:

> God's wisdom is profound, his power is vast. Who has resisted him and come out unscathed?
>
> Job 9:4

> My people have committed two sins: They have forsaken me, the spring of living water, and have dug their own cisterns, broken cisterns that cannot hold water.
>
> Jeremiah 2:13

> You stiff-necked people, with uncircumcised hearts and ears! You are just like your fathers: You always resist the Holy Spirit!
>
> Acts 7:51

God in his wisdom keeps prodding at our hearts. As we encounter the wide array of trials that come at us throughout our lives, both relatively minor ones and those as serious as the circumstance I encountered with my dad on Christmas night, we experience our Lord's concern for our sanctification. Rather than ignoring his concern for us and just "muddling through as best we can," he invites us to use a community of faithful friends to look actively and intentionally for the ways he would want to use our pain to shape and reshape our hearts. We can allow him and those in our Christian family to move us from merely *crying out* in pain or shame to a holy *coping*, and from there to humble *confidence*, to an undaunted and proactive *compassion* for others in times of trials—the coping, confidence, and compassion by which we grow more and more like Jesus every day!

THE "HEART—SPIRIT—SANCTIFICATION— SERVICE CONNECTION"

Initially regenerated by the Holy Spirit, we are continually being made more like Jesus, continually being made holy as he lives and works in our hearts. Our hearts grow toward the likeness of Christ's sacred heart, wise choice by wise choice, and by repenting when our choices are not so wise (Matthew 3:8; Acts 26:20; 2 Corinthians 6:14, 13:14; 1 John 1:7).

Little by little, especially as we encounter suffering and allow the Holy Spirit to have his way in our hearts, God works to dissolve our self-sufficiency while increasing our dependence on Christ's sufficiency. He revitalizes and renews us, so that our hearts of stone become hearts of flesh, hearts like those of Jesus Christ himself (Ezekiel 11, 36; Jeremiah 2). And this not for ourselves (Romans 15:1); we are *saved* for the purpose of *being sent out on a mission* to act as Christ's representatives. We are not saved for the purposes of self-help; instead, Jesus invites us to work with him as co-redeemers, as witnesses to his saving work in a world dark and lost. We work to bring light to that world before our Lord comes in final judgment, and it is too late.

GOING DEEPER...

If you would like to explore the ideas from this chapter further, I suggest you read:

Allender, D.B. The Cry of the Soul: How Our Emotions Reveal Out Deepest Questions About God. Colorado Springs, CO: NavPress. 1994.

Allender, D.B. To Be Told: God Invites You To Co-Author Your Future. Colorado Springs, CO, Waterbrook Press. 2005.

Keller, T. J. The Reason For God: Belief In An Age Of Skepticism. New York: Penguin Group (USA) Inc. 2008

Keller, T. J. The Prodigal God: Recovering the Heart of the Christian Faith. New York: Penguin Group (USA) Inc. 2008

CHAPTER SEVEN

RECOILING: RECOGNIZING THE IMPLICATIONS OF THE HEART "LIVING IN A CULTURE OF COMFORT"

We do not necessarily doubt that God will do what is best for us; but we are wondering somewhere deep inside how painful "the best" will turn out to be.

C.S. Lewis, *The Problem of Pain*[16]

I f God's plan for his people is good—and it is—then what keeps us from whole-heartedly embracing his perfect and merciful plan for using suffering for man's good? What inhibits most believers from more fully embracing the ideas we've considered in this book thus far?

Westernized 21st century Christians live a precarious predicament. We enjoy so many "advantages". Most of these advantages lie well beyond the grasp of the majority of people on the planet. Yet these advantages represent a very mixed blessing, a "culture of comfort."

Nearly all of Scripture's sixty-six books include passages that help believers face the challenges a "culture of comfort" presents. God has sent us *into* this world, and yet not *of* it, and commissioned us to carry out an unspeakably meaningful mission here. The entire Bible story is about an intervention from the outside as the first cause and final cure—of God's creating everything in the beginning (Genesis 1) and intervening to take away the sin of the world (John 3:16).

Especially over the past forty-plus years, Christians in the western world have seemed to grow increasingly comfortable with the advantages that this life has to offer. In many ways, we have become a part of the problems engulfing our world, our communities, our families, and even our own hearts. We have bought into the values of the culture around us. We have made it our whole-hearted purpose in life to avoid one thing: *discomfort.*[17]

Not only the unconverted, but the converted heart of the Christian will war against the world's ways, the flesh, and the devil until Jesus returns to make all things new. Christian, be wise, and put on the armor!

DON'T GET COMFY HERE!

Scripture again and again describes the normal Christian life as anything but a life of ease. Consider these examples:

> And not only this, but we also exult in our tribulations, knowing that tribulation brings about perseverance; and perseverance, proven character; and proven character, hope; and hope does not disappoint, because the love of God has been poured out within our hearts through the Holy Spirit who was given to us.
>
> Romans 5:1–5, (NIV)

> In this you greatly rejoice, though now for a little while you may have had to suffer grief in all kinds of trials. These have come so that your faith—of greater worth than gold, which perishes even though refined by fire—may be proved genuine and may result in praise, glory, and honor when Jesus Christ is revealed.
>
> 1 Peter 1:3–7, (NIV)

> But rejoice insofar as you share Christ's sufferings, that you may also rejoice and be glad when his glory is revealed.
>
> 1 Peter 4:12–13

God tells us to rejoice in our suffering. The Bible warns God's people against the dangers of adopting the culture of the world around us, the thoughts and values fueled by Satan and fanned into flame by humanity's rebellion against God and his Christ[18]:

> [Jesus said,] "If you were of the world, the world would love you as its own; but because you are not of the world, but I chose you out of the world, therefore the world hates you."
>
> John 15:19

> Now we have received not the spirit of the world, but the Spirit who is from God, that we might understand the things freely given us by God. And we impart this in words not taught by human wisdom but taught by the Spirit, interpreting spiritual truths to those who are spiritual.
>
> 1 Corinthians 2:12–13

Our God knows, loves, and cares for our hearts. Remember, he notices when even one downy feather falls from a bird's wing or a blade of grass quakes in the wind (Luke 12:22–31). Not only that, he sent his own Son to die for us! Surely he does not allow his own redeemed sons and daughters to suffer pointless pain! God does not needlessly deny relief and comfort to his children or to the world he so loves (John 1:12; 3:16).

Instead, he uses the weeping and the heartbreak we experience to protect us from the dangers of a culture that opposes the salvation he has begun in us. God uses our suffering to refine our hearts, to temper them so that we adopt the temperament of Jesus himself, who "suffered not so that we would not suffer, but that we would become more like him."

To illustrate the dangers posed by our culture of comfort, let's begin with examples drawn from a global perspective, then the dangers posed for the church, and finally, the dangers a culture of comfort poses for individual hearts. As we consider these examples and a few of the implications, temptations, and consequences embedded in them, we will more thoroughly understand the dangers we face.

> Because we are so inclined to put our own comfort and advantage first and avoid adversity... Our most merciful Father comforts us by this teaching: that he promotes our salvation (and sanctification*) by inflicting the cross upon us. (*What Calvin calls "furthering our salvation.")
>
> John Calvin, parenthesis added

Our culture of comfort directly and indirectly:

- Promotes *humanism,* a humanity-centered (vs. Christ-centered) view of the universe, of laws and other governmental regulations; a culture of comfort also creates habits of the heart to match that view.

- Welcomes widespread *secularism* (e.g., "This world is all that exists") with its corresponding rejection of a godly perspective on human behavior (i.e., no shame, no toleration for religion, no ultimate accountability to a super-natural authority).

- Encourages rampant *pluralism* which is often quickly followed by its philosophical cousin—full-blown *relativism* and the denial of absolute truth.

- Justifies society-wide *privatization* with its implication that one's private life has no bearing on one's public life.

- Deceives us into devising simplistic solutions for healing the world's deepest problems. These solutions are ultimately unworkable and fruitless (e.g., education will prevent the spread of HIV/AIDS; family values will reduce the prison population; democracy all around the world will end all wars; redistributing the world's wealth will eliminate poverty). All this conspires to keep us from seeing that the only answer to humanity's plight is Jesus Christ.

- Harms children by undermining Biblical parenting, replacing it with a view of parents and children as "best pals". The parent's God-given responsibilities are made subservient to their needs.

- Promotes people into positions of power before they have faced their emotionally wounded hearts and spirits. These broken leaders then create and/or enable similar wounds in the organizations they try to lead.

- Encourages young people to choose a career based on an idealized identity or on the allure of consumerism and materialism, rather than urging them to create a lifestyle intentionally designed to capitalize on the potential for glorifying God.

- Leads to a degradation of the role of fatherhood, because when one father refuses to face the pain of self-examination, he leaves his children's hearts hiding and hardened to the role of Defender that fathers are created by God to fulfill.[19]

- Endangers the most innocent and vulnerable members of society when "choice" trumps the emotionally challenging but Scripturally mandated need to choose LIFE, from conception to natural death, as the Bible defines it. [20]

- Engenders a pathological and cultural narcissism that treats any threat, large or small, to one's agenda, life, ego, or predetermined comfort zone as a murderous attack on their identity and dreams.

- Supports entire industries that thrive on the creation and distribution of medications that have the potential to suppress a more holistic understanding of the root causes of conditions like depression, attention deficit disorder, anger management issues, and passive-aggressive tendencies.[21]

- Fosters the creation of "seeker-friendly churches" in which leaders and members alike often avoid the painful but necessary process of speaking the truth in love.

- Encourages heart-hardening *remorse* (fear and shame for the consequences) after committing a sin, rather than *repentance* (confessing sin to the Holy Spirit, another believer in Christ, and being accountable for turning from the sin).

- Entices Jesus' disciples to embrace only half the Gospel, either *legalism* (which focuses on the disciple becoming outwardly pious, while encouraging judgmentalism, law-centeredness, and works-based attempts to merit God's favor) or *liberalism* (which focuses on the love of Christ while numbing the heart to the seriousness of sin, denying the truths of Scripture, and counting on God to forgive anyway).

- Creates a kind of amnesia by which Christians forget our unique status as "resident-aliens" in this universe who do not belong here. One day Christ will call us home.

- Tempts even God's people to avoid the kind of long-term relationships that require heart transparency, emotional vulnerability, and sacrifice over time. Creates instead a preference for surface relationships that are anonymous, disposable, and safe, but never deepen beyond what's comfortable.

- Deceives Christians into believing that salvation is the end, rather than the means, which God is using to create and renew communities of faith in anticipation of the New Heavens and New Earth. Such faith communities call for a self-sacrificial commitment of time, talent, and treasure and are thus, almost by definition, emotionally *discomforting*. Disciples of Christ are *saved* and *sent!*

- Promotes a preference even in Christian hearts for convenience over commitment, calm over productive conflict, shallowness over self-knowledge, selfishness over stewardship, and self-protection over self-disclosure.

- Lulls us into spiritual drowsiness that downplays the damage sin has done in our hearts, encouraging us to deny our personal need for confession and repentance. Repentance, of course, is decidedly uncomfortable.

- Leaves us little choice but to avoid being hot or cold about much of anything in life let alone our faith. We become lukewarm in our faith (Revelation 3:16—a very stern warning).

- Provides fertile soil for Satan's various and deceptive schemes to flourish in the human heart, the most problematic of which is at the "core" (e.g., the apple Eve ate despite God's loving command) of the fallen heart, *"Did God really say ... ?"* (Genesis 3:16—when Satan planted the seed of doubting God in Eve's heart which flourished in all hearts thereafter).

In short, the culture of comfort creates a heart-hardening environment. When we allow Christ to care for us through our discomfort, our hearts soften. But when we unknowingly allow or purposely invite the world, our own sinful flesh, or the devil himself to anesthetize our discomfort, it's the hardening process itself that makes us more comfortable. Our heart and our witness become exactly like the cross in the stone seen in the Introduction and Heart Application—encased, impermeable, and hidden from a watching, wounded, yet deeply wanting world.

ESCAPING DISCOMFORT

The human desire to avoid discomfort is both simple and complex. Evading the uncomfortable things in life:

- Gives evidence as to the fallen nature of the human heart.

- Creates unnecessary pain that we ourselves and those around us must endure.

- Potentially sets us on the path that leads toward the only permanent and ultimate cure for our pain—the *weeping/window/way* process by which God uses human suffering to transform human hearts.

I once participated in a weekly forum of executive business leaders who were transitioning in their careers. The forum offered members the opportunity to consider the spiritual component of their lives, especially as it impacted their transitioning careers.

One week, I told a story that exemplified how God had used "the weeping, the window, and the way" to help me through a dramatic transition in my own life and career. Following the session, I noticed a gentleman waiting to speak to me outside the room. Somewhat sheepishly, he approached me to ask, "Do you think that some sort of trial or tribulation is *always* a necessary component of change and growth?" In an instant I saw that he was desperate for a big change in his life, yet he wanted to avoid the pain of digging deep enough to see what his life's delays, dreams, and doubts would say to him. Beyond a shadow of a doubt, he wanted me to say, "Well, I don't think trials are *always* necessary." I did not say that. I could not say that.

Despite the discomfort that he knows we will experience in it, God always intends his *weeping/window/way* for our good. He knows that when we attempt to avoid the pain, we doom ourselves to the same state of heart and spirit experienced by the author of Ecclesiastes:

> "Meaningless! Meaningless!" says the Teacher. "Utterly meaningless! Everything is meaningless ... under the sun."
>
> Ecclesiastes 1:2 (NIV)

Note this truth carefully: If our *weeping,* or for that matter our *prosperities,* are understood apart from God, only on an earthly plane (i.e., "under the sun"), our hearts will harden and continue to harden. We are condemned to living a meaningless life. What's more, we inevitably will choose one of the three worldviews the author of Ecclesiastes explored as he attempted to cope with life lived *only* "under the sun."

Most people live out one or more of these "ism's." Tragically, each injects an equally potent spiritual poison into the human heart:

- *Stoicism*—a lifestyle that denies or avoids emotions, considering them irrelevant. Stoics deal with destructive emotions by means of extreme self-control and inner fortitude.

- *Hedonism*—Stoicism's opposite. This lifestyle focuses on experiencing as much unrestrained pleasure as possible, considering *pleasure* to be life's chief end.

- *Existentialism*—a lifestyle that grows out of despair, based on the belief that existence has no purpose or meaning. Existentialists put on a brave front and face daily life with courage and even lofty convictions, despite the deep despair.

In contrast to these toxic approaches to life's hurts, God calls his people to share in Christ's sufferings. Our tears do not surprise God, nor should we find ourselves surprised by the pain and tears in life.

DISCOMFORT, DISEASE, AND POTENTIAL DELIGHT

Have you ever said, "That experience really touched my heart"? Our weeping touches God's heart, too. The sensory pain we experience as the result of illness or injury, the emotional pain of loneliness, fear, or shock, the repressed pain that shows up in behaviors that lie invisible, all of it touches God's heart. How sad, then, if we waste our weeping, if we fail to let the Holy Spirit use it for the redemptive process and purposes he intends!

By means of his *weeping/window/way*, God, in love and truth, wants to help us crucify our sinful nature. Through our suffering (*weeping*), he opens a *window* into our hearts through which we see both our *sin* and how deeply loved we are in Christ Jesus (Romans 1:18–32; 8:1–39). God intends that this process happen not just once, at our conversion, but in every time of *weeping*, every time discomfort breaks into our awareness and upsets our self-satisfied complacency. Through that window, we spot the specific idols that are causing us pain by resisting their own dethronement. Beloved, when you avoid discomfort with all your heart, you avoid the only comfort God offers for your heart—his forgiveness for your sins, his merciful eviction of those idols, and a supernaturally renewed vitality for God's mission to the world.

I remember one day as a kid when I ran headlong into a field of tall grasses. Great fun, until I realized the field was covered almost entirely in burr-bearing plants. My mother spent a long hour or more teasing the burrs out of my hair. Excruciating pain, but it had to be done.

Similarly today, I would much rather my loving, truth-speaking, and completely empathetic Savior and Lord "tease the sin out of my heart." It is decidedly uncomfortable, but if we resist, we face two extreme dangers:

- The danger of landing in *hell* when sin has taken its natural course and created such hardness of heart that pride now exerts a stranglehold on the unbelieving heart, demanding complete control of that heart—forever! (See Matthew 5:29–30; 10:34–42.)

- The danger of landing in *heaven* in a state short of what God desires because I refuse to offer up my whole heart to Jesus while still here serving him on earth (Philippians 4:17; Hebrews 4:13; 13:17; 1 Peter 4:5).

If the fans of the "loving and peaceful Jesus" in our culture of comfort were to learn the depth of his hatred for sin in our lives, it would shock them into either true faith or rejection of his teaching. After all, the "loving and peaceful" Jesus once counseled his followers:

> Woe to the world for temptations to sin! For it is necessary that temptations come, but woe to the one by whom the temptation comes! And if your hand or your foot causes you to sin, cut it off and throw it away. It is better for you to enter life crippled or lame than with two hands or two feet to be thrown into the eternal fire. And if your eye causes you to sin, tear it out and throw it away. It is better for you to enter life with one eye than with two eyes to be thrown into the hell of fire.
>
> Matthew 18:7–9

Despite our sin, Jesus loves us still—when we repent and believe in faith (1 John 1:5–10). Never forget! He has called us into his family of faith. We are, by faith, his brothers and sisters. He took all our condemnation and guilt upon himself at the cross. Those who trust in him as Savior and Lord need never bear that burden: "There is now no condemnation for those who are in Christ Jesus" (Romans 8:1). Jesus loves us just where we are, but he is not satisfied to leave us there. As firmly as he told the adulterous woman, "Neither do I condemn you. [But,] go, and sin no more" (John 8:11), so he commands us to leave our lives of sin. He has freed us to live for him and leave our sin and guilt behind. You see, Jesus took God's condemnation upon his own shoulders so we wouldn't have to! The discomfort of sin and guilt is gone for those who are in Christ. Yet, salvation, too, can be uncomfortable if we fail to use it for the purposes of a radical intervention in the lives of those around us who are living in a broken world. Consider this equation:

Impression (the entrance of God's Word, an apprehension of his Truth and his will for our lives deep within our heart) *without . . .*

Expression (relentlessly and joyfully releasing God's Truth into the lives of people living in the world of hurt all around us) *will result in . . .*

Depression (the emotional state of the self-oriented, compartmentalized, unused, and hardened heart)[22].

THE CURE?

The final cure for every iota of brokenness of any kind will not come until Jesus Christ returns to make all things absolutely new! In this True Truth we have the most marvelous and unshakable hope:

> Then I saw a new heaven and a new earth, for the first heaven and the first earth had passed away, and the sea was no more. And I saw the holy city, the new Jerusalem, coming down out of heaven from God, prepared as a bride adorned for her husband. And I heard a loud voice from the throne saying, 'Behold, the dwelling place of God is with man. He will dwell with them, and they will be his people, and God himself will be with them as their God. He will wipe away every tear from their eyes, and death shall be no more, neither shall there be mourning, nor crying, nor pain anymore, for the former things have passed away.'
>
> Revelation 21

The heart of mankind restored to God's image and Eden-like state will indeed be one of the most glorious manifestations of God's redemptive plan.

But, until then:

- Double-back and do an honest assessment of the nature of your faith in the midst of a Bible-based community of loving saints. Make sure you have indeed been born again, and are not striving in faith based on a religion of meritorious works, unworthiness, or cheap grace (2 Corinthians 5:17; Galatians 6:15; 1 Peter 1:3, 23).

- Embrace "the big picture fact" that you exist uniquely, and by God's grace, within the big story of his redemptive plan[23]. You have a crucial and special role to play within that plan, but this will remain *unknown* to you if you avoid the "joyous discomfort in your trials" (Philippians 3:10; Colossians 1:24; James 1; Hebrews 5:8).

- Embrace the fact that the primary idols of pride, control, and comfort (worldliness) desire to woo us away from everything and anything that would help us become "those who belong to Christ Jesus"—people who have, by the Spirit's supernatural power at work within our hearts, "crucified the flesh with its passions and desires" (Galatians 5:16–26).

- Embrace opportunities God provides to examine our hearts and discover the places in which we have grown too worldly (Psalm 51; 58; 139).

- Take up the cross and take in the suffering that Jesus endured as he went about his ministry here on earth (1 Peter 4:12; Revelation 2:10).

- Proactively and urgently run towards the chaos of heartbreak in our world to comfort other hearts. (2 Corinthians 1:3–7; Philippians 2; 2 Timothy 3:16–17).

- Involve the counsel of Christ, the Bible and a community of the faithful friends in the proactive pursuit of holiness, maturity, and service (Psalm 119:24; Acts 1:2; John 17; Revelation 3:18).

This is the way, the only way, by which God works in us his unspeakably grand gift of a renovated, restored heart, a heart that is more like Jesus'.[24]

Despite the solution, the redemption for hardheartedness and suffering God has provided, many Christians who live in today's culture of comfort are depressed.[25] Even though there are a variety of reasons for this (reasons both legitimate and sinful), one key cause I would suggest involves a tendency in the church to treat the faith as simply one more self-help strategy. We have failed to identify the True Truth and act on it. We cling tightly to something that was meant to be given away. Impression always happens in the church mainly for the purpose of expression: [Jesus said,] "It is more blessed to give than receive" (Acts 20:35).

Paul addresses this issue as he writes to the church at Philippi, urging them not to look for ways to avoid the difficult obedience that creates joy in the hearts of Christ's followers. Check these commandments and warnings against allowing our hearts to harden by grasping onto Christ's blessings, and not giving them away:

> If you have any encouragement from being united with Christ, if any comfort from his love, if any fellowship with the Spirit, if any tenderness and compassion, then make my joy complete by being like-minded, having the same love, being one in spirit and purpose. Do nothing out of selfish ambition or vain conceit, but in humility consider others better than yourselves. Each of you should look not only to your own interests, but also to the interests of others.
>
> Your attitude should be the same as that of Christ Jesus: Who, being in very nature God, did not consider equality with God something to be grasped, but made himself nothing, taking the very nature of a servant ...
>
> Philippians 2:1–7 NIV

Again and again, God in love holds out the opportunity to choose the way of true and abundant life. But how easily his people choose another path, the path of false comfort, the path that leads to spiritual death, and often physical and eternal death later on:

> But they refused to pay attention and turned a stubborn shoulder and stopped their ears that they might not hear. They made their hearts diamond-hard lest they should hear the law and the words that the Lord of hosts had sent by

his Spirit through the former prophets. Therefore great anger came from the Lord of hosts.

Zechariah 7:11–12 (The Message);

When we know the truth about our own heart's condition at the deepest level, we have a much more finely-honed ability to recognize it in others and, thus, become a more effective agent for compassionate healing!

THE CROSS IN THE STONE

Before we go on, pause for a moment to take a fresh look at the image of the stone at the beginning of the Heart Application section, page 106. Think about it. Do you believe it is possible for a person who has Christ's cross planted firmly in the center of his or her heart, not to fully release the resurrection power of that cross into the world because of the heart's hardness surrounding the cross within?

When one is converted by the supernatural power of the Holy Spirit, one's heart of stone is *removed* and *replaced* by the birth, death, and resurrection of Jesus Christ. When Jesus died, you died; when Jesus was resurrected, you were resurrected; while Jesus followed his father's will instead of his own, you have the power to do the same within you.

As I think about the poor example of my own life, I would have to say that living in the reality of who I *truly* am in Christ is the most difficult aspect of my faith. Most of the New Testament missives to the first century church would support this notion as well: living in faith is hard and we need constant reminding. The Holy Spirit brought one of my favorite Old Testament passages into the New Testament to address the very same "heart problem" we have identified in our own culture of comfort:

Today, if you hear God's voice, do not harden your heart..."

Psalm 95:7–8; Hebrews 3:8, 15

If you look very closely at the picture of the stone in the Introduction and Heart Application segments, you will see a peculiarity, an apparently unimportant detail that speaks volumes about the reality I have been describing. Darker marks in the stone show how the contents of the cavern, the cleft in which the window/cross sits, were slowly yet methodically leached out as the stone hardened.

As I have asserted so far and will continue to repeat throughout the rest of this book, God intends to use the brokenness, suffering, and trials of this world as the *main means* of fulfilling his redemptive plan. If this is true, then what will happen to the faith life and witness of Christians who live deeply immersed in a culture that makes every effort to put off pain, supplant suffering, and deny discomfort of any kind?

Despite our Lord's intention to renovate our hearts, he has freed us to reject the process by which he does this. He will not override our choice to avoid his renovating power. Like the way of salvation as our Lord described it in Matthew 7:13–14, God's cleansing process for renovation, "the *weeping, window,* and the *way,*" is narrow. It leads to a circumcised heart and to True Life, a life of service not based on duty, but anchored in delight. Few find or follow this path.

TRICKLES OF GRACE... OR THE OVERFLOW OF JESUS CHRIST?

As I consider all of this, I think about the impact of Christ's cross on our culture and how his Truth can merely seep out from the church, and the hearts in which Christ has planted his cross. God intends that the power of the cross burst forth from our hearts with the supernatural power that raised Christ from the dead! That is the power that has been released into the hearts and spirits of all who know Christ. He calls us to live radically uncomfortable lives, animated by deep and personal thankfulness for the message of the cross.

Paul writes, "for just as the sufferings of Christ flow over into our lives, so also through Christ our comfort overflows" (2 Corinthians 1:6, NIV). If this is true, then its inverse is true as well: *For just as the sufferings of Christ [do not] flow over into our lives, so also through Christ our comfort [will not] overflow [into the lives of others]*". This is indeed a dreadful description of what happens when a Christian ignores, circumvents, or even knowingly rejects the plan God has put in place for giving us resurrection power, true peace, and eternal comfort.

When any of God's people grow so self-satisfied, self-indulgent, and self-centered that they can no longer "weep in dust and ashes" (cf., Psalm 102:9) over the brokenness all around, and when they cannot weep unashamedly over the joyous things that reflect the character of God in his creation despite the brokenness all around, then the intended overflow of comfort from those believers into the lives of others will not occur.

Why not? Because even as Christians, we can be tempted into keeping the comfort God has given us to ourselves. This is due to the residual sin within the born-again person as well as the foibles of living in a self-help system: it's all about me. But if we make this choice, it will slowly but surely harden and eventually destroy our hearts.

The "joy of... salvation" (Psalm 51:12) God has given us will shrivel up and die. We will lose the joy that comes from sacrificial service here on earth. Over time we will lose the miraculous blessing of seeing God's Shekinah glory—a sense that one is in the presence of God—in the redemptive outcome of every person to whom we choose to minister. We will also lose the position of higher authority in heaven when Jesus Christ stands face-to-face with us and asks: *"How did you use the faith in me, given you while on earth?"* (Hebrews 4:13; 13:17; Romans 14:12; 1 Peter 4:5).

The apostle Peter spent his dying breath writing to the followers of Christ about the dangers of allowing the heart to harden.

I intend always to remind you of these qualities, though you know them and are established in the truth that you have. I think it right, as long as I am in this body, to stir you up by way of reminder, since I know that the putting off of my body will be soon, as our Lord Jesus Christ made clear to me. And I will make every effort so that after my departure you may be able at any time to recall these things. I will always remind you of these things, even though you know them and are firmly established in the truth you now have.

2 Peter 1:12

Even our redeemed hearts are forgetful and prone to wander. We need continual reminders that we were created to love, serve, and share the message of salvation. As we have seen before, our forgetfulness is seldom innocent, but rather an outgrowth of the heart's sinful condition. One of the main roles of God's prophets in Old Testament times was to help God's people remember the True Truth. Today's prophets carry that same responsibility. You and I carry out a similar charge as we remind, encourage, exhort, and offer the hope of the Gospel of Jesus Christ to others.

FRUITFUL WEEPING

So I [God] weep, as Jazer weeps, for the vines of Sibmah. O Heshbon, O Elealeh, I drench you with tears! The shouts of joy over your ripened fruit and over your harvests have been stilled. Joy and gladness are taken away from the orchards; no one sings or shouts in the vineyards; no one treads out wine at the presses, for I have put an end to the shouting.

Isaiah 16:9–10

In what ways does it help you to know that God and his son (Isaiah 53:3; Luke 19: 21; John 11:28) weep much in the Bible?

The things that bring us to tears stir the deep places of our hearts. Weeping, and the circumstances that accompany it, insist that we stop our busy lives. Weeping cuts open the encrusted places of our hearts, making invisible things visible, opening up things unseen for our inspection. Until this happens, repentance, renewal and growth towards maturity and effectiveness remain impossible. We remain in large part resistant to God's will.

On the other hand, if we refuse to waste our weeping and use our trials as opportunities to listen to the Holy Spirit, we will find that he has "worked in us a heart of flesh to replace our heart of stone". We will have hearts that become increasingly more like Jesus' heart (Romans 6:14; 10:5–13; Hebrews 1; Ephesians 4:15–16; 1 John 5:4).

Hearts that have experienced the comfort of Christ's presence and power during times of weeping gain another great blessing. Such hearts are more readily able to run toward the chaos and discern the needs of others whom God has providentially placed in their proximity. Such hearts tend to recognize the hurt, self-deceit, and loneliness in others. This opens doors of opportunity for sharing Christ's love and peace.

Jesus knew well the hearts and spirits of those around him (Matthew 12:25; Mark 2:8; Luke 5:22; John 2:24). But I do not believe that he acquired this knowledge solely by accessing his supernatural, all-knowing nature as God. Nor did he need to do so. Why? Because Jesus suffered as we do. He monopolized on his own suffering as we should. He embraced his role as a suffering servant, and regularly called out to his Father, obeying out of destiny, love, and gratitude. Jesus responded to those in his midst out of their deepest need for spiritual re-creation and renovation.

Jesus knew human suffering, because he suffered, just as we do. I truly believe that Jesus understands God's plan for growth from the inside out (Hebrews 5:8), not simply in the abstract but through his own Way, Truth, and Life. He invites us into the same process so that we learn to know, grow, and sow a true and comforting intimacy with God the Father into both our own hearts and lives and the hearts and lives of others.

My own experiences early in life, and on that Christmas

night with my dad, absolutely revolutionized the empathy and compassion of my own heart and spirit. In ways I would not have believed possible, I know far better the hearts and spirits of others around me—those of complete strangers and of the people in my own family. I can personally testify to the fact that this protocol works! I point not to pride, but rather the process. Still, I resist it at times. Competing "truths" war for supremacy within our hearts. We believe many lies. Our emotions-will never fully align with the True Truth of God's Word and manifest in his Son Jesus, the Word Incarnate. We need his cross and his forgiveness.

Recently, I explained to a new friend—a warm-spirited woman in her mid-sixties—that I was completing the process of writing this book. I shared the title and explained that the story of my dad's suicide lay at the center. She looked at me for quite some time and said nothing. I waited. Finally she spoke, sharing a truth that was evidently lodged deep in her heart. "I cannot cry," she admitted. "I just can't."

I offered a question that invited her to take the risk of going with me to a still deeper place: "Would you like to be able to weep?"

She thought a moment, then replied haltingly, "Yes ... yes, I think I would."

Little did my friend know that in her desire to release her tears, God himself patiently waited, intent on helping her know him and his love. Releasing ourselves to our need to weep can be so *freeing* and yet so *fearful* if we can't trust God!

A SUMMARY: THE GOD OF ALL COMFORT

In review, why would an all-powerful Creator of an originally perfect, but now rebellious and broken world, care so much about our weeping and our comfort? The answer to that question helps to unlock the still deeper significance of our tears.

God cares about our weeping and about our comfort, first,

because God knows well what the heart was like "in the beginning;" he plans to bring it back to perfection "in the end." He sees the whole of his redemptive plan from beginning to the end, and he yearns for the day it is finally complete.

Second, God cares about our weeping and our comfort because that is who the Triune God revealed in the Bible is. Perfect love in community cannot help itself as it is drawn inexorably to the aid of those who weep in pain and in joy. Just as human fathers run to their children to hold them as they cry, to hug them as the tears flow, so the Triune God longs to comfort his children as well. God offers his soothing love to us, simply because we need it as we weep, mourn, and woefully wax under the yoke of brokenness of this time in which we live, the time between Adam's Fall and Christ's return. In this time, God's comfort is our only hope.

Still, we dare never forget God's intention that we give his comfort away to others in their need. We dare not hold onto that comfort as if it were the ultimate self-help program. As we will see in more detail later, God redeems our weeping, not simply to make us feel better, but with the intent that with him we become "co-redeemers" of others' tears. Just as the planets influence one another's orbits, so the people of God find themselves drawn towards one another in times of weeping.[26]

Third, God cares so deeply about our tears and our comfort because he has given his word, his promise to help us. We live in a horribly broken world. Suffering and trials of all kinds confront our senses constantly. God knows this, and he also knows that his fallen creatures—you and I included—must take full responsibility for creating that suffering and chaos to begin with (Genesis 3). And yet, he has promised somehow and always to incorporate the brokenness, the tears, the trials into his eternal and redemptive purposes for his glory and our good. He will keep that promise (Psalm 23, 119:50; Romans 8:28).

Finally, God cares deeply about our tears and our comfort because the salvation he has provided in Christ, our salvation from sin and our ultimate deliverance from all our tears (Revelation 21:4), is not an end in itself. Rather, it is the means to the brand new community, the new family, he is bringing into existence (Isaiah 56:1–8; Acts 2:40–47; Hebrews 11:13–16; 13:10–16).

As he comforts us in our times of weeping through his presence and promises, the Holy Spirit deepens our communion with him. At the same time, he draws us into a larger community of faith where weeping is best cared for, where it can be redeemed, and where we can then, as God's instruments in turn, use it in a way so that others experience his comfort. In doing so, our communion with one another deepens and community naturally, dynamically, and organically grows. This is all part of God's Redemptive Plan—of which you are a vital part.

GOING DEEPER...

If you would like to explore the ideas from this chapter further, I suggest reading:

Spiritual Depression: Darkness Before the Dawn: Overcoming Spiritual Depression, Tabletalk Magazine, March 2008, Ligonier Ministries, Orlando, FL

Guiness, O. Steering Through Chaos: Vice and Virtue In An Age Of Moral Confusion. Colorado Springs, CO: NavPress. 2000.

Cloud, H., & Townsend, J. Boundaries. Grand Rapids, MI: Zondervan. 1992.

Sproul, R.C. The Consequences Of Ideas: Understanding The Concepts That Shaped Our World. Wheaton, IL: Crossway Books. 2000.

Schaeffer, F.A. Death in the City. Wheaton, IL: Crossway Books. 2002.

Guiness, O. Fit Bodies, Fat Minds. Ada, MI: Baker Books. 1994.

Crabb, Dr. L. J. The Silence of Adam. Grand Rapids, MI: Zondervan Publishing House. 1995

Zacharius, R. Cries of the Heart. Nashville, TN: W Publishing Group (Thomas Nelson, Inc. 2002.

GOD'S PROTOCOL FOR REDEMPTIVE SUFFERING: THE WEEPING. THE WINDOW. THE WAY.

The six chapters you are about to read (Chapters 8–13) will apply what I have called "God's protocol" for allowing and using our suffering to bring about a deeper relationship with him, spiritual transformation, and increasing Christ-likeness.

The three phases of that protocol correspond to the principles of God's "three-step process" for sanctifying our suffering (See: Appendix "B", especially #6.) and the specific biblical passages the Holy Spirit brought to my remembrance as I knelt and cried out to God next to Dad as he lay dying in the snow.

My own personal experience—on Christmas night and elsewhere—provides a real-life illustration of the linear, yet cyclical and ascending protocol by which God would re-create in each of us the sacred heart and holy life of Jesus Christ himself. Each phase—the weeping, the window, and the way—is vitally important.

It's critical that we not short-circuit the process in a misguided attempt to "get back to normal", or be tempted by other such worldly advice. Heartbreak, challenges, and tragedies—be they everyday frustrations or massive catastrophes—each call us to pause, stay put for a time, remember, and mark well what God wants to tell us about the state of our hearts.

The Cycle of Redemptive Suffering

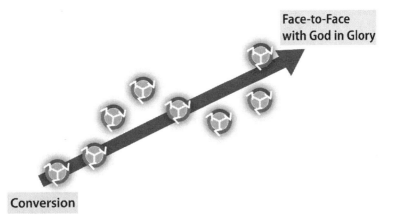

The Ascending Journey of Sanctification and Christ-Likeness

JESUS AND THE BIBLE: APPLYING THE WORD TO YOUR SUFFERING, HEART, SPIRIT, AND LIFE

Anyone who lives in our broken, sinful world should expect to suffer. While some try to deny this truth, sooner or later reality catches up with them. Christians can expect to endure additional suffering through persecution for Christ's sake. God can redeem all of our suffering, using it to glorify himself and accomplish his purposes in our lives.

To understand and live this more deeply, we apply the Word to our suffering hearts—the Bible, which is God's Word, the person of Jesus, the Word Incarnate, and words exchanged within a community committed to encouraging growth in faith and in world-redeeming effectiveness in one another. The next six chapters will help you do this.

"And I will give them one heart, and a new spirit I will put within them. I will remove the heart of stone from their flesh and give them a heart of flesh" (Ezekiel 11:19).

FROM ANOTHER WHO HAS
SUFFERED MUCH...

As we move forward and see how the stewardship of suffering can impact so many aspects of our life, I'm reminded of a quote from one who has endured much. Joni Eareckson Tada suffered a broken neck and paralysis when diving into a pool many years ago. But she, like few others we have seen, has been an awesome steward of her pain. She encompasses much of what we have learned so far in one sentence:

> God uses suffering to purge sin from our lives strengthen our commitment to him, force us to depend on grace, bind us together with other believers, produce discernment, foster

sensitivity and compassion, discipline our minds, spend our time wisely, stretch our hope, cause us to know Jesus Christ better, make us long for truth, lead as to repentance of sin, teach at us to give thanks in times of sorrow and blessing, increase faith, and strengthen character.

Joni Eareckson Tada, Stephen Estes, *When God Weeps*[27]

ALL WEEPING: ALL TEARS, ALL TRIALS, AND ALL FREEFALLS ARE GOD'S OFFER FOR FIRMING UP THE FOUNDATIONS OF FAITH

It's not the things in the Bible I don't know that frighten me; it's the things I do know!

Dwight L. Moody

Shortly after the 9/11 tragedy, I experienced a church service that included a guest pastor to help the congregation work through the trauma and grief evoked by those awful events. His sermon began something like this:

"Are you shocked and broken-hearted about this tragedy? I completely understand your shock and surprise. But, please know, my friends, that God is as surprised as are we. He is reeling as well!"

What about that? Are we to be consoled by the fact that God is as confused, surprised, and chaotic as his human creations? I don't think so! Only if we accept the premise that misery loves company does the consolation of God's supposed confusion give comfort.

To the contrary, Scripture clearly portrays the Lord as a God of supreme wisdom and absolute control (Psalm 139; Matthew 10; John 6:37). Nothing takes him by surprise, least of all human sin and the weeping that results from it. Scripture assures us that God is *not* the author of confusion, darkness, or frustration of any sort. He delights in truth, love, wisdom, and peace. These attributes of God increasingly come into our hearts, in part, as we allow him to help us discern the meaning of the confusion, darkness, and frustration we face as we live here in a broken, sinful planet.

What our Creator God understands is the genesis of our pain, confusion, and tears. The Scriptures reveal much about the causes of human suffering and the ways in which God mercifully intends to use it for our good. That revelation carries with it the ability to make us both wise and willing to cooperate with his design. (See, for example, John 14; and Philippians 2). God's True Truth makes it possible for us to place all of human history into the context of God's redemptive plan. This includes our individual and family histories—past, present and future, as well as each and every one of our personal tears and trials, joys and laughter. God's True Truth helps us see how all the pieces of history fit together—from the creation, to the fall, to Christ's birth, death, and resurrection, to his return to make all things new (2 Corinthians 2:11; 11:3; Revelation 1:1–22:21).

In the light of God's revealed wisdom, the Bible admonishes us to not be surprised when evil attacks or when sin eats away at our individual lives or in God's good creation. We need not find ourselves in shock when bad things happen to us, to the members of our own family, or to the rest of humanity. Those who live without Christ are often surprised because they live without the benefit of knowing the truth God has revealed to us (1 John 1:2). The surprise of unbelievers is predictable. But Christians should not be caught off guard when sin and suffering erupt, disturbing our fragile peace:

- "How could someone as nice as Harry leave his wife and family?"
- "This city's crime stats are simply shocking! I can't believe it."

- "The leadership of that big bank was so smart. How could they have let that happen?!"

- "They lived right next door to me. Their house was a meth lab?! It's mind-boggling!"

- "Our pastor did *what?*"

Especially in times of trial and tragedy, God wants to find in his people hearts both *wise* and *willing*, that trust his purposes and graciously submit to them, even when those purposes involve experiencing times of trial and suffering. Christians are not surprised by suffering; we anticipate it. And as we grow in grace, we are more fully prepared to run toward it, not away from it.

As you have grown in faith, have you noticed how you're more and more compelled to run, not walk, to the needs of others whose weeping has opened a window into their heart where you might be able to comfort, encourage, and help them see the way?

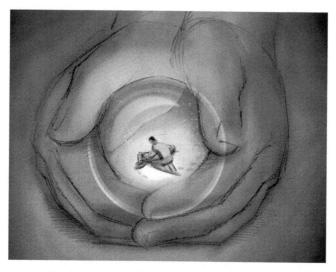

Dad and I on Christmas night protected
by God's presence and care.

Whether my Dad and I on Christmas night, or EveryMan experiencing a trial of some sort, all forms of suffering result from living in a broken world—and are lovingly allowed and used by God to draw us closer to his only son Jesus Christ.

HAPPY WEEPING

> Blessed are the poor in spirit...Blessed are those who mourn...Blessed are the meek. Blessed are those who are persecuted because of righteousness...Blessed are you when people insult you, persecute you, and falsely say all kinds of evil against you because of me...Rejoice and be glad...!
>
> Matthew 5:3–11

Really? Did Jesus Christ actually say, *"Rejoice and be glad..."* when life's circumstances crush our hearts and bring our spirits down to all-time lows? We perhaps expect something more like, "Hang in there," "Keep a stiff upper lip," or even, "I'm with you, and I understand. I'll take care of it. You get back to work." But, *"Rejoice and be glad...?"* It seems just a bit much, don't you think?

Then, just as now, the people who first heard Jesus' teaching hoped for more than a mere attitude adjustment from their Messiah. But Jesus knew that true life (Deuteronomy 30) centers on the heart and on developing the fruit that grows out of hearts that are engrafted into Jesus (John 15), hearts that trust in him alone for Life and abide in him. None of us are born with these kinds of hearts. Sinful and fallen, all human hearts need to be stripped of self and filled with Christ.

As previous chapters have pointed out, the blessed process Christian theologians call sanctification or purification takes place within a three-step process I have been describing throughout this book as *the weeping, the window,* and *the way.* Using this life-long process, God sets us apart for his service and sends us out on a mission for Christ with open-handed patience coupled with a near-fanatical urgency rooted in a twofold fact:

- Jesus is coming quickly to usher in the end of the redemptive age; time is very short (John 14:18, 28; 21:22–23; 2 Peter 3; Revelation 7).

- Satan, now released into the world, rages against Christ and seeks to discourage Christians and to keep non-

Christians from coming to faith; our adversary is blazing with anger, he knows his time is short, and he intends to go down swinging, taking with him every human soul he can manage to enslave (Revelation 12:13–17).

God intends to recruit our hearts—our whole selves—for works of justice and mercy. The Gospel of Jesus Christ is not some kind of divine self-help program. Weeping initiates the process God uses to transform our trials into triumph and our tears into the means by which our hearts are ultimately transfixed upon Jesus Christ. If we commit to not using trials for Christ's triumph both in and through us we have missed the point of God's entire redemptive plan.

Until we realize this and keep on reminding ourselves of it, God appears detached, indifferent to our pain. If we love God only for the ways he can help us advance our own agenda and enhance our own comfort, we miss what he wants to do both in and through us. If that is our objective, then achieving our own agenda has manifestly become our god. When our plans for life go south, we will find ourselves bewildered and then blame God as our faith falters. Those who look to us as God's people for wisdom and help in their own times of weeping will look in vain.

BLESSED TO BLESS

Pain—and the tears that come with it—are a fact of life in our broken universe. Too often as we experience this brokenness, God's people behave like the storybook character Chicken Little, who runs from one end of the farmyard to the other shouting: "The sky is falling! The sky is falling!" Despite our frequent shock when trouble and turmoil transpire, we can be certain our wise and gracious God has absolutely figured the disasters, tears, and pain of a fallen creation into his awesome plan of redemption. After all, what does the word redemption refer to if not the present day's utter ruin, and God's perfect plan to remake it all for time and eternity—through Christ in YOU!

In the face of our inevitable tears, some well-meaning Christians would advise: "When suffering overtakes us, we are not called to try to understand it. We simply 'fall upon God,' and trust him in the trial." To this counsel, I would offer a crucial amendment: the Bible makes it clear that God wants us to enjoy a wise and informed faith, infused with insights from God's inspired Word.

The Lord wants his people to have a firm enough grasp on his marvelous redemptive plan that we are enabled by that understanding and the gracious work of his Holy Spirit through it to join him in a purposeful lifestyle, in which we engage in the process of advancing his redemptive plan

When we feel confused or even paralyzed by suffering, Scripture calls us to remember that we live in an utterly broken world. The war with evil has been won by Christ on his cross, and yet the "clean up action" continues. Unexploded mines litter the landscape and sometimes spontaneously blow up, and many pockets of enemy resistance remain (John 19:30; Revelation 12:7–16). And yet in a way both profound and mysterious, our Lord's mercy extends so far that he uses the world's brokenness. He uses our brokenness for his glory and for our blessing, until Jesus returns again to wipe away every tear with his own hand (Isaiah 25:4–8; Matthew 11:28–30; Revelation 21:1–4).

When we grasp this True Truth, it conveys marvelous benefits, and we become more willing to fall on God in our own times of trial. We wisely understand and anticipate the weeping of others, seeing it as God's call for us to proactively act as his agents in their lives.

Conversely, surprise at our own weeping or "paralyzing shock" at the world's tears is one of the deadliest forms of Biblical foolishness. It prevents the Body of Christ from fully and immediately engaging in the task God has given us, the Christ-based triage of heart and spirit so necessary in times when those around us suffer. Weeping is the doorway to a form of ministry that is uniquely ordained by God for the offering of his comfort in the flesh—meaning you and me. Have you accepted and embraced this amazing call upon your life? Are you less surprised by suffering and more super-charged to be a redeeming force within it?

Our Redeemer intends that we accurately anticipate the effects of the Fall in our own lives. He also intends that we anticipate the effects of the Fall in the lives of others in our sphere of influence. Our Redeemer-God intends that we walk through the doors the Holy Spirit opens, speaking truth, love, and peace to *any* hurting heart.

FAITH'S FOUNDATION

As the Book of Hebrews begins, the author addresses a community of believers who face a severe trial. Disillusioned and distraught, they are almost ready to jettison their faith in the living God. They are ready to give up the True Truth and go back to their former faith system, a socially appropriate, though false, set of beliefs. With this in mind, consider the blessed reminder the writer of Hebrews offers:

> In the past God spoke to our forefathers through the prophets at many times and in various ways, but in these last days he has spoken to us by his Son, whom he appointed heir of all things, and through whom he made the universe.
>
> The Son is the radiance of God's glory and the exact representation of his being, sustaining all things by his powerful word.
>
> After he had provided purification for sins, he sat down at the right hand of the Majesty in heaven. So he became as much superior to the angels as the name he has inherited is superior to theirs.
>
> Hebrews 1:1–5

Think about this! Those weeping first century Christians needed more than anything else a foundation, a secure place on which to recover from the freefall of their fear. And so the Holy Spirit took them back to the beginning, to the foundational truths that underlie the Christian faith. These struggling believers needed to be reminded that only by fixing their eyes on Christ would they have the clearest possible view of God. Persecuted for faith in the Savior who once and for all time removed their sins in the blood of his cross, they needed to remember that Jesus Christ is God himself, the very God who forever reigns over the universe to bring glory to his name. Their suffering was not out of God's control, nor had it taken him by surprise.

The struggling present-day church needs to hear this same True Truth. We, too, need to go back to the beginnings, back to the creation and to the God who loves us more deeply than we could ever imagine, even though we have turned our backs on him (Romans 5:8). This God treats all our tears, whether of pain or joy, in a very special way. He intends to use them all to draw us closer to himself and to one another (Matthew 22:36–40).

As our trials and troubles strip away our self-sufficiency, the Holy Spirit wants to help us know more deeply his True Truth, grow in spirit toward emotional maturity and more Christ-like affections, and sow the love of Christ into the hearts of others who suffer. We sow that love as we witness to them about God's mercies and look for ways to comfort those who weep. Our good and gracious God wants to use our weeping in such a way that:

- We *know* Christ and our need for him more profoundly, even as learn to know our own hearts more thoroughly. In times of weeping, the Holy Spirit kneads the Gospel more deeply into the hidden recesses of our hearts where faith resides, calling and empowering us to live in willing obedience and submission to the One who made the Gospel possible—Jesus Christ.

- We *grow* in the grace and truth he offers and then intentionally look for ways to follow him more nearly, love him more dearly, and serve him more willingly by serving others in joyful obedience to our Redeemer.

- We then *sow* words and actions of witness into the lives of others as we seek out ways we might provide comfort to other sufferers. Consider the promise the Holy Spirit has attached to this sowing in Psalm 127 verses 5–6: *Those who sow in tears will reap with songs of joy. He who goes out weeping, carrying seed to sow, will return with songs of joy, carrying sheaves with him.*

This is the Ecosystem of Eden Redeemed that God created in Christ within our hearts after the Fall. Heaven dwells here among us because the hearts of those who know and love Christ, having been redeemed are also now being re-shaped. Following are some Bible verses I have paraphrased:

The God of all restoration wants to bring his people back to himself so that our hearts can be healed, more and more fully restored.

Deuteronomy 30; Romans 10

The God of all re-creation wants to use our times of weeping in redemptive ways *so that* the organic knowing-growing-sowing cycle can be released in our hearts and lives in greater power in future trials, future times of weeping.

Romans 8:28; Hebrews 4:14, 5:7

The God of all reassurance wants to pour his comfort and peace out into our hearts so that his comfort and peace can more freely flow out from our hearts into the hearts of others who weep.

2 Corinthians 1:3–7

CHARLIE: A GLIMPSE OF GRIEF FROM A MOTHER'S PERSPECTIVE, BY ZOE GLIK

"The weeping, the window, and the way?" Oh yes, I've been there. I am there. In the days and months after July 17, 2006, I'd try with all my heart to remember that life is precious and fleeting and not to take a single moment of it for granted...in a matter of seconds, my life had changed forever. Nothing, no word or warning could have prepared me for the horrific day we learned of our eldest son Charlie's sudden and tragic death.

The two police officers came to our front door to tell us he had been killed in a car accident. Upon hearing their explanation, my knees collapsed to the floor, my chest caved in, and my heart broke, just as my husband and other son, Billy's had, shattered into a million pieces. Shortly after the officers left, I remember the three of us in a huddle, making a promise, sealing a covenant that no matter what, we would not let what had happened ruin the rest of our lives.

Clearly and not so clearly, a foundation was laid under our feet and it was strong enough to get us up and moving toward a recovery from the hell we were living. How often it's been said, we were recovering from "every parent's worse nightmare". Life up until that day was so good. We were coasting along with our share of problems and obstacles, but with a relative level of happiness and peace. We had everything going for us, our health, security, and wonderful families to share our joys and sorrows too. My husband and I were doing our best to raise the boys with faith in God, loyalty to family and sound character. We had each grown up with supportive and loving parents. Our lives and our world were as perfect and comfortable as could be...and then the officers arrived.

To describe the experience of losing a child in a senseless tragedy is difficult. I knew deep down that this event had the potential to destroy me and that it would take every ounce of strength to weather this inescapable storm. One of the hardest things was to see my elderly parents trying to help me, but seeing me so wounded in body, mind and spirit, they were tempted to despair ... my parents taught all six of us that your faith is the absolute most important aspect of your life.

My dad is my hero. To see that much unfamiliar sorrow in his eyes was simply heartbreaking. Later, he would encourage me and advise me in ways only he could do. My dad is a faithful, righteous and wise man. God was I glad he was there for me in the worst of the dark suffering. I remember calling one morning to tell him we had found a grief counselor. He responded, "Great, honey, we have one two. His name is Jesus Christ and he's free." What a relief it was to laugh.

The magnitude of the loss and the depth of the pain was apparent in all aspects of my life. I walked with a limp and felt like I had a sand bag on my right shoulder. When I cried, it seemed I had a hot pinball lodged in my throat, and the effort it took just to swallow was huge. I groaned because there weren't any other adequate things I could do. The tidal wave of grief takes over crashing and receding in its own good time. Later, I would remember what Charlie had told me as a little boy ... he said, "Don't cry, Mom ... don't worry. God would never leave you alone." He was five and he was right. At times I'd cry, "God help me, I can't do this, Lord, Jesus help me." He answered my prayer by giving me a quiet courage that would sustain and help me through some excruciating times. I'd make it somehow, this much I knew. I'd make it by the grace of God, by His grace alone.

The "if only's" and guilt were killer but didn't plague me for too long. These are the things you think you could have controlled to stop the accident. For as many of these that existed there were "thank God's" too ... he didn't suffer, no one else was hurt, no one killed him, he wasn't angry or troubled. Charlie's life was filled with joy right up to the end. As hard as it was to believe and accept, he was in Heaven, the safest place of all.

Two things that continue to inspire me: First, the people from our past and present lives came in droves to comfort us. They offered us every imaginable aspect of help and support they could. And they prayed for us just shy of unceasingly. They prayed with hope and conviction. We had been sustained by the power of prayer, period.

Secondly, healing takes time and the path I was on lead to more healing. As a Mom, I didn't have too many choices or alternatives. I had to rely on the courage and truth God has been so gracious in giving me. And I trusted the intricate plan He has for me with more faith. The road to my healing has been giving back, offering a hug or a word of encouragement to the people in my life, friends and strangers. I believe in God's promise of eternal life through his only Son's life and death. Jesus Christ is at the center of my life. Without Him and His word, I'd be nowhere.

I will never look at any human being—every Image Bearer of God—the same again. For me, the fruits of this trial are more patience; more compassion; to live life for all it's worth each day; to treat my time, my gifts, and my treasure as precious in the sight of God; more assurance of my temporal and eternal destiny than ever before; more time with the person of the Holy Spirit . . . and much more!

Charlie used to tell me, "You have to live for today; tomorrow is never promised!" Truer words were never spoken by a young man who lived them out, and left behind a testimony to their vitally important power and truth.

I miss Charlie more than words could ever express. I miss his smile, his spirit for life, the gleam in his eyes, his humor and energy. All the things only a mother could know about her son. Just as the many who loved him for the treasure he was, I loved him too. Charlie had a heart of gold. I'll see him again. Of this I am most certain.

Please, beloved of God, do not waste your weeping. As C.S. Lewis warns in *The Four Loves*[28]:

> Love anything and your heart will be wrung and possibly broken. If you want to make sure of keeping it intact you must give it to no one, not even an animal. Wrap it carefully round with hobbies and little luxuries; avoid all entanglements. Lock it up safe in the casket or coffin of your selfishness. But in that casket, safe, dark, motionless, airless, it will change. It will not be broken; it will become unbreakable, impenetrable, and irredeemable. To love is to be vulnerable.

The titanic struggle of our wounded hearts involves the Christian's earnest desire that our hearts become more like the sacred heart of Jesus Christ. On the other hand, the Christian often avoids the weeping that we must embrace as an inherent part of growth towards Christ-likeness. As we desperately avoid the weeping, there can be no open window into our hearts, and thus, no way to grow in loving Jesus. Our hardened hearts remain locked up safe in the casket of our selfishness. In Chapter 9 we will further explore the protocol our Redeemer-God has set in place so that his children may avoid that casket.

GOING DEEPER...

For further reading, see:

Tada, J.E., & Estes, S. When God Weeps. Grand Rapids, MI: Zondervan. 1997.

CHAPTER NINE

YOUR WEEPING: STOPPING THE FREEFALL, AND RESETTING THE FOUNDATIONS OF THE FAITH—APPLYING GENESIS 1:1, JOHN 1:1, DEUTERONOMY 31:6

In my distress I called upon the LORD; to my God I cried for help. From his temple he heard my voice, and my cry to him reached his ears.

Psalm 18:6

My heart is in anguish within me; the terrors of death have fallen upon me.

Psalm 55:4

I waited patiently for the LORD; he turned to me and heard my cry. He lifted me out of the slimy pit, out of the mud and mire; he set my feet on a rock and gave me a firm place to stand.

Psalm 40:1–2

THE UPSIDE-DOWNNESS OF
GETTING IT RIGHT-SIDE-UP

The intermingling of our Godliness as Image-Bearers of the Creator and our idolatrous grasp of worldly things has, over time, blinded, deafened, and dumbed us to how it was in the beginning. Therefore, when God works to get things back in order, it can easily appear to us as though he's getting it all wrong.

Despite the testimony of God's people through the ages, we find ourselves tempted to live forgetfully. We can be blind to the paradoxes, ignorant of the counterintuitive principles and processes God masterfully employs to redeem us from the curse of sin. Ironically, God uses the very curse itself as a means by which to show us our core needs and drive us to himself for the redemption he has provided in Christ—and continued growth into the likeness and impact of Christ until he comes again.

Our forgetfulness does not change the truth that we live life entrapped, caught up in the matrix of a horribly upside-down world. Don't let it surprise you, beloved, that suffering is the door to joy; weeping leads to an increase of wonder and worship of God; sadness the entrance to happiness; rainy days the doorway to rainbows; tears the prelude to triumph; and the cross the gateway to the resurrection.

Viewed from a mere earthly plane, suffering will always seem upside-down. Sin has so completely infiltrated our universe that no human being can see things right-side-up without being born again from above (John 3:1–21). Only when we have become the new creations Paul describes in Galatians 6:15, only when God has begun the process of restoring his image in us, do the scales begin to fall from our eyes and our perceptions begin to clear. Only when we rest on a firm foundation can the freefall caused by traumatic circumstances stop, and the next stage in God's protocol begin.[29]

As we have already seen, the creation God himself described as "very good" fell into decay as a result of sin. Death invaded God's perfect creation in the Fall. Every tear ever shed in the centuries since Eden has fallen as a result of human sin. God's treatment of those who have turned back to him as the one and only true God is as tender and intimate as one could imagine:

> You [God] have kept track of my every toss and turn through the sleepless nights, each tear entered in your ledger, each ache written in your book.
>
> Psalm 56:8 (The Message)

The Freefall: All weeping, whether in joy or in sorrow, results in a "freefall of faith" and the opportunity to know for the first time, or re-establish, our foundations!

FREEFALLS AND FOUNDATIONS

As you recall in Chapter One, I fell into a terrifying freefall of heartbreak as I knelt next to my Dad's body. I cried out to God in terror for him to stop the freefall before I couldn't take it anymore. God answered this prayer by and through his Word in the Bible. His words of hope encircled-enfolded me with these words:

- *In the beginning … God said, …* (Genesis 1:1)

- *In the beginning was the Word …* (John 1:1)

- *Be strong and courageous. Do not fear or be in dread … for it is the* LORD *your God who goes with you. He will never leave you or forsake you* (Deuteronomy 31:6).

In the upcoming chapter, we will not only see exactly why the Holy Spirit provided me these specific passages from the Bible but how they might apply to your experiences of freefalls, of suffering trials of any kind.

Whether we want to admit it or not, this is the state of every human being when weeping occurs in varying levels of intensity. Heart-shattering circumstances can cause this, yet so can life's smaller hurts and challenges. Simply trying to live life apart from the True Truth can send anyone into a daily freefall. The teenage prostitute, forgotten by her parents, addicted to drugs, and focused on simply turning the next trick experiences freefall. But so does the apparently successful businessman who detests getting out of bed each day to face the purposelessness of his life. Only the foundation of a Biblical faith can prevent the freefall I've been describing.[30]

The experience of freefall, like all the other parts of my journey, was unique and personal. And yet, as I've noted earlier, Soren Kierkegaard, the Danish philosopher, once said, "That which is most personal is also most universal." Embracing this Truth empowers us to embrace other people—highly flawed image bearers of God like us.

My experience in Dad's garden was unique to me, yet you likely recognize it in your own life, too. Something like this has probably happened to you, more or less. The True Truths the Holy Spirit used to "catch me," as it were, and then plant my feet firmly on the Lord's foundation, apply in a universal way to all shattered and weeping hearts, all suffering spirits.

1. Please record any experiences in your life where you were in an emotional, psychological, or spiritual *freefall* that was tied to circumstances such as a sudden death, a broken relationship, a loss of a job, confronting an addiction of some sort, hearing the news of a life-threatening disease, etc. What, if any, *foundational* beliefs did you land on that stopped the freefall? Or, perhaps, did you ever land at all?

2. Is it possible that you are, to one degree or another, still in a freefall related to a time of sudden suffering or an unredeemed trial in your life? Or perhaps the experience has been somehow compartmentalized within your heart?

3. If and when you have experienced a freefall of suffering of any kind, could you recollect what sort of *foundation* may have stopped your freefall, and given you the sort of hope that you were going to be alright?

_____

_____

_____

_____

4. Were your foundations sure, rock-solid, and unshakeable? Or perhaps only a temporary form of foundation like distraction, denial, or delusion like "time heals all wounds", or "I'm fine ... really"!

_____

_____

_____

_____

With this in mind, let's take a more in-depth look at the Scriptures God brought to our attention during my own freefall. As we do that, we will consider three foundational truths that can also provide the springboard for the next important step in the journey. The three foundational truths are the "Creation Foundation," the "Christ Foundation," and the "Covenant Foundation."

The Foundations: No human being can be fully human without foundations of some kind. And no worldview except a Biblical worldview offers a foundation of faith that is rational, personal, foundational, and grace-full.

FOUNDATIONAL TRUTH 1: "CREATION FOUNDATION"–"IN THE BEGINNING"

Bang! A blow to the heart! A gunshot? A divorce? An unexpected phone call from the police? A crushing career-path disappointment? A fiancé who drops off the face of the earth without warning? An accidental or unexpected death in the family? A missed opportunity to comfort a friend—and then the discovery that it's too late? An unexpected pregnancy or late-term miscarriage? A sudden and terminal disease? A loved one offended by your faith who refuses to return your phone calls? A realization that there's got to be more to life than working, spending, saving, vacationing, retiring, and dying? A parent who has deeply disappointed you yet again? A cherished pet passed away?

With events just like these, the freefall begins in every human heart. And just as quickly, the Counselor, the Holy Spirit is always "timelessly present" in the "eternal now" (Tillich) to initiate or continue his work in our hearts. This is not an afterthought. It's not God's act of desperation in an "Oh, my goodness, what do we do now?" moment. No, it is the work by which the Holy Spirit has been reclaiming, reshaping, and re-animating human hearts since the Garden of Eden. The first foundational truth the Spirit used as he began that work in on Christmas night came from Genesis 1:1. Here are those words in their context:

> In the beginning, God created the heavens and the earth. The earth was without form and void, and darkness was over the face of the deep. And the Spirit of God was hovering over the face of the waters. And God said, "Let there be light," and there was light. And God saw that the light was good. And God separated the light from the darkness. God called the light Day, and the darkness he called Night. And there was evening and there was morning, the first day.
>
> Genesis 1:1; 2–5

Creation leapt into existence at the bidding of the Triune God. Theologians refer to this creation as happening *ex nihilo,* a Latin term meaning "out of nothing." The Father imagined the universe. The Son spoke the Father's mind, putting into words the universe the Father imagined. The Holy Spirit made these thoughts and words manifest in material ways by fluttering over the uncreated to create (Genesis 1:2).

In the very beginning, words mattered—literally! Through words, creation came to be. And words matter still today.

The Bible is replete with content that underscores the claims of Genesis 1 and the importance of those claims to the faith. Many of these carry special importance to those in freefall, who are faltering in their faith. There are well over five hundred Old Testament passages that refer to creation, one hundred of these in the emotional songs of Psalms and over seventy-five of them in the wisdom literature of Proverbs. Wisdom and emotional self-awareness are reclaimed and refined in sanctified suffering. And then consider the fact that the converse is also true: foolishness and emotional blindness are engendered by avoiding sanctified suffering.

In addition, these passages undergird each other as essential and foundational creation doctrines:

- The one, true God is eternal, perfect, infinite, and tri-une—one God in three distinct persons, co-equal in majesty: "Have we not all one Father? Has not one God created us?"

  Malachi 2:10

- Jesus' role in all things, not just some things: "In the beginning was the Word, and the Word was with God, and the Word was God. He was in the beginning with God. All things were made through him, and without him was not any thing made that was made."

  John 1:1–3

- God's creation out of emptiness leaves nothing out: "For by him [Christ] all things were created, in heaven and on earth, visible and invisible, whether thrones or dominions or rulers or authorities—all things were created through him and for him."

  Colossians 1:16

- God planned before time or creation to give to his elect, via his Holy Spirit and Son, your new heart: "Father, I desire that they also, whom you have given me, may be with me where I am, to see my glory that you have given me because you loved me before the foundation of the world."

  John 17:24

- God-centered faith begins with the foundation of his act of creation: "Now faith is the assurance of things hoped for, the conviction of things not seen. For by it the people of old received their commendation. By faith we understand that the universe was created by the word of God, so that what is seen was not made out of things that are visible."

  Hebrews 11:1–3

- God has linked his first and prefect creation inextricably to re-creative redemption, when all things will be made new: "The creation waits with eager longing for the revealing of the sons of God."

  Romans 8:19

- God plans to re-create the human heart: "Neither circumcision counts for anything, nor uncircumcision, but a new creation."

  Galatians 6:15

- God's final act in his Christ-centered plan to make all things new: "John to the seven churches that are in Asia: Grace to you and peace from him (God) who is and who was and who is to come, and from the seven spirits who are before his throne, and from Jesus Christ—the faithful witness, the firstborn of the dead, and the ruler of kings on earth."

Revelation 1:4–5; see also Revelation 21; 22; and 2 Peter 3:13

It is no small matter, then, that many today, even in the evangelical church, are playing fast and loose with the creation account in Genesis. As Tim Keller, pastor of Redeemer Presbyterian Church in New York City, has said, *"If you came from nothing, and you end in nothing, at least have the integrity to admit that your life 'in between two nothings' cannot possibly amount to anything."*

Is the creation account from Genesis some sort of metaphor or hocus pocus mythology that we can interpret any way we please? Can we ignore the question of the origin of the universe without chipping away at the foundation on which we stand in times of distress and weeping, the foundation that supports us even in our times of praise and thanksgiving? Absolutely not, beloved. The Bible's beginning sets the stage for the Bible's ending, and for everything in between.

When we embrace the True Truth that the Triune God made everything out of nothing in the beginning, then we will also fully appreciate his magnificence, especially his wisdom and power. We will see ourselves as image-bearers of this same God. And we see those around us as image-bearers of their Creator, too. Perhaps most important of all for those who find themselves in the free fall of fear and pain, taking Genesis 1 at its face value leaves us with great peace in regards to questions about all other True Truth revealed by God in Scripture. God, in love and truth, sustains the universe he has made and in that sustaining providence, holds us securely.

Beginnings really matter. If you describe yourself as a follower of Jesus Christ and yet have somehow come to accept an anti-theistic form of evolutionary or naturalistic creation, then you are straddling two incompatible belief systems.

The incompatibility of these systems can resolve itself in only one of two ways. You can submit to the divine revelation from the Bible, or you can suppress the Truth and harden your heart.

THE CREATOR AS SUSTAINER

My wonderful 103-year-old grandmother, Mimi, used to pine away in her nursing home bed, "Oh Johnny, I just can't understand why God is leaving me here so long. I just want to go and be with him. I know, I know, he's got a lot going on. I know he's too busy with the really important things to take care of little 'ol me."

Many people living in our postmodern culture have embraced this false theology. They believe that God got things started just fine, but has since abandoned the helm of the ship, leaving us to flounder in a sea of chaos and randomness. Even committed Christians sometimes fall prey to a worldly view of God as benevolently indifferent, distractible, or even sadistic.

The idea that the Creator has adopted a policy of benign neglect toward his universe could not be further from the truth. Nor could it be more frightening! In times of weeping, we have no other foundation than to cry out to a God who is near. Consider these True Truths, all revealing our dependency on the Triune God as creator and sustainer, inspired by God and drawn from the Bible:

- Our own personal control over our destiny is limited and yet empowered by free will: "Will your cry for help avail to keep you from distress, or all the force of your strength" (Job 36:19; see also Proverbs 11:4)?

- God's omniscience, apart from a personal relationship with the Savior, is convicting and frightening: "No creature is hidden from His sight, but all are naked and exposed to the eyes of him to whom we must give account" (Hebrews 4:13).

- The human lifespan is brief; our strength, insignificant: "The grass withers, the flower fades when the breath of the LORD blows on it; surely the people are grass" (Isaiah 40:7).

- Wealth, no matter how much we amass, will not keep death at bay: "The sun rises with its scorching heat and withers the grass; its flower falls, and its beauty perishes. So also will the rich man fade away in the midst of His pursuits" (James 1:11).

- We cannot save ourselves (or anyone else) in the Judgment: "No man can redeem the life of another or give to God a ransom for him" (Psalm 49:7).

- The War of All Wars is over, but skirmishes for souls will continue until Christ returns: "Now the salvation and the power and the kingdom of our God and the authority of His Christ have come, for the accuser of our brothers has been thrown down" (Revelation 12:10; see also verses 7–17).

In short, the human condition is bleak apart from Christ. Yet, we need not weep alone. Our fears need not overwhelm us. Not only did God create a magnificent universe for us, beautiful beyond our wildest dreams, he also sustains that universe in an even more magnificent fashion. He does this under the influence of the reality of the resurrection and the finished-but-not-yet-complete (until Jesus returns) work of Christ. He rules it, directing events in it for the good of his people. Because he does, we can trust him, even when we weep in frustration, loss, pain, and suffering. These foundational promises can slow and then halt freefalls of any kind:

- God sustains us in every trouble: "Blessed is the one who considers the poor! In the day of trouble the LORD delivers him; the LORD protects him and keeps him alive; he is called blessed in the land; you do not give him up to the will of his enemies. The LORD sustains him on his sickbed; in his illness you restore him to full health" (Psalm 41:1–3).

- God keeps a close eye on us and supports us: For the eyes of the LORD run to and fro throughout the whole earth, to give strong support to those whose heart is blameless toward him" (2 Chronicles 16:9).

- God's Son is always with us to counsel and comfort: "For to us a child is born, to us a son is given; and the government shall be upon his shoulder, and his name shall be called Wonderful Counselor, Mighty God, Everlasting Father, Prince of Peace" (Isaiah 9:6; Hebrews 13:5–6).

- Jesus has sent the Counselor, the Holy Spirit, to direct and sustain us: "If you love me, you will keep my commandments. And I will ask the Father, and he will give you another Helper, to be with you forever, even the Spirit of truth, whom the world [those who haven't put their faith in Jesus] cannot receive, because it neither sees him nor knows him. You know him, for he dwells with you and will be in you. I will not leave you as orphans; I will come to you" (John 14:15–18; 17–parenthesis added).

- The God of the Bible is unique, altogether transcendent, imminent, infinite, and intimate with those who love him: "I love the LORD, because he has heard my voice and my pleas for mercy. Because he inclined his ear to me, therefore I will call on him as long as I live. The snares of death encompassed me; the pangs of Sheol laid hold on me; I suffered distress and anguish. Then I called on the name of the LORD: "O LORD, I pray, deliver my soul!" (Psalm 116:1–4).

- God's Word sustains forever, giving us wisdom: "Your testimonies [the Word of God both in Christ and in the

Bible] are my delight; they are my counselors" (Psalm 119:24–parenthesis added).

- God pours out his love for us in Christ. No circumstance or power, not even the most dire, can pluck us out of his hand: "For I am sure that neither death nor life, nor angels nor rulers, nor things present nor things to come, nor powers, nor height nor depth, nor anything else in all creation, will be able to separate us from the love of God in Christ Jesus our Lord" (Romans 8:38–39).

- God's person, presence, and power sustain us: "The Lord is faithful. He will establish you and guard you against the evil one. And we have confidence in the Lord about you, that you are doing and will do the things that we command. May the Lord direct your hearts to the love of God and to the steadfastness of Christ" (2 Thessalonians 3:3–5).

- We are not alone, even when we feel alone: "Be strong and courageous ... for it is the LORD your God who goes with you ... He will never leave you or forsake you" (Deuteronomy 31:6).

Is it time to stop the freefall and shore up the foundations of your faith? Here are some questions you may find helpful as you think through the first foundational truth:

1. Do you believe with all your heart that the words with which the universe began are true? Explain.

_____

_____

_____

_____

_____

2. "The Bible's beginning sets the stage for the Bible's ending—and for everything in between." To what extent do you believe this to be true? Why does it matter?

_____

_____

_____

_____

_____

3. If you were to believe in the deepest recesses of your heart that the God of the Bible was the perfect, all-loving, all-truthful, all-knowing, all-powerful, all-present Creator and is presently the Sustainer of the Universe, what difference would it make in how you dealt with life's trials? (See: Philippians 3.)

_____

_____

_____

_____

_____

4. Would it help or hurt you in your suffering to know that the God of the universe created you and loves you? (See: Genesis 2; Psalm 139.)

_____

_____

_____

_____

_____

5. Consider Job, quite possibly the most afflicted person other than our Lord, described in Scriptures. In chapter

after chapter, his friends and family chided him. When he finally presented his case before God, what answer did he receive?

_____

_____

_____

_____

You might remember Job's comeuppance from God begins by, *"Where were you when I laid the foundation of the earth?"* and continues along these lines for two entire, and long, chapters! (See Job 38. Consider also Psalm 104:5; Proverbs 30:4; and Proverbs 8:24–29).

- Why did God give this specific reminder of love and truth to Job, do you think?
- How do God's words to Job further illuminate the concepts you have read so far in this chapter on freefalls and foundations?

FOUNDATIONAL TRUTH 2: THE CHRIST FOUNDATION

FOUNDATIONAL HOPE FROM HEBREWS

Christ Our King ... Come Down:

Now in putting everything in subjection to him, he left nothing outside his control. At present, we do not yet see everything in subjection to him. But we see him who for a little while was made lower than the angels, namely Jesus, crowned with glory and honor because of the suffering of death, so that by the grace of God he might taste death for everyone.

Hebrews 2:8–9

Christ Our Captain ... Having Conquered Death:

> For it was fitting that he, for whom and by whom all things exist, in bringing many sons to glory, should make the founder of their salvation perfect through suffering. For he who sanctifies and those who are sanctified all have one source.
>
> Hebrews 2:10–11

Christ Our Brother ... Christians Engrafted into the Family Tree of God:

> That is why he is not ashamed to call them brothers, saying, "I will tell of your name to my brothers; in the midst of the congregation I will sing your praise." And again, "I will put my trust in him." And again, "Behold, I and the children God has given me."
>
> Hebrews 2:11–13

Christ Our Suffering Servant ... Our model prophet, priest, and purpose:

> Since therefore the children share in flesh and blood, he himself likewise partook of the same things, that through death he might destroy the one who has the power of death, that is, the devil, and deliver all those who through fear of death were subject to lifelong slavery. For surely it is not angels that he helps, but he helps the offspring of Abraham. Therefore he had to be made like his brothers in every respect, so that he might become a merciful and faithful high priest in the service of God, to make propitiation for the sins of the people. For, because he himself has suffered when tempted, he is able to help those who are being tempted.
>
> Hebrews 2:14–18

The Bible includes many therefores. The word connects ideas to their logical conclusions. God's logic is perfect logic. As we begin to think about what I am calling "the Christ Foundation," consider this therefore from 2 Corinthians 5:17:

Even though we once regarded Christ according to the flesh, we regard him thus no longer. Therefore, if anyone is in Christ, he is a new creation. The old has passed away; behold, the new has come.

As we saw in Chapter 1, the first creation was totally ruined by sin. Human hearts were hardened and damaged beyond recognition. They were left in a state far different from what God had intended. But just as the Father, Son, and Holy Spirit cooperated in the beginning, to create our universe, the Triune God works continuously to win our redemption.

Jesus Christ condescended to remove himself from the timeless community of the Trinity, to live the sinless life that we should have lived, and then to die an excruciating death on a cross in our place. Just as in the beginning, the Son had spoken the Father's mind, putting into words the universe the Father imagined, so now the Son entered that universe as The Word Incarnate. He came to explain his Father's mind and heart.

In his gospel John calls Jesus the Word. In doing so, he uses the Greek word, "logos." This term carries the connotation of abstract reason. The more philosophical Greeks thought of it as a force that brought order and harmony to the universe. To the Jew, the word would have connoted the revelation of God throughout the Holy Scriptures. To both readers, John portrays Jesus Christ as the incarnation of God's revelation of himself in the Hebrew Scriptures, and as the center, order, and reason of the entire universe!

Both of John's audiences had a great stake in the claims he was making about Jesus Christ. We do too. As the Word of God, Jesus embodies God's intentions toward us. He embodies God's decrees and moral precepts. He embodies the plan of the Godhead to save humankind from our sin. Consider the wonder of it all. God himself entered the time-space continuum he created and we contaminated. He entered it to save us from the destruction we rightly deserved for our disobedience:

In the beginning was the Word, and the Word was with God, and the Word was God. He was in the beginning with God. All things were made through him, and without him was not any thing made that was made. In him was life, and the life was the light of men. The light shines in the darkness, and the darkness has not overcome it.

John 1:1–5

Jesus Christ often asserted his eternal coexistence with the Father and the Holy Spirit. Yet he did it in such an off-handed and understated way that we might fail to notice the jaw-dropping significance of what he said about himself. Note, for example, the words in italics below:

- The seventy-two [disciples sent by Jesus to evangelize] returned with joy, saying, "Lord, even the demons are subject to us in your name!" And he said to them, "*I saw Satan fall like lightning from heaven.* Behold, I have given you authority to tread on serpents and scorpions, and over all the power of the enemy, and nothing shall hurt you. Nevertheless, do not rejoice in this, that the spirits are subject to you, but rejoice that your names are written in heaven" (Luke 10:17–20; emphasis added).

- [Jesus said,] "*All things have been handed over to me by my Father;* and no one knows who the Son is except the Father, or who the Father is except the Son and anyone to whom the Son chooses to reveal him" (Luke 10:22; emphasis added).

- [Jesus said,] "*I and the Father are one*" (John 10:30; emphasis added).

- [Jesus said,] "*Whoever hates me hates my Father also*" (John 15:23; emphasis added).

- Jesus remained silent and gave no answer. Again the high priest asked him, "*Are you the Christ, the Son of the Blessed One?*" "*I am,*" said Jesus. "*And you will see the Son of Man sitting at the right hand of the Mighty One and coming on the clouds of heaven.*" The high priest tore his clothes. "Why do we need any more witnesses?" he asked. "You have heard the blasphemy. What do you think?"(Mark 14:61–64; emphasis added).

A good question, with consequences both now and forever! What do you think of Christ Jesus? Do you consider Jesus to be a liar? A lunatic? Or the Lord he claimed to be? Please think closely about this crucial question. There are no other choices. He alone is qualified to do the work of salvation within your heart, beloved.

After having made the claim that Jesus Christ is "the Word," God incarnate, John continues the first chapter of his Gospel by making a claim for the legitimacy of Jesus' mission on earth: to abolish the requirement that we merit God's favor by obeying the law perfectly, and to offer himself as the sacrifice for our sin in our place. Jesus came to earth to become the perfect lawbreaker on our behalf in order that we could be saved by his grace and truth. He did not, of course, abolish the law. Rather, he fulfilled it:

> From his [Christ's] fullness we have all received, grace upon grace. For the law was given through Moses; grace and truth came through Jesus Christ. No one has ever seen God; the only God, who is at the Father's side, he has made him known.
>
> John 1:16–18

The New Testament clearly shows that Jesus' claims were fully consummated. After Jesus' crucifixion, resurrection, and ascension to glory, John witnessed and described the Savior's eternal majesty:

> And he [Jesus] who was seated on the throne said, "Behold, I am making all things new." Also he said, "Write this down, for these words are trustworthy and true." And he said to me,

"It is done! I am the Alpha and the Omega, the beginning
and the end. To the thirsty I will give from the spring of the
water of life without payment."

Revelation 21:5–6; see also 2 Corinthians 5:17

In times of weeping, Christians can remember these precious truths: first, God created and sustains it all; second, Jesus Christ's birth, death, and resurrection secures the faithful one's temporal and eternal destiny; and third, God's covenant promise is as unbreakably secure as the Trinity itself.

We can rest on this firm foundation and respond in our distress as Jesus himself empowers us to respond. When the world, the flesh, or the devil tempt us to believe that our disobedience has drawn God's wrath, or that we are being punished for our sins, that we aren't really secure in God's promises, or that we need to merit God's favor by somehow being good or offering up good works—when any or all of these temptations come flying our way as we weep, we can look to Jesus and his cross. That cross became the lightening rod for all of God's justifiable anger at human sin. There on the cross Jesus endured the punishment we deserved.

Since that is so, it would be unjust of God to demand that we, too, pay for our sins. No, God is not unjust. Instead, God intends that our weeping produce purification, not somehow complete our justification.

True enough, while we live here on earth, our sins will usually lead to unpleasant consequences—the bank robber goes to jail, or the drug addict loses her job and perhaps her family. But these troubles do not result from God's anger. Even when we sit in a pool of tears as a result of our own sin, we can turn to our Savior for help. Such is the enormity of his grace that he will help us bear even the consequences of our own disobedience, as he gives us the gift of repentance (Acts 5:31) and brings us back into fellowship with himself. He is always full of grace and truth for us.

Is it time again to shore up the foundations of your faith? Here are some questions you may find helpful as you think through the meaning of "The Christ Foundation" for your own times of tears:

1. In the passages above from John 1:1–5 and 1:16–18 to whom does the name "the Word," refer? What precisely do these two passages claim about "the Word" (pp 212-213).

_____

_____

_____

_____

2. Do you believe with all your heart that these words about Jesus Christ are true? Explain why or why not. Why does it matter to you personally? How could it provide a foundation in those times when you find yourself in freefall?

_____

_____

_____

_____

3. Consider more deeply John 1:1–5 and the verses that follow it.
   • Who is "the true light" (verse 9) of your life?

_____

_____

_____

_____

- What claim must one make to be counted among "the children of God" (verse 12)? What does it mean to be "born of God" (verse 13)?

_____

_____

_____

_____

_____

4. How did Jesus Christ perfectly embody "grace and truth" (verse 14) when he "became flesh and dwelt among us" (verse 14)? Why is this a vitally important issue as you grow to become more like Jesus Christ?

_____

_____

_____

_____

5. In what ways do your heart, your words, and your life "bear witness to Jesus Christ as the son of God" (verse 15)? Can you give at least five examples?

_____

_____

_____

_____

6. Where do your story and your tears fit within God's story of creation and redemption, as you consider your calling as one of Jesus' disciples (verses 35–51)?

_____

_____

FOUNDATIONAL TRUTH 3: THE COVENANT ASSURANCE FOUNDATION

Have you ever visited a carp pond? Visitors often toss handfuls of food pellets into a teeming horde of fat, yet malnourished fish. The foam and froth on the top of the water clearly communicates the frantic, famished state of the fish.

When I visit the self-help section of bookstores today, visions of carp ponds come to mind. Dropping a book with the designated purpose of self-help into our freefalling culture of comfort can create a similar feeding frenzy. Pushing the analogy a bit further, a freefalling person can be as indiscriminate about what he or she is gobbling-up as one of those malnourished carp I've just described. We are what we eat—at least, our hearts reflect what we eat, and this truism applies whether we are describing our spiritual, emotional, intellectual, or physical selves. Our hearts are what we gobble-up, ingest, and live out of—whether it be the True Truth or the falsehoods of our faith.

In the Bible, God has spread out a banquet for us, replete with promises that hold out enormous hope, even in times of deepest weeping. Nothing provides a firmer foundation for those who love the Lord than his covenant promises. Why? Because these promises reflect God's character, not our own. They are not conditional, based on what we do or have done. Rather, they come to us purely by God's grace, via what Jesus Christ has done, and we could never do on our own.

They flow out of his heart of perfect love and truth toward us in Christ. This makes the Covenant Assurance Foundation essential in every human circumstance, but especially during the freefall of trauma, trial, and distress. Our most frightening, anxiety-provoking, and horrific experiences cannot trump the promises God has made to us.

The language of covenant sits uncomfortably on contemporary ears. We encounter the word seldom in our culture. Yet, the concept of the covenant crisscrosses the Bible from page to page, from Old Testament to New.[31] The covenants that that God makes with his people in Scripture communicate "unconditional love" through sending his one and only son to die a horrible death on the cross. In our fallen world, we often experience the conditional love of the people around us. Most people remain committed to us so long as conditions of convenience and control remain in place. But as soon as love gets tough, as soon as the relationship fails to fulfill our needs or ceases to be what's best for us, the pledges of unconditional love are often broken.

The astounding and glorious details and implications of God's unconditional love deserve much deeper study. Whole books have been written about them. For our purposes in this chapter, I invite you to consider the covenant promise God made to Abraham and to all who shared his faith (See Romans 4, especially verses 15–17).

Genesis 15 records a strange ceremony indeed, one drawn from the culture in which Abram, later known as Abraham, lived. The Chaldeans who lived in Canaan at that time often made covenants with each other, taking a particular kind of blood oath. To seal a covenant, an animal was slaughtered in a particular way and the parties to the covenant would walk between the pieces, in this ceremonial way acting out their oath. By walking through the path of blood, the parties to the covenant were pledging their lives. If they were to break their promises, they would pay with their blood. They would be cut in two, just as the animals had been.

With that background in mind, Genesis 15 makes a good deal more sense with a God-sized caveat! Abraham slaughtered the animals and laid them out on the ground, following the Chaldean custom. But God himself was the only party to the oath. Instead, as verse 17 tells us, a "smoking firepot" and a "flaming torch" moved across the path of blood. God the Father and Jesus—the Light of the World—made a covenant with themselves. In doing so, God swore to Abraham and all of his spiritual descendants that God would be cursed if he broke his covenant promises. But God also swore that he would be cursed if Abraham or his spiritual descendants broke the covenant!

We have, of course, broken it again and again just as Abraham did. But God accepted our curse, Jesus taking it into himself as he hung on our cross.

Christ's sacrifice is the basis for every promise God has ever made. By it, he kept the law undefiled, fulfilling the requirements of justice, even as he continued to love his people unconditionally. By it, he remained both "just and the justifier of the one who has faith in Jesus" (Romans 3:26).

God's New Covenant with us in Christ, and the fulfillment of the "Old" Covenant he cut with Abraham in Genesis 12, will never be broken. Right from the beginning, God knew he was making personal, intimate promises to a fallen race. Yet, as we saw above, he swore by himself (Hebrews 6:13) and to himself that he would forever fulfill the legal, yet loving relationship the covenant represented. In Christ, God kept the covenant he made with the people of every century, every nation, who are *by faith* children of Abraham.

I find it wonderfully ironic that the third and last word of hope God brought to my heart on Christmas night, is a True Truth that encompasses and supersedes the previous two. Consider all three words of hope together:

- In the beginning, God created the heavens and the earth (Genesis 1:1).

- In the beginning was the Word, and the Word was with God, and the Word was God (John 1:1).

- Be strong and courageous. Do not fear or be in dread... , for it is the LORD your God who goes with you. He will not leave you or forsake you (Deuteronomy 31:6).

"THE THREE C'S": AN EVERLASTING FOUNDATION

In Creation, the triune God made a covenant with himself to create a reflection of his glory in the universe; human beings were to bring glory to him and receive his blessings.

In Christ—the only sinless, perfect human being ever to walk the planet, God was glorified and a sinful humanity was infinitely blessed.

In Covenant, now, by faith in Jesus, I receive the irrevocable promise of God's presence moving out into the chaos before me, comforting and encouraging me, despite my fears and tears. This promise belongs to all who cling to Christ by faith.

As we have seen in previous chapters, the remarkable True Truth is that the holy, omniscient, eternal, and omnipotent God has condescended in Christ to enter into covenant with sinful, feeble, flawed, and weak people like you and me. This is one of the very basic truths of the Christian faith. Yet in the freefall of deep suffering, it's one of the first things we forget. We find ourselves flailing in despair, feeling very out of control, and we begin to think that not even God could be in control of our circumstances.

But those feelings cannot negate God's promises to us. God's Word will never be broken—for his character is absolute and unchanging. He has sealed his promises to us in the birth, death, and resurrection of his own Son! He has sent the Holy Spirit to live in us, to assure our hearts that he will move out into the chaos that lay ahead. He will never leave or forsake us, just as he could never leave or forsake himself (2 Timothy 2:11–13)!

Over the next hours, days, months, and years, the Lord kept his promise that he would never leave me, bringing rock-solid assurance and peace to my heart, and the strength I needed to redeem the circumstances I encountered. This verse of God's encouragement and promise to never leave or forsake me under any conditions has become so important to me.

It has greatly encouraged me in so many ways as I rested on

God's character and promises to me. I know how totally undeserving I am of these blessings, but they have come to me because of God's plan and love for me, evidenced in the creation and, especially, in Jesus Christ who paid for all my sins on his cross.

When this verse (Deuteronomy 31:6) of promise is read in its context, we can see that the Holy Spirit has included it in a larger section of covenant promises to Moses and to the people of Israel:

> The LORD your God himself will go over before you. He will destroy these nations before you, so that you shall dispossess them, and Joshua will go over at your head, as the LORD has spoken. And the LORD will do to them as he did to Sihon and Og, the kings of the Amorites, and to their land, when he destroyed them. And the LORD will give them over to you, and you shall do to them according to the whole commandment that I have commanded you.
>
> Deuteronomy 31: 3–5; emphasis added

The Covenant God of ancient Israel continues his unbreakable promises to all who trust in him today. He goes before us, with us, and within us into any and every situation, especially those that require us to wrestle, not "against flesh and blood," but rather "against the rulers, against the authorities, against the cosmic powers over this present darkness, against the spiritual forces of evil in the heavenly places" (Ephesians 6:12). Consider:

- God has promised to go before us today and every day in every circumstance: "Know therefore today that he who goes over before you as a consuming fire is the LORD your God. He will destroy them and subdue them before you. So you shall drive them out and make them perish quickly, as the LORD has promised you" (Deuteronomy 9:3).

- God has promised to be our help and our hope forever: "Do not put your trust in princes, in mortal men, who cannot save. When their spirit departs, they return to the ground; on that very day their plans come to nothing. Blessed is he whose help is the God of Jacob, whose hope is in the LORD his God, the Maker of heaven and earth, the sea, and everything in them—the LORD, who remains faithful forever" (Psalm 146:3, NIV).

- God's promises are steadfast and trustworthy: "LORD, God of Israel, there is no God like you, in heaven above or on earth beneath, keeping covenant and showing steadfast love to your servants who walk before you with all their heart" (1 Kings 8:23).

- God has promised redemption in Christ and has kept that covenant promise: "For to us a child is born, to us a son is given; and the government shall be upon his shoulder, and his name shall be called Wonderful Counselor, Mighty God, Everlasting Father, Prince of Peace"(Isaiah 9:6; see also Luke 2; 7:22).

- The Triune God of the Bible has made us his very own people and has written his name, his True Truths, on our hearts: "For this is the covenant that I will make with the house of Israel after those days, declares the Lord: I will put my laws into their minds, and write them on their hearts, and I will be their God, and they shall be my people" (Hebrews 8:10).

- God promised that the sufficiency and effectiveness of his Word, the True Truths proclaimed in the Bible are available and must be worked through, but will endure and encourage every person of God: "All Scripture is breathed out by God and profitable for teaching, for reproof, for correction, and for training in righteousness, that the man of God may be competent, equipped for every good work" (2 Timothy 3:16–17; Isaiah 55:10–11).

Is it time to stop your own freefall and shore up the foundations of your faith? Here are some questions you may find helpful as you think through the third foundational truth, the Covenant Assurance Foundation:

1. Can God lie? Or promise something and then not deliver on his promises?

_____

_____

_____

_____

_____

2. Which promises from Scripture prove foundational for you when you experience emotions like fear, anxiety, worry, self-doubt, or trepidation of any kind? When has God kept his promises to you personally? Name several specific events.

_____

_____

_____

_____

_____

3. What are the roadblocks that keep you from trusting in God's promises more? When and where did those roadblocks originate? What experiences, doubts, falsehoods, or betrayal of promises, perhaps in childhood, erected them?

_____

_____

_____

4. Imagine Jesus Christ sitting right next to you as you think about the faith, courage, and strength you need in order to move out into all of life. As you listen to him, what are his words of promise, remembrance, encouragement, hope, and exhortation to you?

5. Jesus has a covenant with you—you personally—in his promise, "I will never leave you or forsake you" (Deuteronomy 31:6; Hebrews 13:5). What explicit difference do these words from Jesus Christ make in your life? What additional assurances from Jesus help as well?

6. To what community of faith do you relate? Do the people there know you? Can they remind and encourage you in the promises God has made to you for life here on earth and for life eternal? If so, how do you invite their encouragement and counsel? If not, how could you find such a community, a local manifestation of the Body of Christ? What will your first step in that search be?

_____

_____

_____

GOING DEEPER...

For further reading, you might want to explore:

MacArthur, J. (1980). *The Beatitudes: The Only Way to Happiness.* Chicago, IL: The Moody Bible Institute.

CHAPTER TEN

ALL WINDOWS: BLOWN OPEN INTO THE HEART BY THE TRIAL TO DISCERN THE TRUTHS FROM THE FALSEHOODS WITHIN THE HEART

Search me, O God, and know my heart! Try me and know my thoughts! And see if there be any grievous way in me, and lead me in the way everlasting!

Psalm 139:23–24

If we confess our sins, he is faithful and just to forgive us our sins and to cleanse us from all unrighteousness.

1 John 1:9

Resolved, whenever I do any conspicuously evil action, to trace it back, till I come to the original cause; and then both carefully endeavor to do so no more, and to fight and pray with all my might against the original of it.[32]

Jonathan Edwards

Weeping, suffering, and trials of any and every kind offer us a unique opportunity. We can stay put in the pain for as long as it takes to get to know ourselves better, to see our heart, our spirit, our deepest desires and motivations as God sees them. Such self-examination is the means by which we begin the process of offering ourselves more fully to God for his purposes.

Suffering and self-examination are inextricably linked. We cannot serve God more thoroughly without allowing him to sanctify our suffering and use it to make us more holy and fully committed.

We will not seek to know ourselves better unless life circumstances confront our sense and sensibilities. Every human being who has ever lived has experienced times of weeping. No one has to explain tears to us. Perhaps a few of us, though, have considered the possibility that we can waste our tears. Not many of us have considered how we might engage God's know, grow, and sow process that yields the fruit of redemptive weeping and sanctified suffering. Fewer still look forward to the joy the apostle James suggests our trials can bring (James 1:1).

How do we peer through the window that weeping opens into our hearts as the next step in God's journey for heart transformation? How might we better recognize it as a window of opportunity, to redemptively mourn the losses in our lives? How might we even come to celebrate our times of mourning as God's Old Testament believers did, seeing them as unique stepping stones along the path to knowing and trusting God more deeply? As we begin to answer those questions, I invite you to join me in an imaginative exploration, which grows out of the Truth revealed in Scriptures like John 14:16, 26, 15:26; and 17:1–26. I believe that all weeping of any kind opens a window into our hearts. By opening that window, God the Holy Spirit signals his yearning to begin a heart-to-heart conversation with us.

"Beloved, I'm here. Dear child of mine, I'm right here beside you. You are going to be okay. You are resting on the foundation of my never-ending love for you. I am here to enlighten, encourage, and embolden you. I am The Counselor Jesus sent when he ascended. I am the person of the Trinity who points to Jesus, in any way I'm allowed to do so by the heart I occupy.

I am with you in this sacred place. I want to sit with you, to peer with you into the window of your heart. Take a deep breath. Stay with me in this place for a while. Abide. Trust me to help you see your heart in the way I see it. Look. Listen. I want to remind you of something vitally important, something you may have forgotten in this time of freefall and pain.

Since I have given you new birth, you are a new creation. On his cross, Jesus released you from the debt of your sin. As he died, he announced, "It is finished!" Paid in full! Justice will never demand more. So, since all of your sins—past, present, and future—are erased, why might your loving God have allowed this weeping to occur? To further punish you? No! That would be unjust. It would mean that I have broken my promises to you. I am righteous, and a righteous God will never ask for a double payment of your sin.

No, this time of trial was not for punishment, but rather for purification, dear child of mine! I want to use it to help you move further along the road that leads to holiness. Through it, I want to work in your heart a closer likeness of the One who lives within you, Jesus Christ. I want to heal and transform your heart. I want to help you sweep out the idols of worldliness, the fleshly habits of your former rebellious self, and the Satanic deceptions to which you still cling.

I want to clear away the destructive emotions that flow out from those deep recesses of your heart. I want to help you bring your emotions into concert with your newly refurbished beliefs. This kind of alignment makes for a very happy heart, a heart impassioned, humbled, and yet emboldened to serve!

It's a complicated process, beloved. It will take time and patience—a lifetime, in fact. It's a journey. But I will help you. I will never leave you, no matter how ugly the muck and mire, how deep the pain. I am committed to working through this process with you. You are mine in Jesus—for now and forever.

Now look with me, precious one. Can you see the hardness of broken dreams and disappointments over there? And here, do you see here the stain of that deadly sin you have tried to cover over? Do you understand that, despite your efforts to hide it, your anger, silence, and inability to hear constructive criticism belies your denial of its existence? Can you see the decay and corruption your sin has caused in this part of your heart?

Now look here. Do you see the place where my grace and your deepest loves have healed some ugly wounds? Isn't that awesome? There is nothing that I cannot heal and use for your refining.

Look deeper. Stay here with me long enough to see, not simply a particular sin, but the sin beneath the sin—your deepest motivations that have animated your beliefs and actions. I can help you go there without fear. I will not accuse or blame. Take the time you need to open this door, one that you have barricaded so heavily, the door that bears the placard: "Childhood."

Will you let me open that door? When I do, can you see how the shame, mistreatment, or neglect of your heart has scarred it? Do you understand that those scars often now keep you from sharing your heart's deepest desires? Do you recognize your fear that those desires will be treated with the same disdain you experienced in childhood? Do you recognize the fear that you will become anonymous yet again? Can you see how hiding your shame and trying to control every outcome shuts you off from a closer relationship with me and with others I have put into your life?

I want you to see even more, my beloved. I want you to know at a much deeper level that the things which hurt your heart, hurts my heart, too! I truly understand your weeping. I weep myself as I witness so many hearts falling in love with lesser gods and idols. I weep as I see those false gods taking the place of Jesus Christ in your heart, as I watch them demand of you the same devotion I demand. I know they will never show the mercy I graciously offer. They take life, my beloved. They do not give it.

Like you, I weep at the sting of decay and death that sin inflicts on all of life. Jesus wept in love and truth all of his life.

Do you see the guilt that lies over there in the shadows, both false and very real, that is eating away at your heart because you will not allow my light, truth, and grace to reveal the True Truth? Remember the sword always precedes the peace. The surgery I will do will hurt only for a moment, my beloved, I promise. But the healing will last for time and eternity.

Take another deep breath as you remember my promises and love. These will never end. I know you completely, and I love you infinitely. Let me tell you the truth about what your tears reveal. Then we can see the Way by which I will lead you out of this place of tears and toward a deeper love for me and for others.

Over time, if you will trust me to use your tears, if you will let me teach you to hate sin, and if you will bask in my love, I will do what I have promised. I will turn your heart of stone into a heart of flesh. I will soften and re-shape your heart, making Jesus the center of your existence and the reflection of your faith in action.

You will leave this place wiser, more mature, more joyful, more secure, and completely unafraid of death. You will leave ready to risk everything, knowing you can lose nothing, offering the comfort I have given you to others who need my comfort. Jesus' compassion is becoming your compassion; Jesus' ability to empathize with the heart and spirit of others is becoming yours; Jesus' hatred of sin and love for the sinner is becoming yours.

You are free! Awesomely free. Yes, free indeed. But now I see tears of another sort, tears of joy. Let them flow. Consider it all joy, beloved.

Please, don't ever short-circuit a time like this with me. And please, never forget the Gospel truth that you are more sinful than you ever dared imagine, and yet you are also more loved than you could ever dare hope. Go now, confident that as you do, I will stay right beside you. I live in you, resurrected, completely unafraid of death, enabling you to show the courage and compassion of Jesus himself as you move back into the chaos to put flesh on my supernatural forces and calm the storms in other hearts."

_____

WISDOM: THE ANTIDOTE FOR WASTED WEEPING AND HARDENED HEARTS

The apostle James wrote the words below to followers of Jesus who, like the first believers to read the Letter to the Hebrews, faced various degrees of trials and persecution. Notice the way in which James links trials and his readers' need for an open window into their hearts:

> Count it all joy, my brothers, when you meet trials of various kinds, for you know that the testing of your faith produces steadfastness. And let steadfastness have its full effect, that you may be perfect and complete, lacking in nothing. If any of you lacks _wisdom,_ let him ask God, who gives generously to all without reproach, and it will be given him. But let him ask in faith, with no doubting, for the one who doubts is like a wave of the sea that is driven and tossed by the wind. For that person must not suppose that he will receive anything from the Lord; he is a double-minded man, unstable in all his ways.
>
> James 1:2–8—emphasis added

A church living in a culture of comfort might well forget or flounder upon the True Truth. The tempering of our faith (some Bible versions use the word "testing") results in lasting joy, because the tempering transforms your heart and mine, as it works in us the temperament of Jesus Christ. Joy results as we grow more like Christ with every trial.

If that is true, just imagine how deeply the Holy Spirit yearns to help you discern your biases, blind spots, denials, and the untruths you believe. Just imagine how much he wants to show you his own perspective on the "truths" you hold so dear, the ones you refuse to scrutinize yourself and protect from the scrutiny of others. Imagine how deep his desire is to open the window into your heart so that he can make the invisible visible as he talks to you about his love for you, his purposes for your life!

Do you imagine he intends to shame you? Far from it. He wants to begin in you a personal revival, one that will far outstrip your own puny efforts to make yourself more acceptable to God by mustering up more good works which are motivated by an increase of pride, guilt, or need to control your life. No, not that way!

But these results come only in the midst of suffering, as we endure the daily frustrations of living in a fallen world, as we undergo persecution for the name of Christ, and as we weep over all the many other losses and pain experienced in a world broken by sin. How can I make such a broad assertion, such an apparently outrageous claim? Because it is only as we suffer that our hearts are most fully available to God. Suffering sanctifies and sets apart the saints for works of divine origin and nature, beloved (Romans 1:1, Hebrews 3; 1 Peter 3:15).

Consider, for example, the tears of joyful worship. Wouldn't you agree that we weep because we approach the throne as less than what God intends for us? We are all saints by God's declaration, but yet also sinners, still burdened by temptations and by less than holy attitudes and motives. Don't we weep in worship because we feel our spirits, deep inside, enlivened by the melodies and words of praise, and yet we continue to long for the day when we will see God face-to-face together with all the saints—the family of God, home at last, our sanctification fully realized in glorification.

Do you believe this to be true? Use the Bible or your own life story as the proof text. And then consider how much damage we inevitably do to our hearts and spirits as we twist and squirm, trying to slam the window shut as soon as possible, as we avoid exploring our response to trials.

OPEN THE WINDOW! OR NOT?

My grief all lies within; and these external manners of laments are merely shadows of the unseen grief that swells with silence in the tortured soul.
William Shakespeare, Richard II, Act 4, Scene 1

When the weeping comes, we can choose to join the Holy Spirit at the window opened by our tears. We can also refuse to do so. God creates opportunities and through them offers us more of himself. These opportunities are an invitation to a life that takes the shape of a cross as we grow upward in our relationship with God and outward in relationships toward others.

Shakespeare captures what happens to the human heart that rejects such opportunities by suppressing the truth. When our beliefs and agendas are shredded by life, when the resulting emotions are trapped unexpressed or unredeemed in the airless vacuum of a hardening heart, a spiritual abscess forms. Our focus turns inward toward the tortured heart, rather than outward by serving others who weep, mourn, or suppress the truth as we have.

The Holy Spirit will not force us to commune with him or conform to the One to whom he points—Jesus Christ. Love simply doesn't work that way! Offer he will. Draw he will. Coax and woo, he will. Create or allow the conditions whereby we might be more apt to pay attention, he will. Even weep he will. But he will not force.

Many do reject God's invitation to use their trials for receiving the treasure trove of benefits stored up for those who trust him. Many refuse to allow the Holy Spirit to use their pain as the means of circumcising their hearts. Yes, even born-again Christians can choose to harden their hearts. They can choose to remain in the lonely and unfulfilling place of worldliness, fear, pain, and disillusionment.

Please don't join them there! Don't waste your weeping by

refusing to join him at that window! Don't take the risk of losing the abundance of joy, purpose, love, and wonder God offers you as you move forward, taking the way back into the world!

> This is my comfort in my affliction: that your promises give me life.
>
> Psalm 119:50

GOING DEEPER...

For further reading, see:

Lewis, C.S. The Problem of Pain. New York: HarperCollins. 1940.

Lewis, C.S. A Grief Observed. New York: HarperOne. 2001.

CHAPTER ELEVEN

YOUR WINDOWS: FALLEN. FORGIVEN. FREE. APPLYING ROMANS 1:18, ROMANS 8:1

> Man's walled mind has no access to a ladder upon which he can, of his own strength, rise to knowledge of God. Yet his soul is endowed with translucent windows that opened to the beyond.
>
> Abraham Heschel
> God in Search of Man: A Philosophy of Judaism

> Search me, O God, and know my heart! Try me and know my thoughts! And see if there be any grievous way in me, and lead me in the way everlasting!
>
> Psalm 139:23–24

In the garden on Christmas night, the freefall of heartbreak and emotional chaos had stopped. The Lord had placed his everlasting arms beneath me (Deuteronomy 33:27). I knelt, by faith, on a solid, three-pillared foundation—the True Truths of Creation, of Christ, and of the Covenant promises God has given in the Bible. A weeping servant of God can rest. Now I could abide for a while (John 15:1–11) communing with the Holy Spirit as he comforted me and as he invited me to peer through the window that suffering had blown open in my heart.

THE WAVES OF WOULD-A, COULD-A, SHOULD-A'S

Recall that it was in the place of security, resting on God's foundational love and truth, his rock-solid promises impossible to break, that I began to feel the reality of my regrets about my relationship with my father. Remember, resting on the security of our salvation, this time is for purification, not punishment. This all-important fact is easily forgotten for many Christians, but not for Satan: he wants us to remain immature and as ineffective as possible.

The Waves of Would-a, Could-a, Should-a's: All trials of any kind are accompanied by truths and falsehoods that can either be *discerned* and offer glory to God, or *disregarded,* and offer glory to self—and result in a hardened and bitter heart.

There were no more second chances or tomorrows for Dad and me. Wave after wave of true and false guilt pounded me until I cried out to God to stop the pain and forgive me. God most mercifully answered my cries for his mercy by reminding me of "the bookends of the Gospel":

- The wrath of God is being revealed from heaven against all the godlessness and wickedness of men who suppress the truth.

  Romans 1:18

- Therefore, there is now no condemnation for those who are in Christ Jesus.

  Romans 8:1

It is very likely that the proverbial "Waves of Would-a, Could-a, Should-a's" is one of the most prevalent and debilitating realities in the life a non-Christian and Christian alike.

Now, it is perfectly logical that guilt should cast a shadow over a non-believer's life. For every human being ever born since Adam has been declared guilty before an utterly holy God (Romans 3:23). But for those who are in Christ Jesus, all guilt and estrangement from God has been paid for by Jesus Christ on the cross. What God offered me on Christmas night is not only at the centerpiece of his entire redemptive plan—the reality of sin and salvation—but the prerequisite disposition of the heart and emotion for the forgiven Christian to inventory and cleanse the heart from all forms of guilt.

Even though we are saved for eternity in heaven (Romans 8), we still sin—and sin left unseen and unconfessed will destroy our fellowship with the Holy Spirit, will harden our hearts, and greatly diminish our witness and effectiveness as a disciple of Christ.

This is huge! And we'll now spend some time unpacking the truth and love of God for you and me in how God uses the Gospel to save *and* sanctify the Christian.

THE HOLY SPIRIT: GET TO KNOW HIM BETTER!

The Holy Spirit could be called the supernatural heart-changer. And that is one of the unique purposes for which he had brought me to this place, a change of heart that glorifies God and blesses his beloved children.

It was especially important that I rest, remain, and abide in The Spirit. It is equally important for you to know that you do not sit at this window alone. Satan would, of course, prefer that you isolate and deafen yourself to God's voice and blind yourself to his purposes. Your own fallen hearts, likewise, will pull you in these directions. But Jesus tenderly invites you to hear his voice and receive his counsel: "Today, if you hear his [God's] voice, do not harden your hearts ... " (Psalm 95:7–8).

Here in the place of rest, the Counselor will come to you:

When the Counselor comes, whom I will send to you from the Father, the Spirit of truth who goes out from the Father, he will testify about me (John 15:26 (NIV); John 14—where Jesus calms the hearts of his troubled disciples; identifies himself most clearly; and then promises the Holy Spirit).

I tell you the truth: It is for your good that I am going away. Unless I go away, the Counselor will not come to you; but if I go, I will send him to you.

John 16:7 (NIV)

Make them holy—consecrated—with the truth; Your word is consecrating truth.

John 17:17 (The Message)

Jesus, who is himself the Wonderful Counselor of Isaiah 9:6, now sits at the right hand of the throne of God, making intercession for us (Romans 8:34). He sends the Holy Spirit to facilitate sanctification, spiritual growth, and an increase of compassion in our hearts.

Instead, the Holy Spirit offers his counsel to our hearts through his Word, prayer, the community of faith, the sacraments, and service to others. He points us to his love and truth demonstrated in Jesus Christ, the Word Incarnate. And he points us to the Bible, his written Word of love and truth.

We need the Spirit's counsel every day, but all the more so when suffering and trauma of any kind begins to crush our hearts and stir up pain and grief in our spirits and emotions (See chapter 2).

As we have seen, weeping opens the window of the heart to the light, love, and truth of God himself so that any and all opportunities for growth, maturity, and increasing compassion can occur. In fact, a holy renovation of this kind cannot occur until suffering of some sort has blown open the window of the heart! Why not? Because, as we have already seen in several previous chapters, our sinful hearts tend by both nature and habit to keep those windows closed and locked![33]

Circumstances associated with living in a very broken world, or even God himself (Psalm 107; 139), will blow the window open. But we can choose to slam it shut again. Choice is an implicit requirement of love: we can always choose to not love God or anyone else in return, right?

Without God, there is only one other choice. We can choose the self-help route or resort to the wide array of other avoidance mechanisms our culture holds out to us. Such is the depth of our unwillingness to open the window of the heart that we will do almost anything to avoid the Lord's loving, but truthful scrutiny. We know full well we need help. But we tend to look for it in all the wrong places, don't we? It's the spiritual equivalent of trying to perform heart surgery on our own heart!

MORE SINFUL...YET MORE LOVED...

It is indeed a fearful thing for a soul to be living in "a fool's paradise," persuading one's self all is well while in reality the wrath of God abides on him. But is it anything less tragic (even though less dangerous) for a child of God to live in "the slough of despond," passing sentence of Divine condemnation upon himself when in fact God has blotted out his transgressions?

A.W. Pink, *An Honest Heart*[34]

We could avoid so much unnecessary suffering if we would invite God's presence right away, asking him to befriend us in our times of greatest need. Our Lord Jesus is the only one equipped to do the kind of surgery that is required. He made your heart and loves it in ways you cannot even imagine! He offers you real and eternal life, as you entrust your broken heart to him.

The surgeon's knife always precedes the healing of a wound. Similarly, the sword of True Truth (Matthew 10:34) and the pain of confession and repentance precede the peace of pardon and growth.

> How can I know all the sins lurking in my heart? Cleanse me from these hidden faults.
>
> Psalm 19:12—NLT

> Although the Lord has various ends in view in bringing his people under the cross, yet we ought to hold fast the principle, that, as often as God afflicts us, we are called to examine our own hearts and humbly seek reconciliation with him.
>
> John Calvin, Commentary on Psalm 25:18

COMMUNITY: STRENGTH FOR THE JOURNEY

The journey into truth is one best taken with companions we can trust, who have plumbed the depths of their own hearts and know the True Truth. These friends will, in love, strengthen us for our journey toward spiritual maturity by reminding us of what I am calling in this chapter the "Gospel Fact." Companions like that encourage us as we grow in greater and greater holiness and they push us forward into increasing "Gospel Fortitude." Let's look briefly at each of these three attributes.

First, and most importantly, the "Gospel Fact" is that Jesus Christ is who he said he is, and we can fully rely on the forgiveness God gives in Christ's cross. Our resurrection from death is as certain as Jesus' own bodily resurrection.[35] God cannot lie!

Anxieties and worry of any kind, even death, need not dominate our faith walk, and fear need no longer dictate our actions. Yet many Christians live debilitated and anxious about yesterday and worried about tomorrow. This steals much of the comfort the presence and power of the risen Christ can bring into our lives today! We can turn from this kind of lifestyle, living instead out of a heart passionately committed to transforming the world for Christ, one heart, one day, at a time.

This is not a fantasy or some flighty feeling. It is not a fiction or an "I wish it were so" hope. It is the heritage of each of the heavenly Father's born-again sons and daughters. And it creates in us "Gospel Fervency" that is the engine for all that the disciple does each day. The Fact of God's redemptive plan in Jesus Christ will have an organic outgrowth of excitement and intentional contagiousness one might call Fervency!

Second, those in whom the Holy Spirit has worked "Gospel Fervency" then, live the Christian life with a surpassing zeal, a sense of life and death urgency, single-mindedness and wholeheartedness. Such a life focuses on the shape of the cross every day, loving and serving God (cf., Deuteronomy 6:5; 11:18) and our neighbors (Mark 12:31). Those who are in Christ seek to love and serve like there's no tomorrow, while remembering there is an eternity of perfection that awaits us.

In contrast, the degree to which we lack this kind of Gospel Fervency correlates directly with our refusal to handle our weeping, and the suffering we endure, in the way prescribed. Consider the priorities expressed by the apostle Paul in this regard:

> Indeed, I count everything as loss because of the surpassing worth of knowing Christ Jesus my Lord. For his sake I have suffered the loss of all things and count them as rubbish, in order that I may gain Christ and be found in him, not having

a righteousness of my own that comes from the law, but that which comes through faith in Christ, the righteousness from God that depends on faith.

> Philippians 3:8; see also Jeremiah 9:23–24;
> John 17:3; Romans 8:18; and 2 Corinthians 5:15.

In the passage above, by "count," Paul and others refer to an important aspect of what it means to be a Christian: "counting" means, "I've given reality very careful and close consideration, and in light of all the facts, I deem everything fodder compared to what Jesus Christ means to and in my life."

Clinging in faith like our brother Paul to the "Gospel Fact" and buoyed up by "Gospel Fervency," we have all we need to live with "Gospel Fortitude." James describes this fortitude perfectly as he heartens his readers with these words:

> Count it all joy, my brothers, when you meet trials of various kinds, for you know that the testing of your faith produces steadfastness. And let steadfastness have its full effect, that you may be perfect and complete, lacking in nothing.
>
> James 1:2–4; see also Philippians 2 and Hebrews 11

"Gospel Fortitude" speaks to the connections we have made between the heart and spirit (see Chapters 5 & 6). With those connections in mind, think about fortitude, sometimes defined as the "strength of mind that enables a person to encounter danger or bear pain or adversity with courage." Gospel Fortitude results from a growing commitment to sound doctrine in the heart. That True Truth in turn generates emotional resonance so that heart and spirit are aligned with one another to an ever increasing degree and the fruit that flows from a life of discipleship—love, joy, peace, patience, kindness, goodness, faithfulness, gentleness, and self-control as described in Galatians 5:19–24—creates a feast for a famished world.

Jesus Christ epitomized the "Gospel Fortitude" every Christian needs to understand and push toward, every day of our lives.

The Window: All weeping opens a widow into our heart so we can see our hearts as God does. Spent time with The Holy Spirit, and a community of faith—so that sanctification can occur and we become more like Jesus Christ.

A GLIMPSE THROUGH THE
WINDOW—GUILTY AS CHARGED

Many Christians choose to repeatedly close the window to their hearts. It's more comfortable, in a hellish sort of way, to live a lukewarm Christian life than it is to live on the extremes of the Gospel—knowing and embracing the depth of the sin *and* the heights of God's love. In that middle, neither hot nor cold place, we soothe ourselves with platitudes and untruths like these:

- I know I'm sort of sinful, but I'm not as bad as Hitler.

- I've been told God loves me, but then I don't suppose he knows about all the really bad things I've done.

- I sense that there needs to be some heart-cleansing, but I'll tend to it tomorrow.

- How could I ever allow someone else to see the darkness of my heart?

- Time heals all wounds.

- I'm not perfect but I live a good life; I've paid my dues; I'm a very charitable person!

Here's the rub, beloved: Any choice to live as a Christian in conformity with the culture of comfort is to choose to live as an orphaned son or daughter of the living God. It's spiritual suicide—an accusation I, of all people, do not make lightly. What begins as spiritual suicide will incrementally result in living a purposeless life as a dead man walking.

In addition, that choice commits you to what we might call a daisy chain theology, a "he loves me, he loves me not" uncertainty. Such a theology damages your heart, kills your spirit, and saps all joy and contentment from life, all while replacing it with fear, envy, and a fragile identity. Such a life recreates the realms of hell on earth for the Christian. It delights Satan, who wants more than anything to keep God's sons and daughters miserable and make our service for Christ as ineffective as possible.

In contrast with this tepid and tenuous response to God's mercy, look with me at how amazingly and clearly David applies "the weeping, window, way" paradigm. These are words spoken from the depths of the heart and spirit by a man whose heart and spirit are in alignment with the True Truth, a man who sees himself as thoroughly ruined by his sins, yet fully and utterly redeemed by his Savior. Having humbly yet boldly seen reality for what it is, David is sent out on his way to minister to the world:

The Weeping:

> Have mercy on me, O God, according to your steadfast love; according to your abundant mercy blot out my transgressions. Wash me thoroughly from my iniquity, and cleanse me from my sin. Psalm 51: 1–2

The Window—opened to reveal the reality of sin:

> For I know my transgressions, and my sin is ever before me. Against you, you only, have I sinned and done what is evil in your sight, so that you may be justified in your words and blameless in your judgment. Behold I was brought forth in iniquity, and in sin did my mother conceive me. Behold, you delight in truth in the inward being, and you teach me wisdom in the secret heart. (Psalm 51: 3–6)

The Window—opened to reveal the reality of salvation:

> Purge me with hyssop, and I shall be clean; wash me, and I shall be whiter than snow. Let me hear joy and gladness; let the bones that you have broken rejoice. Hide your face from my sins, and blot out all my iniquities. Create in me a clean heart, O God, and renew a right spirit within me. Cast me not away from your presence, and take not your Holy Spirit from me. Restore to me the joy of your salvation, and uphold me with a willing spirit. (Psalm 51: 7–12)

The Way—of moving back into the chaos of the world as a witness and co-redeemer:

> *Then* I will teach transgressors your ways, and sinners will return to you. Deliver me from blood guiltiness, O God, O God of my salvation, and my tongue will sing aloud of your righteousness. O Lord, open my lips, and my mouth will declare your praise. For you will not delight in sacrifice, or I would give it; you will not be pleased with a burnt offering. The sacrifices of God are a broken spirit; a broken and contrite heart, O God, you will not despise. (Psalm 51: 13–18— emphasis added)

Please look closely at the progression and the promise of David's transforming trial and time with the Holy Spirit, which he then redeemed by being a powerfully-used healer in the lives of countless people. The heart/spirit/life alignment the Holy Spirit had brought about in David made it possible for him to face the True Truth about his guilt and God's goal in revealing it the way he did.

Make careful note that the primary audience of the passage from Romans 1 below is applied to the non-believer who is as yet unconverted. However, the heart, spirit, and life of the believer in Jesus Christ benefits from the same message:

> For the wrath of God is revealed from heaven against all ungodliness and unrighteousness of men, who by their unrighteousness, suppress the truth.
>
> Romans 1:18

Suppressing the True Truth always results in a hardened heart (Romans 1:21–22). And God loves us so much he knows that a hardened heart will always result in: our harm, estrangement from him, and less saltiness and light to a decaying and dark world.

By means of the key verses God gave me on Christmas night, a process similar to the one David must have experienced was begun in me. I began to see the necessity and the possibilities of living the Christian life on the extremes of the Gospel, rather than absorbing the values offered by the culture of comfort.

The Spirit opened my heart to see the idol work that would be necessary for my illumination, repentance, sanctification, and growth (Romans 1:18 ff). And, what's even more important, he also opened my heart to see ever more clearly the reality of my condition as a redeemed, and unconditionally accepted son of God (Romans 8:1 ff).

SITTING AT THE WINDOW: SEEING TRUTH AND FALSEHOODS

Sitting with the Holy Spirit at the window of my heart that night, and many times thereafter, I have concluded that suppressing the truth is the most fundamental articulation of the impact the Fall has had upon the human heart. At its core, the phrase describes a twofold assault on the True Truth:

- The truth about God—which leads to the heart-destroyers of idolatry and ingratitude.

- The truth about death—which leads to an unrelenting denial of death and striving to make our lives in this world amount to something lasting.

This double-edged suppression results in the utter chaos Paul describes in Romans 1:21–32. The human heart is indeed capable of true evildoing and wickedness. The human heart is utterly depraved:

> For although they knew God, they did not honor him as God or give thanks to him, but they became futile in their thinking, and their foolish hearts were darkened. Claiming to be wise, they became fools, and exchanged the glory of the immortal God for images resembling mortal man and birds and animals and creeping things.

Therefore God gave them up in the lusts of their hearts to impurity, to the dishonoring of their bodies among themselves, because they exchanged the truth about God for a lie and worshiped and served the creature rather than the Creator, who is blessed forever! Amen.

For this reason God gave them up to dishonorable passions. For their women exchanged natural relations for those that are contrary to nature; and the men likewise gave up natural relations with women and were consumed with passion for one another, men committing shameless acts with men and receiving in themselves the due penalty for their error.

And since they did not see fit to acknowledge God, God gave them up to a debased mind to do what ought not to be done. They were filled with all manner of unrighteousness, evil, covetousness, malice. They are full of envy, murder, strife, deceit, maliciousness. They are gossips, slanderers, haters of God, insolent, haughty, boastful, inventors of evil, disobedient to parents, foolish, faithless, heartless, ruthless. Though they know God's decree that those who practice such things deserve to die, they not only do them but give approval to those who practice them.

Romans 1:21–32

As you allow the True Truth about the ways in which the human heart suppresses the truth to saturate your own heart and spirit, do you get a better idea about what's going on in the world in which we live today?

In his book, *Body Life,* Chuck Colson tells the story of a Jewish survivor of Auschwitz, Yehiel Dinur, called to testify against Adolf Eichmann. As the two men locked eyes, Dinur began to shout and sob. Finally, he collapsed, falling to the floor. Observers concluded that a flood of horrific memories had overtaken Dinur and had rendered him unconscious.

Dinur later said no. Rather, he had seen Eichmann as simply an ordinary human being, a person in whom sin and evil were at work as they are in all of us. Dinur said, "I was afraid about myself. I saw that I am capable to do this ... Eichmann is in all of us." This is an amazing insight that all of us would be well-advised to heed.

- What do you find most interesting or applicable to your own life in this story? Perhaps you've come to a similar place of self-awareness about the nature your own heart? Of EveryMan's heart?

But for the grace of God, the seeds of evil in our own hearts could be watered to the point that sin blooms in exactly the same way. You and I have no idea what we are capable of doing. We cannot even imagine what the headlines would include were God to lift his hand of providential protection off the powder keg of sin in our hearts. The consequences in the world would be beyond horrifying.

Please know this again: God's merciful providence prevents the vast majority of potential chaos that is pent up in the heart of mankind. His grace keeps wickedness from running rampant through the world in which we live. Why? Because he wants with all his heart to save as many sinners and sanctify as many saints as possible before the curtain descends on human history and Christ returns in judgment.

We live in a culture that has made an art form of suppressing the truth. Unregenerate people suppress the truth about God, because they do not want to be held accountable to anyone for their behavior. Human beings are, at heart, rebels. Then, having killed God, as Nietzsche said, they must also suppress the truth about death. They must find a way to disguise the fact that they don't know what their lives amount to, where they will spend eternity or, in fact, the simple inevitability of their own death. Unless these truths are suppressed, the fear will suffocate them, or so their spirits tell them. Solomon had it right when he observed that the stained conscience is a merciless taskmaster: "The wicked flee when no one pursues, but the righteous are bold as a lion" (Proverbs 28:1).

The wicked Solomon describes are those who insist on their right to look down upon others and insist on total control of their own lives. The righteous are those who see God through the lens of Christ's cross and who have the assurance that he has applied the blood of the eternal covenant to their hearts. The righteous know and trust the True Truth the Bible has revealed. As a result, they can sit boldly near the window of their hearts. In full assurance of the Savior's love, they can sit with their Counselor and Friend, taking the time and bearing the pain involved in replacing the lies with the True Truth.

With David and all the righteous, saved sinners of every place, society, and language, we plead:

> Create in me a clean heart, O God, and renew a right spirit within me. Cast me not away from your presence, and take not your Holy Spirit from me. Restore to me the joy of your salvation, and uphold me with a willing spirit.
>
> Psalm 51:10–13

Much of the difficulty in the task of cleansing hearts comes in the fact that the sins we readily detect on the surface of our hearts rest on the more fundamental or primordial sin buried deep within. We need to unearth and deal with the sin beneath the sin. As Calvin once observed, the human heart is an idol factory.

IDOL WORK[36]

David quickly gets to the sin beneath the sin in his heart as he prays in Psalm 51:4, "Against you, you only, have I sinned and done what is evil in your sight..." David saw, as did I on

Christmas night while with my dad, that the fundamental sin is the sin of substituting something else for the sufficiency of Christ in the center of our hearts. Once that happens, all hell breaks loose, and our hearts conspire with hell to manufacture all kinds of other evil thoughts, words, and actions—just as Romans 1 warns.

"Idol work" centers on evicting the false gods from our hearts and replacing the lies that enticed us to invite those idols into a position of dominance in the first place. St. Augustine described this as "making good things the only thing."

This tendency in human hearts points to the fact that Satan has no creative power of his own. As C.S. Lewis often pointed out, Satan has never come up with a new and original evil. Instead, he twists the things God has made good, tempting us to worship the creations instead of the Creator. Sexuality is good. Twisted by the evil one, it becomes pornography. Work is good. Twisted by the evil one, it becomes workaholism. Fitness and sports are good. Twisted by Satan, they become compulsive addictions. What is good becomes bad.

This was an all-too-familiar sin in my life as I ran sixty to seventy miles a week in the Colorado Mountains while claiming I ran "in praise of God's creation." In reality, I had pushed the Creator aside entirely and lied to myself about his creation, all while I gobbled-up the praise of men concerning my high alpine feats.

Eventually my idols betrayed me when I went to them again and again for my ultimate worth: I destroyed my own heart and health, but God graciously saved me when I cried out to him even as I was still a sinner (Romans 5:8). It was only when I saw how much God loved me that I could see how blind I was to my idols.

Our pride, fear, and insistence on making *good* things the *only* things drives us to continually usurp the honor and worship that rightly belong to God alone. A fallen, unregenerate heart has no other choice. Even the born-again, regenerate heart can encase the cross of Christ inside its own compartment, meanwhile allowing any number of idols to maintain residence in other, adjoining compartments. Do you see yourself in this picture? Ask yourself the following questions. They may reveal how you might be consciously or unconsciously avoiding suffering so that you might maintain the idol structure within your heart:

- Do you insist on knowing everything, on being right at all times? Do you feel bad when you didn't know something? Then you're encroaching on God's domain of *omniscience* (See 1 Samuel 2:3; Matthew 10:29; 24:36).

- Do you try to be everywhere at the same time, overly worried or anxious that you're somehow missing out? Then you're trespassing on God's domain of *omnipresence* (See Psalm 139:7–12; Hebrews 4:13).

- Do you strive to gain all the power you can, to control life's circumstances or maintain your right to look down on others as much as possible? Then you're treading on God's domain of *omnipotence* (See Isaiah 40:21–31; Revelation 19:6).

- Do you deny the inexorable cycle of earthly life and death by thinking of yourself as everlasting or unbreakable? Are you so afraid of death that there's nothing worth really living or dying for? Then you're taking on only God's domain of *self-existence* (or "Aesity" of God) (See Psalm 90:2; John 1:1–3).

It's a cosmic flip-flop of the grandest kind made by hearts living out of alignment with the True Truth. It can only be turned right side-up again by God using the inevitable trials of living in a broken world, purely by his mercy at work through the True Truth of the Bible and the process the Holy Spirit uses to transform hearts. "Idol work" is about seeing the truth, whole truth, and nothing but the True Truth from God's perspective, not our own. We need help, and lots of it, to make this possible.

A threefold partnership between the Holy Spirit, Holy Scriptures, and "holy friends" must be forged as a transparent and trusted bond in Christ. Such friends focus on spiritual direction and spiritual friendship.

They are willing and able to encourage one another with biblical wisdom in truth and in love. They are essential in our day by day journey of faith, especially when the window of our hearts has been blown open by the storms that bring us, weeping, to our knees. If we are to grow better rather than bitter in these storms, if we are to benefit spiritually in them, the process of grieving, healing, and redeeming must take into account the "idol work" necessary at that point in our journey. This is the centerpiece of heart transformation and "the weeping, the window, and the way" protocol Scripture describes.

REPENT—AND BELIEVE THE GOOD NEWS!

FORGIVEN AND FREE

There is therefore now no condemnation for those who are in Christ Jesus. For the law of the Spirit of life has set you free in Christ Jesus from the law of sin and death. For God has done what the law, weakened by the flesh, could not do. By sending his own Son in the likeness of sinful flesh and for sin, he condemned sin in the flesh, in order that the righteous requirement of the law might be fulfilled in us, who walk not according to the flesh but according to the Spirit.

Romans 8:1–4

We can enlist the help of our holy community in evicting the idols whose presence in the center of our hearts always leads to other, outward sins. Someone has rightly written, "There is no holiness without repentance, for we begin in sin and move towards holiness by the cycle of repentance, forgiveness, and life change alone."

Your heart, born-again in grace, delights in obeying Jesus, but a war between desire and the will rages until Jesus returns. Even so, you can be sure that Jesus Christ has delivered you from the condemnation of your momentary failings. As the reformer Martin Luther recommended, "All of life is repentance ... Sin boldly and repent more boldly still." There is no condemnation left for those who are in Christ Jesus:

> For I delight in the law of God, in my inner being, but I see in my members another law waging war against the law of my mind and making me captive to the law of sin that dwells in my members. Wretched man that I am! Who will deliver me from this body of death? Thanks be to God through Jesus Christ our Lord! So then, I myself serve the law of God with my mind, but with my flesh I serve the law of sin.
>
> Romans 7:22–25

A process of joyful obedience unto repentance and sanctification that enables us to identify our idols and refuse to serve them any longer promotes the change of heart. This change of heart leads to life—vibrant and unspeakably rewarding and rewarded LIFE! (See, for example, Colossians 3:1–17; Hebrews 11:1 ff.; 1 John 3:1–24).

Gracious obedience and authentic repentance when we slip up and sin, accompanied by sacrificial service in Christ's name and a humble yet bold witness to a weeping world, focused on God and others:

> Therefore I tell you, her sins, which are many, are forgiven— for she loved much. But he who is forgiven little, loves little.
>
> Luke 7:47

The prostitute who washed the feet of Jesus could no more think she was bringing something of merit to Jesus than someone seeking admission to an Ivy League school would consider presenting a tape worm as evidence of merit to the admissions committee. The thought of personal merit was preposterous, both in the abstract, and in the harlot's own heart as well.

In contrast, the people sitting with Jesus at the table apparently knew little of the real depth of their own sin as they were sitting above it all in judgment of Jesus' actions in response to "someone so filthy."

Therefore, in their lofty view of themselves, they could only look at her in contempt. They could also scoff at Christ's claim of authority, his insistence that he was both God and man. They knew nothing of his Lordship, love, or of the price he would pay to make pardon for sin possible. They knew none of these things, because they knew nothing of their own sin-filled hearts and need for a Savior.

This brief account from Luke's gospel underscores a key fact: Our ability to believe that we are fully forgiven, and our ability to offer forgiveness to those who anger or injure us, both develop in direct proportion to the depth to which we grasp our own sin and the enormous price Jesus willingly paid to secure our forgiveness.

The heart and spirit must weep deeply enough from within the heart of the heart to experience a spiritual-emotional catharsis enabling us to see our need for change and our utter incapability of initiating that change from within. Writers and speakers have noted it often that "grace is free, not cheap."

The life and death of Jesus Christ here on earth for your sake and mine crushed and shredded God's heart, beloved. Please don't cheapen the Savior's sacrifice. Recognize the enormity of the sin God has forgiven you. Then freely and fully forgive others as the fruit of receiving God's forgiveness yourself!

When we live on the extremes of the Gospel, fully aware that we "are more sinful ... yet more loved" we see again just how costly grace really is and how unworthy even the best of our good works and self-righteous deeds really are. We can do nothing at all, to curry God's favor. As we repent, we plead only the blood of Jesus Christ, the perfect sacrifice, the one who gave himself into death—even death on the cross—as our surrogate and substitute (John 3:16).

FREEDOM AND ASSURANCE!

FORGIVEN & FREED TO SERVE

Or do you not know, brothers—for I am speaking to those who know the law—that the law is binding on a person only as long as he lives? ... Likewise, my brothers, you also have died to the law through the body of Christ, so that you may belong to another, to him who has been raised from the dead, in order that we may bear fruit for God.

Romans 7:1, 4

Commenting on the blessedness of confession and forgiveness, Eugene de Guerin has written, "When the soul has laid down its faults before God, it feels as though it has wings." The apostle Paul expressed this same exuberant joy in the words of Romans 8:1–2. Additionally, the words of the apostle John in 1 John 1:8–10 said of Jesus' cleansing forgiveness as we confess from the heart:

There is therefore now no condemnation for those who are in Christ Jesus. For the law of the Spirit of life has set you free in Christ Jesus from the law of sin and death.

Romans 8:1–2

If we say we have no sin, we deceive ourselves, and the truth is not in us. If we confess our sins, he is faithful and just to forgive us our sins and to cleanse us from all unrighteousness. If we say we have not sinned, we make him a liar, and his word is not in us.

1 John 1:8–10

These words from Romans offer the believer in Jesus Christ a rock-solid foundation on which to stand. God, who cannot lie, has offered his Son up in complete payment for our sins. The finished work of Jesus on the cross, coupled with his resurrection, ascension, and position of authority at God's right hand have sealed our salvation so securely that no power in any dimension of the universe will ever undo it. That True Truth changes everything. Now we are:

- Redeemed to rejoice
- Redeemed to redeem
- Forgiven to forgive
- Changed to change
- Made dead to bring life
- Enriched to serve the poor
- Saved to save
- Blessed to bless
- Justified to secure justice
- Uprooted to plant
- Washed to wash
- Comforted to comfort
- Healed to heal
- Fathered to ransom the orphans
- Reminded to remind
- Embraced to embrace

Meanwhile, Satan rages with fury. He knows his time is short. Jesus will soon return to cast him into the lake of fire forever. The devil has little time to accomplish his vision—to frustrate Christ's victory and his redemptive work: to keep *unbe-*

lievers from true faith, and to make *Christ's people* as ineffective as possible (See Revelation 13).

We have been set free to weep with those who weep and to rejoice with those who rejoice. Let this truth settle deep within your heart! Time is short. Christ is coming. How will you use your new freedom today?

SITTING AT THE WINDOW

Let the Bible guide your thoughts right now as you stand at the window and, led by the Holy Spirit, peer into your heart.

1. What do you believe mourning has to do with pausing at the window of the heart for a while? Why do you believe that it's so difficult to pause at the window with the Holy Spirit, a trusted fellow Christian, or trained grief counselor?

   _____

   _____

   _____

   _____

   _____

2. Reread Romans 1:18–32. In what ways does the idea of God's wrath strike you as possible? As True Truth? Or perhaps as some sort of throwback theology from another era?

   _____

   _____

   _____

   _____

   _____

3. In what ways do you believe God's wrath could be directed at the believer in Jesus Christ, if there is "no condemnation for those who are in Christ Jesus?"

_____

_____

_____

_____

_____

4. Imagine a window of your heart being blown open by an extreme trial in your life. Explain in your own words what it might be like to sit at the window of your heart with the Holy Spirit. What might you see? How would the Holy Spirit console and counsel you?

_____

_____

_____

_____

_____

5. In the shortest fashion possible, describe what sin means to you—first in the abstract and then in your own personal heart, emotions, and life.

_____

_____

_____

_____

_____

6. What 3–5 things, plainly known about God, seem to be suppressed most commonly in our culture today? In your own heart? What examples can you cite to show how you or someone else has "claimed to be wise, but [instead] became a fool?"

_____

_____

_____

_____

7. What legitimate condemnation have you experienced, perhaps especially from your past? What illegitimate condemnation or false guilt? How would you differentiate between the two?

_____

_____

_____

_____

8. Is it possible for chains of condemnation—legitimate or illegitimate—to have been with someone for so long that they become that person's _"Precious?"_ (See Chapter 5.) Might that have happened or be happening to you? How would you know? What might you substitute for those chains?

_____

_____

_____

_____

9. In what specific ways might you (with another's help, perhaps) search your own heart for falsehoods or feelings of any heart-hardening, unnecessary, or unhealthy condemnation?

_____

_____

_____

_____

10. Suppose you could hear Jesus say to you what he said to the prostitute, "Neither do I condemn you, go and sin no more" (John 8:11). In light of both your false guilt and your very real sins, what difference would these words make in your life?

_____

_____

_____

_____

11. When have you lived at the extremes of the Gospel—known the depth and depravity of your sin _and_ the supreme and unending love of God for you, personally? How might you do that more consistently?

_____

_____

_____

_____

GOING DEEPER...

For further reading you may want to explore:

Allender, D.B., & Longman, T. Breaking the Idols Of Your Heart: How To Navigate The Temptations Of Life. Downers Grove, IL: InterVarsity Press, 2007

Nouwen, H. Life of The Beloved: Spiritual Living In A Secular World. New York: The Crossroad Publishing Company. 1992.

Blackaby, H.T. and Blackaby R. Hearing God's Voice. Nashville, TN: Broadman and Holman Publishers. 2002.

Packer, J. I. Growing in Christ. Wheaton, IL: Crossway Book Publishers. 2007.

CHAPTER TWELVE

ALL WAYS: MOVING BACK INTO THE CHAOS OF THE WORLD ... RADICALLY CHANGED TO BE AN AGENT OF CHANGE

Teach me your way, O Lord, that I may walk in your truth; unite my heart to fear your name.

Psalm 86:11

Resolved, after afflictions, to inquire, what I am the better for them, and what good I have got by them.

Jonathan Edwards[37]

A true faith in Jesus Christ will not suffer us to be idle. No, it is an active, lively, restless principle; it fills the heart, so that it cannot be easy till it is doing something for Jesus Christ.

George Whitefield, preacher in the
Church of England, 1714–1770

The weeping. The window. The way. Jesus is the way, the truth, and the life (John 14:6)! God himself descended into this world's time and space as a human baby. How amazing is the cross of his sacrifice! More awesome still is his resurrection from the dead and through it, his defeat of death itself. He is indeed our life!

The Holy Spirit works this faith in us, convincing us of these True Truths. But the Spirit's work in our hearts does not stop there. The apostle Paul calls attention to this profound mystery: *Christ in you, the hope of glory* (Colossians 1:27). Elsewhere, Paul tells God's people that he finds himself enduring the agonies of childbirth, "*until Christ is formed in you!*" (Galatians 4:19). That formation—a supernatural heart transformation—is the purpose the Holy Spirit has in mind for us. Jesus' person and character shining through us! Jesus' comfort flowing from us! Jesus Christ in us—the hope of glory. Jesus himself, the continuation of our redemptive story mysteriously carried out by God's will and our cooperation.

It seems unbelievable, but despite what God has done for us in Jesus, our hearts easily forget these truths. Our hearts forget that all life, both temporal and eternal, centers in Christ Jesus. If we're completely honest with each other, we know how readily other realities push the True Truth aside to take their place in the forefront of our daily lives. In fact, one of the most grievous implications of sin is the forgetfulness that is so often its hallmark! This forgetfulness, in turn, leads us in one of two directions: humanism or materialism. Someone has called humanism the world's second oldest religion. It all started with the infamous question in the Garden, "Did God really say . . . " (Genesis 3:1).

Ever since Eve and Adam fell for Satan's deception, our sinful hearts have doubted God and doted on our own agendas. Our hearts default toward measuring everything and everyone we encounter through the lens of human values and human interests. By our fallen nature, we want to focus on the dignity, worth, and supposed self-sufficiency of those of us who are apart from Christ and his sacrifice for our sins. We rebel at his demand that we give him control of our lives, even while we know that insisting we're in control is madness.

In a similar way, materialism takes our focus off supernatural reality, especially the cross of Christ and the miracle that God worked. Materialism then fills the vacuum it creates in our hearts with a preoccupation on things we can see, touch, and taste.

Materialists scheme and plot, creating ever more complex ways by which to avoid the inevitability of a meaningless death and seize hold onto this world's trinkets, to amass more possessions, collect more honors and awards, and achieve more recognition, all while avoiding the only recognition that really matters! Unaware that this striving is at heart an effort to prove self-worth and earn God's favor, materialism forgets God and our need for him, while at the same time striving zealously to appease him.

Richard Sibbes, a Puritan cleric and theologian of the late 16th and early 17th centuries, describes the dangers of materialism and the rescue God provides to those who suffer this way:

> Christ chiefly manifests himself to the Christian in times of affliction, because then the soul unites itself most closely by faith to Christ. The soul in time of prosperity, scatters its affections and loses itself in the creature, but there is a uniting power in sanctified afflictions by which the soul (as in rain, the hen collects her brood) gathers his best affections unto his Father and his God.

Both humanism and materialism contain within themselves a fundamental contradiction that, once rooted in the human heart, will eventually destroy it. That's why God must use weeping and windows. By this process, he breaks the crust of ice that forms over our hearts the moment we are left to our own devices.

That ice forms every day and must be broken every day. If you don't yet know this truth, if you have not yet experienced it, you simply don't know yourself very well. Perhaps the brokenness of this sinful world hasn't yet crushed your heart and spirit. Perhaps you haven't yet been both blasted and blessed by seeing the utter depravity, the desperately lost state of your own or another's heart. Just wait—you will encounter it soon enough. Just wait, but please don't forget.[38]

FRESH WINDS OF GRACE

The Holy Spirit providentially prepares each window opened by weeping for the express purpose of working in our hearts a fresh understanding of the way of the cross and of the Christ who was resurrected and victorious over death. That process is sequential, linear, and repetitive. It is the path by which God leads us to a higher, holier, and more helpful place. Ultimately, it is the way by which we more fully and freely live in Jesus Christ and he lives more freely and fully in and through us. Do you grasp that? Do you see how merciful God is to use the brokenness that we sinful human beings have created as a means by which to heal not only our personal brokenness, but the brokenness of the world? Do you comprehend the mercy by which God uses the broken body of his Son on Calvary as the means by which to save and sanctify our broken hearts for the healing of the human race?

This is outrageous mercy and a completely counterintuitive approach on God's part. It should break our hearts and stir our desire to receive even more of God's love and trust his promises and purposes in our lives. If it does not do that, please keep on considering it before it's too late.

On the other hand, if this mercy does melt your heart, even a tiny bit, then the Holy Spirit has begun a work in you and wants to bring it to completion. It's one or the other. No gray area exists. The Holy Spirit either wants to begin a good work in you by helping you repent of the sin of hating God as you put your faith in Jesus for the first time. Or the Spirit wants to continue that good work, already begun in your heart, as he cultivates your faith and growth in Christ.

Either way, the Holy Spirit intends that the *weeping* of our lives will open a *window* into our hearts that will make it possible for us to see the *way* of the cross anew each day. That way is renewed and enlightened day by day.

That way is renewed, because the Holy Spirit continually shows us new ways to detach ourselves from the influence of the world around us, from the grip of the flesh (our own sinful nature), and from the temptations of the devil. Each new day we need a fresh understanding and cleansing of the heart. We need these desperately, and we receive them as God immerses us again and again in his mercy, his gracious forgiveness and help:

> I thought that I had crossed the line, walked away from love one time too many. I thought I'd used up all the grace, set aside for my mistakes … so many. On my knees I found to my surprise that your mercy renewed with the sunrise. You make your mercy new every day!
>
> Phillips, Craig, and Dean, from "New Mercy"
> Phillips, Craig, and Dean. Where Strength Begins
> Album. Starsong / EMD Label. 1997

That way is enlightened, because the Spirit has laid out a path by which we move closer toward God's goals for us. Greater holiness. Greater purity. Greater devotion. Deeper worship. More willing obedience, sacrifice, and selflessness. More intense compassion. Bolder humility. More zealousness for renewing communities which point to the new heaven and new earth—here and now, today.

As we have seen, the Holy Spirit continues to transform our hearts throughout our lives, making them the mirror image of Christ's own heart! To live the Christian life is to become more and more like the Son of God, Jesus Christ! Growth in likeness of Christ is the only reason God allows us to experience the pain of weeping. It's the reason he opens the window into our hearts—to point us to the way. The weeping and the window are only means to an end.

The way is the path of perfect freedom earned for us by the perfect obedience of Christ. He took the punishment in our place and purchased for us the freedom to live a life transformed and to serve others materially and spiritually. This life, so mercifully and miraculously given to us, is a true metamorphosis—

we are like a caterpillar turning into a beautiful butterfly. As Jesus himself has assured us in Revelation 21:4–5: "The old order has passed away ... For I [Jesus] am making everything new."

Perhaps Spurgeon summed it up best in these words:

> I wish, brothers and sisters, that we could all imitate "the pearl oyster:" A hurtful particle intrudes itself into its shell, and this vexes and grieves it. It cannot reject the evil, but what does it do but "cover" it with a precious substance extracted out of its own life, by which it turns the intruder into a pearl! Oh, that we could do so with the provocations we receive from our fellow Christians, so that pearls of patience, gentleness, and forgiveness might be bred within us by that which otherwise would have harmed us.

NOT THE WAY OF THE WORLD! (OR EVEN THE CHURCH?)

With all this in mind, beloved, pause for a moment to consider the requests commonly given and prayed for in the Church, week-by-week in prayer services and by members of a prayer chain. In all but rare instances, these lists consist of requests that God would remove the sources of suffering, alleviate pain, and heal the disease the person is experiencing. In essence, we ask that God would so influence our circumstances that we would pray for the suffering to end, both for others and ourselves. We ask that persecution disappear, weeping cease, and opposition dissolve.

Asking for relief is not a bad thing, but it is definitely not the main thing! Does that surprise you? Then consider the prayers recorded for us in the New Testament. Reading what St. Paul prayed for all born-again believers in Jesus Christ staggers our imagination when we consider his words in light of the approach the Church today has adopted for prayer:

For this reason I kneel before the Father, from whom his whole family in heaven and on earth derives its name. I pray that out of his glorious riches he may strengthen you with power through his Spirit in your inner being, so that Christ may dwell in your hearts through faith. And I pray that you, being rooted and established in love, may have power, together with all the saints, to grasp how wide and long and high and deep is the love of Christ, and to know this love that surpasses knowledge—that you may be filled to the measure of all the fullness of God.

Now to him who is able to do immeasurably more than all we ask or imagine, according to his power that is at work within us, to him be glory in the church and in Christ Jesus through-out all generations, for ever and ever! Amen.

Ephesians 3:14–21; emphasis added

We ought always to thank God for you, brothers, and rightly so, because your faith is *growing* more and more, and the love every one of you has for each other is *increasing*. Therefore, among God's churches we boast about your perseverance and faith in all the persecutions and trials you are enduring. All this is evidence that God's judgment is right, and as a result you will be counted worthy of the kingdom of God, for which you are suffering.

1 Thessalonians 1:3–5 (NIV), emphasis added

Having trusted God's promises that the events that bring us to tears are ordained by him for our purification, we can see the deeper purposes for our pain and can thank him for revealing the truths and falsehoods of our heart, that we may live more consistently in his Son, who is the way, the truth, and the life. This, then, is cause for great joy and the fully realistic expectation that even the bitterest experience of tears will eventually yield sweet and abundant fruit! In your weeping, God is inviting you to the banquet, so bring a friend along.

AFFLICTIONS REDEEMED:
THE WEEPING, THE WINDOW, THE WAY—
SOME EXAMPLES FROM SCRIPTURE

As this chapter closes, I would like to offer several examples of the pattern I have been explaining and the ways in which God has mercifully used this protocol throughout history. Seeing these, you will likely be able to suggest many other examples of your own, both from Scripture and your own life experiences as you have walked with your Savior through the valley of the shadow.[39]

KING DAVID

The Weeping [of David in seeing his sins of adultery and murder]: *Have mercy on me, O God, according to your steadfast love; according to your abundant mercy blot out my transgressions.*

The Window [in David's heart as the Holy Spirit reminds him of the calling to live as a man after God's own heart]: *You, [Lord,] delight in truth in the inward being, and you teach me wisdom in the secret heart.*

The Way [as David sees the Holy Spirit reshaping his heart and realigning his emotions]: *Create in me a clean heart, O God, and renew a right spirit within me* (Psalm 51:1, 6, 10).

GOD'S OLD TESTAMENT PEOPLE

The Weeping [as God mercifully brings his repentant people home from exile]:

Behold, I will bring them from the north country and gather them from the farthest parts of the earth, among them the blind and the lame, the pregnant woman and she who is in labor, together; a great company, they shall return here. With weeping they shall come ...

(Jeremiah 31:8–9)

The Window [as the Holy Spirit leads them in an examination of their heart's idols, their dry spiritual cisterns, and their spiritually adulterous ways]:

With pleas for mercy I will lead them back. (Jeremiah 31:9)

The Way [of sanctification, of purified obedience; the way lived on the solid foundation of the True Truth]:

I will make them walk by brooks of water, in a straight path in which they shall not stumble, for I am a father to Israel, and Ephraim is my firstborn. "Hear the word of the LORD, O nations, and declare it in the coastlands far away; say, 'He who scattered Israel will gather him, and will keep him as a shepherd keeps his flock.' For the LORD has ransomed Jacob and has redeemed him from hands too strong for him."

Jeremiah 31: 9–11

JESUS CHRIST'S WEEPING, WINDOW, WAY AT GETHSEMANE

The Weeping [Jesus has come to the point of experiencing the horror that has overshadowed his entire earthly life, and he has chosen to take on the sins of the world and the resulting separation from his Father God]:

Then Jesus went with them to a place called Gethsemane, and he said to his disciples, "Sit here, while I go over there and pray." And taking with him Peter and the two sons of Zebedee, he began to be sorrowful and troubled. Then he said to them, "My soul is very sorrowful, even to death..." And going a little farther he fell on his face and prayed, saying, "My Father, if it be possible, let this cup pass from me..."

The Window [Jesus recognizes that his own heart, spirit, and life are inextricably tied to his Father's love, truth, and will for him. Weeping, Jesus nevertheless submits to the Father's will]:

" ... nevertheless, not as I will, but as you will." Again, for the second time, he [Jesus] went away and prayed, "My Father, if this cannot pass unless I drink it, your will be done."

The Way [Jesus raises his broken, yet submissive heart up to the heavens where he can again see the fulfillment of God's entire plan of redemption. Thus, Jesus moved forward in the way as the Fulfiller and the Fulfillment]:

> Then he came to the disciples and said to them, "Sleep and take your rest later on. See, the hour is at hand, and the Son of Man is betrayed into the hands of sinners. Rise, let us be going; see, my betrayer is at hand ... Do you think that I cannot appeal to my Father, and he will at once send me more than twelve legions of angels? But how then should the Scriptures be fulfilled, that it must be so? ... All this has taken place that the Scriptures of the prophets might be fulfilled."
> Matthew 26:36–46, 52–54

The weeping. The window. The way. Even our Lord himself was not exempt from this protocol. Hebrews 5 reminds us:

> In the days of his flesh, Jesus offered up prayers and supplications, with loud cries and tears, to him who was able to save him from death, and he was heard because of his reverence. Although he was a son, he learned obedience through what he suffered. And being made perfect, he became the source of eternal salvation ...

GOING DEEPER...

For further reading, you might want to explore:

Chapman, S.C. & Smith, S. Restoring Broken Things. Nashville, TN: Thomas Nelson, Inc. 2007.

CHAPTER THIRTEEN

YOUR WAY: BECOMING COURAGEOUS, COMPELLING, COMPASSIONATE CO-REDEEMERS—APPLYING EZEKIEL 11:19, ROMANS 8:28, ROMANS 12:2, JOB 19:25

Let not your hearts be troubled. Believe in God; believe also in me... Thomas said to him, "Lord, we do not know where you are going. How can we know the way?" Jesus said to him, *"I am the way, and the truth, and the life.* No one comes to the Father except through me. If you had known me, you would have known my Father also. From now on you do know him and have seen him."

John 14:1–7; emphasis added.

If you look for truth, you may find comfort in the end; if you look for comfort, you will not get neither comfort or truth only soft soap and wishful thinking to begin, and in the end, despair.

C.S. Lewis, The Problem of Pain[40]

I don't know how long I knelt beside Dad before the sirens began to break into my awareness. I do know that in anticipation of the miraculous space God had created for himself, Dad, and me *dissolving*, I felt a sense of fear in anticipation like never before. As I saw the flashing lights and the amorphous taupe, orange, and blue clad bodies approaching, I began to

273

dread what would surely come next. I cried out to God in near desperation:

What now, Lord? I'm so blessed to have been here in this place, but please tell me, what now? I need your help to get through this, Lord. I cannot do it alone. Please, Lord, please give me the strength, the love, and the heart to move forward from here. Please hold me up. Give me hope and show me the way to make it through.

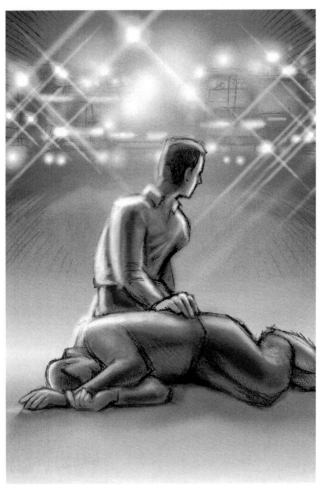

Turned to Anticipate the Way: Anticipating, being wise and faithful, and planning how to return to a world of chaos and suffering is crucially important. Do not rush the process!

As I have already told you, beloved, God answered this prayer by and through his Word in the Bible. For a third time that night, our Redeemer responded to my heart's cry. His words of hope encircled and enfolded me with an extra measure of True Truth from his word:

- I will give them one heart, and a new spirit I will put within them. I will remove the heart of stone from their flesh and give them a heart of flesh (Ezekiel 11:19).

- We know that for those who love God all things work together for good, for those who are called according to his purpose (Romans 8:28).

- Do not be conformed to this world, but be transformed by the renewal of your mind, that by testing you may discern what is the will of God, what is good and acceptable and perfect (Romans 12:2).

- For I know that my Redeemer lives, and at the last he will stand upon the earth (Job 19:25).

That night I learned afresh that he intended to use my suffering to conform my heart, spirit, and will to the image of his Son. I also began to personally and vibrantly see that God intended to use me, his newly transformed son, to work alongside him to accomplish his mission in the world. The changes in my heart were not intended for me alone, but for the hearts of many hurting people. The point was not that I get back to normal as soon as possible. Not at all! Rather, the Holy Spirit wanted me to step back into this world a changed person, as a radical force for change in his world. I could never be the same.

DEAD MEN WALKING?

Sufferers who follow God's protocol for the weeping and the window, and do not waste their tears but let the Holy Spirit use them most redemptively, will likely then find the way forward to the most important phase of the journey. Why? It's the stage that can change the world. But it's also the stage that our own flesh resists, the devil abhors, and the world shuns! The way forward is the "Now What?!" part of the journey, which begins after the freefalling stops, the foundation is renewed, the heart renovation has begun, and we get back to our lives. As we do that, we do it as changed children of God. We are not the same people we were before the heartbreak occurred. Not at all!

First, it's vitally important to mark the differences that have occurred in our hearts and lives, and begin to look for ways to use them for good in the lives of others. This will also help protect us from slipping back into the heart-hardening process Satan would so like to reestablish in our hearts. Reentry is not easy. Remember, you're a different person, plunging back into the culture of comfort, a culture that does not want to notice changes in others for fear they might need to change themselves. This can even happen within the church, where many have become so accustomed to a lukewarm sort of faith that they are skeptical if not resentful of someone whose heart has been set on fire for the things of God.

Following the miraculous experience of being with God and Dad in the garden on Christmas night, I could easily mark the difference in my life in many ways. One very big mark was how radically I saw the need for a sense of urgency to convey the message of the Gospel of Christ in any way I could. Another mark was how I no longer hesitated to run towards the chaos in someone's life because I had seen how quickly one could and would shut the window blown open into their heart, not pausing long enough to peer inside.

Yet another mark was how vitally important it is to never write someone off when they are in a state of unconsciousness and apparent unreachability: God can and does speak and change a heart whenever he pleases. And to somehow short-circuit any opportunity to tell someone the Good News of Jesus Christ, even when all the apparatus says, "He's gone," is a crime of potentially eternal proportions.

Of all the important things I did not do well after Dad's tragic death was to spend time more fully reorienting myself to God, my family, and others who were about to be impacted by the radical changes that had occurred in my life. In many ways, I was a different person after that night in the garden. By not taking the time to mark the manifold changes that had occurred within me in the weeks and months that followed, I did a very grave disservice to God, to myself, and to those around me.

When my wife Peggy and I were in counseling after Dad's death, the counselor once asked Peggy, "Have you mourned the death of the John you knew before his experience on Christmas night?" Intriguing question, is it not? God powerfully and mercifully changes hearts. We need to mark the changes in concrete ways or else our hearts will begin to turn back to stone.

Secondly, the Spirit intends those changes to propel us forward on the way to more authentic "word and deed discipleship." We become near-fanatic, Christ-forwarding people, changed and challenged to pursue the next iteration of heart, spirit, faith, and story. God gives us an undaunted desire to reveal his glory to others, others whom he also intends to convert and conform believers more and more to the image of Christ. All people can be powerfully influenced by God, and by your changed life.

Any time we suffer, the way forward is the way described in the Bible, the way of Christ Jesus and his resurrection, of community impact and renewal. As we explore this in more depth, we should note that the believers described in the New Testament never directly asked God to remove the consequences of living in a broken world. Rather, they asked that God, by means of the inevitable suffering, would transform their hearts to more closely resemble Jesus' heart and then use them to bring the comfort of Christ to others (Ephesians 3; 2 Corinthians 1:3–7; Philippians 2).

Like their world, our world is broken. It will only grow more so, the closer history comes to the culmination of God's redemptive plan and the return of Jesus who will make all things new (See Appendix B). An enraged Satan has been set loose on the earth, and he intends to thwart Christ's cause in every way possible, using every method, weapon, and person at his disposal. He works to keep unbelievers from coming to faith. He works to make those who already belong to Christ as ineffective as possible in the redemptive mission to which Christ has called us. Satan wants to keep us from becoming a more powerful redemptive force in, through, and by Jesus Christ. Don't forget, since sanctified suffering is a key to our growth and effectiveness, The Deceiver and Destroyer will oppose it at every turn!

Thirdly, given this, we remember that the way forward will inevitably involve suffering. Therefore, we must fix our focus on our Savior, our community in the fellowship of the Church, and the Scriptures that reveal him to us. We will then draw resolve, humility, boldness, and peace from it all. Only then can we venture forward in safety and security regardless of what circumstance might befall us.

> So we do not lose heart. Though our outer self is wasting away, our inner self is being renewed day by day. For this light momentary affliction is preparing for us an eternal weight of glory beyond all comparison, as we look not to the things that are seen but to the things that are unseen. For the things that are seen are transient, but the things that are unseen are eternal.
>
> 2 Corinthians 4:16–18

The results? The fruit? That focus and attitude makes it possible for us not merely to endure affliction, but be made better by it. That's what happened in the first century Church. Among other things, they were increasingly unafraid of death! This focus also makes it possible for our ministry to make a real, radical, and lasting difference in the lives of those around us. With hearts transformed by God, we run toward the poor, the orphans, the widows, the prisoners, and the sad and disenfranchised. As we serve we cannot afford to adopt a naïve view of what it will involve, what it will cost. After all, what did it cost God to redeem the world?

Fourth, don't be surprised when sin's brokenness keeps the systems of this world from a healthy responsiveness. Don't be surprised when a Christian brother or sister chooses to remain spiritually stunted. Don't be surprised by mass murder, government graft, or corporate corruption. And don't let "the surprise of sin" paralyze you when it raises its ugly head in any individual or institution. Suffering will continue and escalate, until Christ comes again. Transform your surprise into faith in action.

Fifth, because this is so, we join in Paul's ardent prayer for ourselves and for the hearts and spirits of other believers who, together with us, face life's battles. Together, we pray that all the sufferings we endure will bring about even more thorough sanctification and better works of righteousness.

> So I ask you not to lose heart over what I am suffering for you, which is your glory. For this reason I bow my knees before the Father, from whom every family in heaven and on earth is named, that according to the riches of his glory he may grant you to be strengthened with power through his Spirit in your inner being, SO THAT Christ may dwell in your hearts through faith—that you, being rooted and grounded in love, may have strength to comprehend with all the saints what is the breadth and length and height and depth, and to know the love of Christ that surpasses knowledge, that you may be filled with all the fullness of God.
>
> Ephesians 3:13–21—emphasis added

The way forward involves moving out in faith with Christ, trusting our Redeemer King who has called us to work with him in sharing the Good News of his redemption with our world. As his co-redeemers, we open ourselves to help and be hurt by others. And in obediently and graciously doing that, we take the next steps in the ongoing and upward-bound cycle of sanctification which leads to further sacrificial service. Service involves suffering which leads to further sanctification which results in more service. This simple equation sums it up—when we connect to the person of Jesus, not just a process:

REGENERATION + SANCTIFICATION = JOY... AND REAL (HEART AND WORLD) TRANSFORMATION

Regeneration brings us from spiritual death to eternal life, while sanctification continues throughout our lives, the Holy Spirit working in us to free us from sinful habits and form in us Christ-like affections, predispositions, virtues, and life-changing works. This change is real and palpable. It goes beyond mere feelings of change or the outward appearance of change.

To be sanctified is to be set apart by, and within, the Holy Trinity for his use in a broken and suffering world. This process is vital in the literal sense of that word, as it is necessary for life.

Do you believe this? Do you accept the fact that God has placed within our circle of concern and influence the lives of other human beings, not just for a time, but for *eternity?* This fact should take your breath away. Unless we understand this, embrace it, and live it, we are dead men walking! We shamefully cheapen grace and high-jack the Gospel of Jesus Christ for our own selfish ends (Matthew 3:7ff; 23:25; Romans 15:1–7; 1 Corinthians 13[41]).

We have explored these ideas throughout this book. I pray that as you have pondered them, you have come to discover that to avoid suffering means to avoid sanctification, to avoid becoming more like Jesus Christ. There is no steady state, beloved, no straddle position that will allow us to remain lukewarm or half-hearted. The heart will naturally harden when it is not being softened. This is the law of spiritual entropy! The Good News is that the Holy Spirit is ready, willing, and able to be our constant strength and help. Heart transformation happens as we abide in Christ, submitting to the Spirit's work in us. Read and meditate on Colossians 1:11, Ephesians 5:2, Philippians 2:5–11, and 2 Timothy 1:7; 2:1. Then ask yourself a vital question: What is it that you want, Christian? Do you stand beside Paul, asking for the blessing for which he prayed?

> I want to know Christ and the power of his resurrection and the fellowship of sharing in his sufferings, becoming like him in his death, and so, somehow, to attain to the resurrection from the dead ... let those of us who are mature think this way.
>
> Philippians 3:10; 15

As we reach the third stage in the weeping/window/way protocol, the transformation God has worked in the previous two stages will become apparent in the world. God alone can change your heart, using life's circumstances and his redemptive plan, in connection with his Word to bring about the repentance, faith, attitudes, and actions that will not go unnoticed. But he will not force you to move into the world's calamity, chaos, and change with renewed urgency. You can choose to waste your weeping and debase the suffering of your Savior by focusing it exclusively on yourself. You can live an unchallenged life in an unchanged world, but your troubled heart and spirit will belie your apparently unflappable affections, beloved.

Or you can choose to let the transformation God has worked in your softened heart to bear abundant fruit in your life. What do you want, Christian? How might God use your suffering and heart transformation to make radical changes beginning right now, right where you live? Unless you move forward authentically, deliberately, and proactively into the challenge, the world, your fallen nature, and the devil will certainly find ways to ensure your ineffectiveness.

THE FOUR PRINCIPLES FOR REENTRY

In the end, I was able to do what I considered impossible: I stood up, turned to face the world, and left the garden, the snow, and the miraculous bubble in which God sheltered me during the last minutes of my dad's life on earth.

The passages God had given me lifted me from my knees and enabled me to turn and face the oncoming chaos of the world. Since then, I have come to believe that in a world full of hurt and suffering, we always have a choice. We can perpetually look back at the heartbreak we have endured, scrutinizing little else beyond the wounds that life and others have inflicted on us. In doing so, we refuse to let anything but those wounds define us. Or we can let our Savior redeem our wounds, applying to them the healing power that flows from his Word of True Truth. Then we can move out into the chaos to share this comfort with others who suffer. This is the path of the co-redeemer.

In Philippians, Paul commends both sanctified forgetting and sanctified remembering for the purposes of a super-charged calling:

> Not that I have already obtained this or am already perfect, but I press on to make it my own, because Christ Jesus has made me his own. Brothers, I do not consider that I have made it my own. But one thing I do: forgetting what lies behind and straining forward to what lies ahead, I press on toward the goal for the prize of the upward call of God in Christ Jesus. Let those of us who are mature think this way, and if in anything you think otherwise, God will reveal that also to you. Only let us hold true to what we have attained.
>
> Philippians 3:12–15

As the emergency responders descended on Dad's garden, and the horrific consequence domino game began, the four Bible passages God gave me that night helped me both remember and forget. They helped me identify four keys for using suffering redemptively, for moving back into the chaos of a broken world as a wounded healer. Please, very carefully consider these principles and passages:

The Way Fully Standing, Moving Out Into the Chaos: All of humanity, changed by suffering in some way, must *turn* and *return* to the world. Will we be more like Christ? Will we be bitter or better? The choice is ours to make!

- *Mark the Change of Heart: Less Stone, More Flesh* (Ezekiel 11:17–21; 36)

- *Moan the Purpose of the Spirit: Less Me, More Christ* (Romans 8:18–30)

- *Marvel the Mercy of God: Less Whining, More Worship* (Romans 11; 12:1–3)

- *Move the Mountain with Faith: Less Ruminating, More Redeeming* (Job 9; 19:25)

"Moving back into the chaos, in the way God desires, I will closely consider how I will…"

1. MARK THE CHANGE OF HEART: LESS STONE, MORE FLESH

Take another look at the stone at the beginning of this Heart Application section. Do you see a heart of stone? A window? A cross? Now consider the first Bible verse God gave me as I prayed for help in leaving the garden:

> I will give them one heart, and a new spirit I will put within them. I will remove the heart of stone from their flesh and give them a heart of flesh.
>
> Ezekiel 11:19

This almost unbelievable promise carries two implications. First, in unfathomable mercy, God will use our suffering to supernaturally and naturally re-create within us the heart he intended for us in the beginning. In Chapter Five we imagined God creating Adam's heart as he formed the first human being. We considered the Creator God admiring that heart as it lay, beating for the first time, in the palm of his hand. We saw our Lord taking pleasure as he saw in that heart a perfect reflection of himself. Our God is animating and enlarging exactly that kind of heart in us as we submit to his sanctifying work in our suffering! If this is true, we can continue throughout our lives to mark the change God is making in our hearts, our spirits, and our relationships.

Second, as Christ's graciously obedient heart within us yields to his Spirit's work, we become more like Jesus Christ in word and in deed. This is sanctification—wherein The Westminster Confession of Faith defines as:

I. They, who are once effectually called, and regenerated, having a new heart, and a new spirit created in them, are further sanctified, really and personally, through the virtue of Christ's death and resurrection, by his Word and Spirit dwelling in them: the dominion of the whole body of sin is destroyed, and the several lusts thereof are more and more weakened and mortified; and they more and more quickened and strengthened in all saving graces, to the practice of true holiness, without which no man shall see the Lord.

II. This sanctification is throughout, in the whole man; yet imperfect in this life, there abiding still some remnants of corruption in every part; whence arises a continual and irreconcilable war, the flesh lusting against the Spirit, and the Spirit against the flesh.

III. In which war, although the remaining corruption, for a time, may much prevail; yet, through the continual supply of strength from the sanctifying Spirit of Christ, the regenerate part does overcome; and so, the saints grow in grace, perfecting holiness in the fear of God.

Westminster Confession, Chapter XII, "Sanctification"

We love God, obeying him because we truly want to, love to, not because we have to. The person and mission of Jesus ignites our zeal, strengthens us for the spiritual battle raging within, and we become more obedient to his calling in carrying out that mission with joy! There is no joy—short of seeing God's glory face-to-face when Jesus returns to make all things new (Revelations 21)—better and deeper than the joy of witnessing God illuminating and igniting another's heart who has been saved and sent.

Therefore, beloved, since you are waiting for these attributes of the second coming of Jesus Christ, be diligent to be found by him without spot or blemish, and at peace. And count the patience of our Lord as salvation, just as our beloved brother Paul also wrote to you according to the wisdom given him, as he does in all his letters when he speaks in them of these matters. There are some things in them that are hard to understand, which the ignorant and unstable twist to their own destruction, as they do the other Scriptures. You therefore, beloved, knowing this beforehand, take care that you are not carried away with the error of lawless people and lose your own stability. *But grow in the grace and knowledge of our Lord and Savior Jesus Christ.* To him be the glory both now and to the day of eternity. Amen.

2 Peter 3:14–18—emphasis added

This is no small matter. This is actually the matter of holiness (1 Peter 1:16), the fruit of which is being saved and sent on Christ's mission in the realms of your own sphere of influence. As the Bible describes it, sanctification equates to a change of heart that changes the world—not despite the suffering, but through it!

The context of Ezekiel 11:19 recapitulates the weeping/window/way protocol: a) setting us on the foundation of mercy; b) leading us to remove the idols that reside in our hearts; c) calling us to recommit our lives to God; and d) warning those who ignore such a marvelous and manifold mercy:

FOUNDATIONS OF MERCY[42]

Thus says the Lord God: "I will gather you from the peoples and assemble you out of the countries where you have been scattered, and I will give you the land of Israel."

Ezekiel 11:17

IDOL WORK OF THE HEART[43]

And when they come there, they will remove from it all its detestable things and all its abominations. And I will give them one heart, and a new spirit I will put within them. I will remove the heart of stone from their flesh and give them a heart of flesh ...

Ezekiel 11:18–19

RECOMMITMENT TO GOD[44]

That they may walk in my statutes and keep my rules and obey them. And they shall be my people, and I will be their God.

Ezekiel 11:20

WARNINGS TO THOSE WHO IGNORE SUCH A GREAT MERCY

"But as for those whose heart goes after their detestable things and their abominations, I will bring their deeds upon their own heads," declares the Lord GOD.

verse 21

With this in mind, reflect:

1. What do these verses from Ezekiel 11 say to you about the following questions:

    -   Can you describe a time in your own life when you experienced at the heart and spirit level the sequence of steps described in verses 17–21. Were you converted from being an un-Believer to a Believer? Or from being a "new-born, baby Christian" to a more mature Christian?

        _____

        _____

        _____

        _____

    -   If "Yes," are you prepared to tell someone else the details of your conversion story?

        _____

        _____

        _____

• If "No," would you consider praying to God and telling one other faithful person that you're not certain what the change of heart described really means—in the Bible and in you?

• What does God's yearning after us tell you about him? About yourself (verse 17)?

• Can you define, in your own words, examples of "detestable idols and abominations," and their identification and removal from the heart? What does the description of the heart by John Calvin as an "idol factory" say to you (vv 18–19)?

- What is: a) our responsibility, and b) God's responsibility as depicted in the pronouns found in vv 18–19?

- Does God or man possess the ability to remove a heart of stone and replace it with heart of flesh? What difference does it make either way?

- Describe in your own words your response to God after a heart has been re-created and re-consecrated to him (verse 20)?

- What would be some examples and some of the consequences of continuing to flee from God and chase after idols and detestable things from an obstinate and hardened heart? In your own life, perhaps (verse 21)?

_____
_____
_____

2. When have you experienced the process of the transformation of your heart from stone to flesh? How did that change come about? What stony parts of your life are still in need of transformation?

_____
_____
_____
_____

3. Think of someone who has known your heart in an authentic way for some time. How would this person say your heart has changed over the years?

_____
_____
_____
_____

4. When have you marked the changes God was making and talked about this change of heart with someone else? What happened as a result? Why might a private vs. public affirmation of a change of heart be important?

_____
_____
_____
_____

5. Knowing how important community is to a change of heart, are you part of a committed, life-changing community today? If no, what might be a few first steps? If yes, is there an encouraging story of change that occurred in such a setting for you?

_____

_____

_____

_____

_____

6. Consider how the Prophet Ezekiel was himself, as well as an example to others, of being "A Watchman on the Wall." Please take a close look at what this involves in the "Appendix A" section.

_____

_____

_____

_____

"Moving back into the chaos, in the way God desires, I will closely consider how I will..."

2. MOAN THE PURPOSE OF THE SPIRIT: LESS ME, MORE CHRIST

The second answer God gave as I pleaded with him to prepare me for reentry was a reminder of my Savior and the providential promise God has made with those who cling by faith to his Son:

> We know that in all things God works for the good of those who love him, who have been called according to his purpose.

> For those God foreknew he also predestined to be conformed
> to the likeness of his Son ...
>
> Romans 8:28–29 (NIV)

Nothing can touch the born-again believer except that which God intends to use for his own glory, for our good, and for the good of those whose lives we might influence!

The good promised here refers first and foremost to the fact that our Father intends that we be conformed to the likeness of his son (Romans 8:29) as he works in and through everything he allows to happen in our lives. In giving me this verse, God was saying, "Trust me, John. The heartbreak we experienced together tonight did not take me by surprise. I saw it before time began, and I intend to use it to conform your heart, spirit, and life more to the likeness of my Son. And that's just the start to how I can and will use this tragedy in ways that you may or may not recognize."

Even as this truth washed over me, the Holy Spirit was interceding for me in my weakness. God the Father answered the Spirit's intercession, responding to it perfectly. Through it all, he will continue to point us to Jesus. Within every trial endured and every tear shed by God's suffering servants there exists manifold opportunities to participate in his redemptive work.

Do you see in all this the limitless mercy and wisdom of God? How ironic. How miraculous! As I think about my dad and the tragedy of his death, I am tempted to say to God, "Even this? Even though the heartbreak will disfigure so many?" But whenever I have mouthed that prayer, God has always spoken back to my heart, "No, John, especially this. I re-make broken hearts, but I cannot transform hearts hardened by self-sufficiency, hearts unavailable to me. You will not only see, but will come to joyfully anticipate it as you know, grow, and sow." [45]

With these ideas from Romans 8 in mind, please reflect on these questions:

1. After a tragedy of some sort, it's so easy to stand at a spiritual distance and say something like, *"We know that in all things God works for the good of those who love him."* Or, more commonly in our culture, *"*Everything happens for a reason.*"* In what specific ways, though, have you seen God work through a tragedy for genuine good in your life and through you, in the life of someone you know? Be as specific as possible.

    _____

    _____

    _____

    _____

    _____

2. In times of suffering, like being at a funeral or visiting a fatally ill friend in the hospital, have you heard someone quote this familiar passage?

    _____

    _____

    _____

    _____

3. What has been your response?

    _____

    _____

    _____

    _____

4. What is your reaction when you hear that God intends to use all the things he allows in your life, especially your times of suffering or weeping of any kind, for your good?

5. Does conforming you to the likeness of Jesus Christ and redeeming the ruin in many possible ways appeal to you?[46] If yes, why? If no, why not?

6. Skim back over this section dealing with Romans 8:28–29. What parts cause you the most distress or skepticism? Why might that be?

7. Is God, even now, opening a window into your heart? If so, what do you see through it? Ask the Holy Spirit to show you. Invite a trusted friend to listen as well.

_____

_____

_____

8. Immediately after a trial, words fail. A hug or what some have called "the ministry of presence", is the first step in heart triage. In the longer term, though, in what ways could you come alongside someone whose heart has been crushed, someone experiencing a time of weeping, when God has opened a window into the heart and is ready to show his child the way?

_____

_____

_____

_____

"Moving back into the chaos, in the way God desires, I will closely consider how I will ... "

3. MARVEL THE MERCY OF GOD: LESS WHINING, MORE WORSHIP

God's third response in answer to my prayers came from another part of Romans:

> Do not be conformed to this world, but be transformed by the renewal of your mind, that by testing you may discern what is the will of God, what is good and acceptable and perfect.
>
> Romans 12:2;

I heard in these words an admonition of love for my heart, spirit, and will, directly from God who knows and loves my heart. God was saying, in essence, "Use this time and the trauma of heartbreak as an occasion for remembering, John. Remember the world to which you really belong. Remember you are mine, and you will be richly blessed if you move back into the material world being in it, but not *of* it" (Matthew 16:26; John 1:10; 17; Colossians 2:8).

In Romans 11, Paul describes in detail the hardness of heart shown by those whose hearts should have been the most responsive to the mercies of God. Old Testament Israel had seen that mercy at work on their behalf time after time. Yet, rather than falling to their knees in worship, they fell into the temptation of grumbling and complaining about God's provision for them.

Their hearts became harder and harder, and their tears watered the seeds of idolatry Satan had sown in their hearts. Still, to Paul's stunned amazement, God's mercy was active even as he judged his people. Despite their sins, all Israel, those who live and die in the faith Abraham received as a gift of God's grace, will be saved (Romans 11:26; see also Galatians 6:16).

Not only repentant Jews, but faith-filled Gentiles as well will taste the mercy of God, despite their sinful depravity. Chapter Eleven concludes with an expression of deep worship, and Paul's near-dumbfounded astonishment at this mercy. Like us, Paul knows full well his own heart's utter sinfulness. This leads him to exclaim in worshipful amazement:

> Oh, the depth of the riches and wisdom and knowledge of God! How unsearchable are his judgments and how inscrutable his ways! For who has known the mind of the Lord, or who has been his counselor? ... For from him and through him and to him are all things. To him be glory forever. Amen.
>
> Romans 11:33–36

Know this: we comprehend the experience and measure of God's mercy in direct proportion to the degree we know our own sinfulness and the wrath we justly deserve because of it. Knowing, then, our culpability and its rightful penalty, we join Paul in his hymn of praise as Chapter Eleven ends and Chapter Twelve begins:

> I appeal to you therefore, brothers, by the mercies of God, to present your bodies as a living sacrifice, holy and acceptable to God, which is your spiritual worship. Do not be conformed to this world, but be transformed by the renewal of your mind, that by testing you may discern what is the will of God, what is good and acceptable and perfect.
>
> Romans 12:1; emphasis added

Have you ever made the mistake of forgetting the menace of your own heart while downplaying the depth of God's mercy, saying or thinking something like this:

> *"God is not listening to my prayers or taking my agenda into account! I only want what I deserve! I can't believe this, that, or the other thing is happening to me while heaven remains silent and my prayers bounce off the ceiling of my bedroom. Why can't I get through to him? Why aren't my needs being met for once?"*

I have heard words like these from my own lips and have seen this attitude in my own heart more times than I'd like to admit. The Bible clearly equates my whining with a grumbling spirit and explicitly forbids it (Exodus 16; John 6:43, 61; 1 Peter 4:9). Yours, too. That road will take us nowhere we really want to go.

The alternative—sanctified suffering—transforms our perspective on life and death. It cleanses our hearts of the hardness that leads us to grumble and complain and replaces it with gratitude. Oh what a God-originated blessing an attitude of gratitude really is, friends.

From his admonition to resist worldliness and seek renewal, Paul then goes on in Romans 12 to describe the specific attitudes and actions worked by God as he softens our hearts by pouring out his amazing mercies upon us. These verses show us the way, and they help us identify the lifestyle lived by those who have been transformed by God's mercy:

> For by the grace given to me I say to everyone among you, not to think of himself more highly than he ought to think, but to

think with sober judgment, each according to the measure of faith that God has assigned ... Let love be genuine. Abhor what is evil; hold fast to what is good. Love one another with brotherly affection. Outdo one another in showing honor. Do not be slothful in zeal, be fervent in spirit, serve the Lord. Rejoice in hope, be patient in tribulation, be constant in prayer. Contribute to the needs of the saints and seek to show hospitality.

Bless those who persecute you; bless and do not curse them. Rejoice with those who rejoice, weep with those who weep. Live in harmony with one another. Do not be haughty, but associate with the lowly. Never be wise in your own sight. Repay no one evil for evil, but give thought to do what is honorable in the sight of all. If possible, so far as it depends on you, live peaceably with all.

Beloved, never avenge yourselves, but leave it to the wrath of God, for it is written, "Vengeance is mine, I will repay, says the Lord." To the contrary, "if your enemy is hungry, feed him; if he is thirsty, give him something to drink; for by so doing you will heap burning coals on his head."

Romans 12:3, 9–20

Then, in one simple, culminating sentence, Paul sums it all up:

Do not be overcome by evil, but overcome evil with good.

Romans 12:21

This entire passage makes it quite clear that grace, worship, and Christian growth go hand-in-hand. Their opposites, grumbling and hardness of heart do as well.

In short, in the suffering that automatically comes as we live in the desert wilderness before Christ's second coming, we are either overcome by evil, or we overcome evil with good, just as Paul has written.

After a heart-shattering trial, getting back to normal is not an option. God never intended it to be! Do you believe this deep down in your heart? Instead, suffering offered to God as we die to ourselves will always result in worship and our living more and more for God and others (Luke 10:27). Our lives become cruciform—cross-shaped—as we lift our worship to God and simultaneously reach out to other sufferers near us. Worship, in fact, is best seen as incarnational living. We live worshipfully as we live out Jesus' words:

> Abide in my love. If you keep my commandments, you will abide in my love, just as I have kept my Father's commandments and abide in his love. These things I have spoken to you, that my joy may be in you, and that your joy may be full.
>
> John 15:4

> In this the love of God was made manifest among us, that God sent his only Son into the world, so that we might live [yes, really and truly *live*] through him.
>
> 1 John 4:9; parenthesis, emphasis added

As you can easily see, by worship I mean much more than participating in the Sunday morning gathering of believers, though that certainly plays a central part in the new lives God has given us. True worship involves much more! The Bible properly defines worship as both a lifestyle[47] and an attitude of the heart[48] that, together, result in God's glory and the believer's good:

> Do not be conformed to this world, but be transformed by the renewal of your mind, that by testing you may discern what is the will of God, what is good and acceptable and perfect.
>
> Romans 12:2

With this in mind, let these questions guide your reflection:

1. What evidence can you cite to show that God allows trials, in part, to help us remember we are not citizens of this world but, rather, resident-aliens here?

_____

_____

_____

_____

_____

2. How might personal and holy *remembering* of this kind facilitate community *remembering* as well?

_____

_____

_____

_____

3. In Christ, you bring to the world the best, most enduring solutions to the woes of the world! How does knowing that fill you with a humble confidence? A contented urgency? A passionate compassion?

_____

_____

_____

_____

4. How confident are you that you know God's good, acceptable and perfect will for your life? Explain. How might you cultivate growth in that confidence? How might others help?

_____

_____

_____

_____

5. How passionate are you for God's redemptive plan? In light of the fact that those who follow the patterns of this world are doomed to live lives of failure, frustration, and futility, how do you respond when you see those who don't know Christ making this choice?

_____

_____

_____

_____

6. How do you respond when you see other Christians mirroring the patterns of this world? What might you ask the Holy Spirit to work in you so that your response will become even more like Christ's own heart for the worldly Christian in your midst?

_____

_____

_____

_____

7. When do you most often resort to grumbling and complaining? What might be the sin beneath the sin in this? In other words, what idol in your heart might be stoking the fires of grumbling in your life? List five ways you might investigate and address this.

_____

_____

_____

_____

8. If you were to set a course with a community of Christians you trust, committed to helping one another avoid being "conformed to the patterns of this world," but instead, "transformed by the renewing of your mind[s]," what would it look like? How might you go about it? Be as detailed as possible.

_____

_____

_____

_____

_____

"Moving back into the chaos, in the way God desires, I will closely consider how I will ..."

4. MOVE THE MOUNTAIN WITH FAITH: LESS RUMINATING, MORE REDEEMING

As I stood, turned, and faced the world, God gave me one last passage. It filled me with a reminder of a promise, deep hope, and prepared me to take the first step into the chaos, tender in heart, yet radically tenacious about wanting to see how he would use everything that had happened for the good he had promised:

> [Job said,] "I know my Redeemer lives, and at the last he will stand upon the earth."
>
> Job 19:25

Job arguably endured more suffering than anyone else whose life Scripture chronicles for us, Christ himself being the only exception. As I thought about the words Job wrote so long ago, two key truths echoed through my mind:

1. Jesus Christ, my Redeemer King, lives. He really and truly lives! Death, sin, Satan, and hell could not hold him captive. That's the True Truth.

2. The gift of salvation, and the eventual resurrection with Christ upon his second coming, which I have received by faith in my Redeemer is not an end in itself. Rather, it provides the impulse and the power that enable me to work with Jesus as a co-redeemer in an increasingly broken world. This calling belongs to me until either I die and I am taken up to be with my Redeemer King or he returns at the last to claim his own.

Matthew Henry comments true and well on Job 19:25, and the context in which it's written:

> The Spirit of God, at this time, seems to have powerfully wrought on the mind of Job. Here he witnessed a good confession; declared the soundness of his faith, and the assurance of his hope. Here is much of Christ and heaven; and he that said such things are these, declared plainly that he sought the better country, that is, the heavenly. Job was taught of God to believe in a living Redeemer; to look for the resurrection of the dead, and the life of the world to come; he comforted himself with the expectation of these.
>
> Job was assured, that this Redeemer of sinners from the yoke of Satan and the condemnation of sin, was his Redeemer, and expected salvation through him; and that he was a living Redeemer, though not yet come in the flesh; and that at the last day he would appear as the Judge of the world, to raise the dead, and complete the redemption of his people. With what pleasure holy Job enlarges upon this! May these faithful sayings be engraved by the Holy Spirit upon our hearts.
>
> We are all concerned to see that the root of the matter be in us. A living, quickening, commanding principle of grace in the heart is the root of the matter; as necessary to our religion as the root of the tree, to which it owes both its fixedness and

JOHN O. DOZIER, JR.

its fruitfulness. Job and his friends differed concerning the methods of Providence, but they agreed in the root of the matter, the belief of another world.

Note how Henry acknowledges that Job's faith had a rock-solid foundation before he was sorely tested by God. Job's faith was mightily and deeply rooted by the person and power of The Holy Spirit and an eternal view of life so that the winds of unavoidable suffering could not blow him away. Job was made momentarily bitter by the wrong-headed theology of his "friends," but by Chapter 38 was made much better by God.

WE HAVE BEEN REDEEMED … TO REDEEM

I wish with all my heart there was a stronger way to say this! No aspect of that Christmas night with my dad and God was intended for me alone. No sanctified suffering of any kind belongs only to the sufferer. God redeemed my weeping for the explicit purposes of redeeming and comforting others who weep. God intends that you and I take the presence of our victorious, compassionate, and resurrected Christ to all those around us who suffer in any way. Because he lives in us, we can accompany people who, in tears, sit at the open window of their hearts, seeking the way the Holy Spirit would use to help them live more fully the life of Jesus Christ.

The words *"redeemed, to redeem"* cut though my heart and spirit Christmas night, propelling me forward into the chaos with a grand and renewed purpose of heart. By nature and by habit, I am still tempted into sin by the world, the flesh, and the devil. That's a True Truth. But truer still is the transformation God has worked in me.

That transformation makes it possible to awaken every morning and fall asleep every night, knowing my life's purpose as a co-redeemer with Christ. When we see our suffering through this lens, we can pray as Jesus' taught, "Our Father, whom art in heaven, hallowed be thy name. Thy Kingdom come, Thy will be done on earth as it is in heaven" and then let him make us part of the answer to our own prayer. We see the Kingdom come as the Redeemer works with us and empowers us to cut through the chaos and offer to others the compassion of Christ we ourselves have experienced.

Significantly, Job penned these words not after, but during, his trial. He wrote while he wept. He wrote not in spite of, but because of his suffering! He proclaimed the Word (both written and Incarnate), and so can we:

> Oh that my words were written! Oh that they were inscribed in a book! Oh that with an iron pen and lead they were engraved in the rock forever! For I know that my Redeemer lives, and at the last he will stand upon the earth. And after my skin has been thus destroyed, yet in my flesh I shall see God, whom I shall see for myself, and my eyes shall behold, and not another! My heart faints within me!
>
> Job 19:23–27

Yes, Job wavers and yet, in the end, remains faithful even as he endures suffering of which we cannot imagine. And it transforms his heart. He grows more deeply rooted in the reality that God has adopted him as his very own child and heir, all while pointing us to the person of Jesus Christ as our ultimate source of saving grace. He invests energy in recording the True Truth and ensuring it will remain accessible forever. He sees millennia into the future, prophesying about the Messiah's victory over suffering and death.[49] He finds comfort and hope in the certainty of his own resurrection.

The apostle John remarks of the same Bible truth concerning the Believer's assurances by using a word that is packed with theology, application, and promise: abide. Come hell or high water, abide in Christ. John remarks of such an assurance as an organic, living, engrafted relationship with Jesus Christ:

I am the true vine, and my Father is the vinedresser. Every branch in me that does not bear fruit he takes away, and every branch that does bear fruit he prunes, that it may bear more fruit. Already you are clean because of the word that I have spoken to you. Abide in me, and I in you. As the branch cannot bear fruit by itself, unless it abides in the vine, neither can you, unless you abide in me. I am the vine; you are the branches. Whoever abides in me and I in him, he it is that bears much fruit, for apart from me you can do nothing.

If anyone does not abide in me he is thrown away like a branch and withers; and the branches are gathered, thrown into the fire, and burned. If you abide in me, and my words abide in you, ask whatever you wish, and it will be done for you. By this my Father is glorified, that you bear much fruit and so prove to be my disciples. As the Father has loved me, so have I loved you. Abide in my love. If you keep my commandments, you will abide in my love, just as I have kept my Father's commandments and abide in his love. These things I have spoken to you, that my joy may be in you, and that your joy may be full.

John 15:1–11

Job endures the worst possible outward maladies of a life lived in a broken, sin-filled world. He also suffers from the inward affliction imposed by the words of unsympathetic and hard-hearted friends. And yet Job had begun his journey equipped with the faith God provided, a faith that proved nearly unshakable. Job abided in God!

Has the Redeemer begun his radical transformation in your heart? Have you begun to act as a co-redeemer with Christ, as one who lives out the True Truth that the Triune God lives in you, that your Redeemer lives forever, and that weeping has opened a window in your heart and you have seen the way God intends to use your tears for his divine purposes?

You have been redeemed—by God, in Christ, through the power of the The Holy Spirit—to move mountains, beloved.

Every person who has ever walked into your life has been sent by God to receive a compassionate and redemptive word or deed from Jesus Christ through you. Every person! Think of it!

When our self-focus or fear causes us to pass up these opportunities, we can develop a sense of deep remorse. I know. I've been there often. But I do it a lot less often today, because by God's grace at work in my heart, I'm more wholly conformed and committed to step into the chaos.

Praise God he used the weeping, the window, and the way to revolutionize my life. He can revolutionize yours, too. I pray he does by way of your unavoidable suffering and sanctification therein. I pray with all my heart that all of God's people will engage less in useless ruminating and grow more redemptively responsive to his call: "Today, if you hear God's voice, do not harden your heart … " (Psalm 95:7–8; Hebrews 3:7, 15).

Let the questions below guide you as you reflect on action steps God might be asking you to take as his agent, a co-redeemer with Christ. You may find it helpful to journal your thoughts!

1. In what ways do you see yourself as a person being "redeemed to redeem?" Comforted to comfort? Saved to save? Freed to free? Made joyous to make joyful? Plucked out of hell to help rescue others? Fed to feed? Served to serve? Given grace to give grace? Given truth to give truth? Given love to give love? Having had tears wiped away to wipe away other's tears? Accompanied by the Wonderful Counselor at the window of your own heart to accompany others as they do the same?

_____

_____

_____

_____

_____

2. How might better knowing the Redeemer energize you for your daily calling as a co-redeemer? What's at the heart of any ruminating, resistance, or reluctance you may feel when considering this possibility?

_____

_____

_____

_____

_____

3. Job, in faith-filled suffering, wrote, *"Oh that my words were written! Oh that they were inscribed in a book! Oh that with an iron pen and lead they were engraved in the rock forever!"* If you were to feel a passion like that about your life in Christ the Redeemer, what would you write?

_____

_____

_____

_____

_____

4. When have you seen the way closer to Jesus in a time of deep weeping? What was that like for you? How might God want to use you to comfort others by means of your own experiences with weeping and windows?

_____

_____

_____

_____

_____

5. Do you think it's possible to muster-up or manufacture more faith without having experienced heart-trans-forming, redeemed suffering of some sort? How might a regular time set aside for fasting, adoration, confession, thanksgiving, and supplication help you?

---

6. In what ways would you most like to be more like Jesus as your heart is conformed to his likeness? (Consider Galatians 5:16–26.)

"The human spirit will not even begin to try to surrender itself as long as all seems to be well with it. Now error and sin both have this property, that the deeper they are the less their victim suspects their existence; they are masked evil. Pain is unmasked, unmistakable evil; every human being knows that something is wrong when he or she is being hurt and pain is not only immediately recognizable evil, but evil impossible to ignore.

As I am progressing along the path of life in my ordinary contentedly fallen and godless condition, absorbed in merry-making with my friends for the morrow, or a bit of work that tickles my vanity today, a holiday or a book... When suddenly a stab of abdominal pain that threatens serious disease, or a headline in newspapers that threatens us all with destruction, sends this whole pack of cards tumbling down.

At first, I'm overwhelmed, and all my little happiness's look like broken toys. Then, slowly and reluctantly, bit by a bit, I try to bring myself into the frame of mind that I should be in at all times: *I remind myself that all these toys were never intended to possess my heart, that my true good is another world, and my only real treasure is Christ!*

But the moment threat is withdrawn, my whole nature leaps back to the toys: I'm even anxious, God forgive me, to banish from my mind of the only thing that has supported me under the threat because it is now associated with the misery of those few days.

Thus, the terrible necessity of tribulation is only too clear!

God has had me only for forty-eight hours—and then only by dint of taking *everything else* away from me! Let him but sheathe the sword for a moment and I behave like Poppy (the dog) when the hated bath is over: I shake myself dry as I can and race off to reacquire my comfortable to dirtiness, if not in nearest manure heap, at least in the nearest flower bed. And that is why tribulations cannot cease until God either sees us remade, or sees that our remaking is now hopeless."

C.S. Lewis, *The Problem of Pain*[50],
Chapter 6; emphasis added

COMMUNITY IS KEY TO APPLYING THE PROTOCOL

Armed with these principles and the weeping, the window, and the way protocol, you may well treat your future occasions of suffering far differently than you have treated them in the past. This protocol holds out much hope for healing and redeeming past wounds, for using the weeping you have experienced as an integral part of your present-day giftedness and unique passion to serve. God mercifully and passionately wants to see the life of his Son recreated within every re-born heart. He wants to use these transformed hearts then, in turn, in the lives of other sufferers, and by continuing this process, he wants to change the world for time and eternity.

He does this most often as his people live out the protocol within community. A loving, truthful, patient, compassionate, wise, Christ-centered, and Bible-based community of spiritual friendship and spiritual direction can provide much help as you explore your own as yet unopened windows, and work through your own way forward.

As you examine your story, beloved, you will discover Christ's resurrection power in it. Few Christians understand the details of their own life's story and God's redemptive glory within it. Our stories remain untapped veins of pure gold, just waiting to be explored and then redeemed as we use them for good in the lives of others.

The Story of the Stone is my story. But it's also yours. It's the story of all those whose hearts God held in his hand in the beginning, hearts that he wants to transform from stone to flesh by sanctified, redemptive suffering. As you think about that story now, take whatever time you need to skim back over this book. Reread your notes and those sentences you've underlined, notice where you've turned down a page corner. Share these with others who travel the path of faith with you. Commit to help one another avoid the hardening that suffering can produce.

By the power of the Holy Spirit, commit to living as the sort of sufferers Jesus Christ wants you to be day by day, and for each today you encounter along life's pilgrimage:

> Jesus Christ suffered, not so that we might not suffer, but so that when we do suffer, we could become more like him.
>
> *The Sufferer,* Sermon by Pastor Tim Keller

The Cycle of Redemptive Suffering

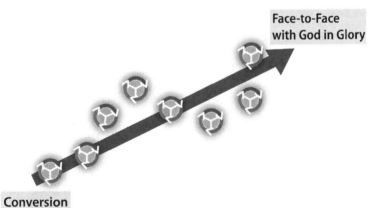

The Ascending Journey of Sanctification and Christ-Likeness

GOING DEEPER...

For further reading you may want to explore:

Bonhoeffer, D. Life Together: The Classic Exploration of Faith in Community. New York, NY: HarperOne (Div. of Harper Collins). 1978.

Crabb, Dr. L. J. Becoming a True Spiritual Community: A Profound Vision of What the Church Can Be. Nashville, TN: Thomas Nelson, Inc. 1995.

TOOLS, NOTES & RESOURCES TO HELP YOU GO DEEPER

This material is a series of brief articles, recommended reading, and additional material from Scripture intended to help interested readers explore more fully the ideas presented in the chapters above.

While none of it is essential to an understanding and application of those ideas, I urge you to take full advantage of the insights such exploration will open up to you! As you might imagine, this resource is not meant to be exhaustive.

As you share this book within your community of faith, be sure to suggest to others any additional resources you have found helpful in your faith journey, particularly those that address issues and questions raised in The Weeping, the Window, and the Way.

AN IMPORTANT CONSIDERATION FOR THE WAY FORWARD: EZEKIEL AND THE ROLE OF "THE WATCHMEN ON THE WALL"

The prophet Ezekiel points to the prophetic role God calls all Christians to play in a culture that strays from God in all sorts of awful ways, a culture very much like the one in which Ezekiel and the other prophets ministered. Regularly applying God's protocol, the weeping, the window, and the way helps transform our hearts in such a way that we become "watchmen on the wall," just as Ezekiel was.

Perhaps this is obvious, but let me remind you that the watchman's audience is primarily the church, not the world. Some of God's people there have, to be sure, devoted themselves to faithfully following God's will. But others have gone astray, drifting from the True Truth. And some, sad to say, have become as worldly and corrupt as the culture of comfort all around us. But all tend toward forgetfulness. All need constant reminding.

- *Watchmen* are called by God. This calling does not ordinarily come with dramatic fireworks or a striking vision but rather as we are born again, as we become new creations in Christ. With the new birth comes a new direction.

- *Watchmen* love Christ and his followers in a way that provides a covering of God's person and provision, especially in times of wandering away from God, which happens in every generation! Therefore, Watchmen continually remind God's people of who he is in every way possible, while also encouraging fellow believers of the many and multifaceted provisions God has mercifully promised to his people.

- *Watchmen* remain well-aware of the ways in which God has radically transformed their own hearts, emotions, and lives. They are also aware of their ongoing need for further transformation. This awareness creates deep humility, and a broken-heartedness that makes it possible to serve in joy, entrusting the results of their service to God.

- *Watchmen* live in the world, but are not of it (cf., John 17:15–17). They stand on the wall, as it were, serving as a lookout for approaching spiritual dangers. This provides a unique and much-needed perspective unattainable by those who do not regularly separate themselves from the distractions and deceptions of the world.

- *Watchmen* take full advantage of the heart transformations God offers. Through this cyclic process, they become more compassionate. They also grow increasingly passionate in their role as watchmen, offering God's perspective and counsel to his people in: a) *remembering* who they are, b) *warning* them of the dangers they face, c) *encouraging* them in God's pardon and unconditional love, d) *exhorting* them toward increasing holiness, Christ-likeness, and e) *sharing the hope* that flows from Jesus' open tomb and impending return to rescue his bride.

- *Watchmen* love the Church Universal as the bride of Christ, the body of true believers scattered throughout the world, God's people of every tribe, language, and nation. Watchmen also love the church on earth as the institution Jesus has set in place to steward the mysteries of God (cf., 1 Corinthians 4:1–2). While imperfect and flawed, the church on earth is vitally important to our Lord's mission here on earth. Watchmen stand on the wall, committed to love the church in truth, and to speak truthfully about the church in love.

- *Watchmen* do not shrink from their God-given responsibilities because of any push-back from the world, the flesh, or the devil, knowing all of these are pitted against God's plan of redemption.

- *Watchmen* regularly and intentionally spend time with the Triune God of the Bible: Father, Son, and Holy Spirit. Watchmen rise early in the day to be with God and in his Word. Watchmen also surround themselves by a community of spiritual friendship and direction, because they know their own hearts and refuse to allow isolation to damage either their faith or their effectiveness in ministry.

Having read this description, in what ways do you believe God has called you to be a watchman for his people? Why? How does your personal story relate to a universal need for Watchmen?

1. _____

2. _____

3. _____

4. _____

5. _____

GOD'S REDEMPTIVE PLAN

HAVE PEACE: THERE'S A PERSON, A PROMISE, AND PERFECT PLAN IN PLACE

One of my favorite passages of the Bible is a simple, yet supremely important promise, "For God is not the author of confusion but of peace, as in all the churches of the saints" (1 Corinthians 14:33, KJV). No, the God of the Bible is not a God of chaos or disarray, he is the God of order. His plan for our salvation creates peace within our heart, our spirit and our life. Do you want God's person, peace, purpose, and plan in your heart?

A variety of issues at work in our culture, our churches, and our own hearts today can give the impression that the people of God are as uncertain and confused as the world around us about the Bible, the God who inspired it, and his redemptive plan. Sometimes, this uncertainty and confusion tempts the church to entertain substitute theologies or to flail in antagonism at those who espouse the True Truth of the Bible.

Uncertainty and confusion, along with their first cousins, worry and anxiety, are killers of the human heart. God created us in his image, to love him with all our heart, mind, soul, and strength. Our hearts were not made for confusion. Please, beloved, don't blame God for the confusion and uncertainty his people sometimes express. And don't let it stir up doubts in your heart concerning his plan for your salvation. God has made nothing truly important to be a mystery to us. He does not intend to confuse you.

The fact is, God loves the world and has devised a very specific plan for it—the Plan of Redemption. How illogical would it be for the one who so carefully created you, the one who made you the culmination, the pinnacle of his creation, to leave you twisting in the wind, confused and despairing, over issues of eternal life and death!

No, God has displayed the truth about his awesome person, plan, story, and glory in what he has done to rescue us, his beloved image-bearers, from the misery, pain, shame, and fear that befell us when we fell into sin. Human beings have long tried to resolve this problem by creating religions and schemes by which we reached out to God, presenting to him supposed "good works" by which to merit his favor. These efforts never provided more than momentary, hollow relief. And they resulted in only hearts more hardened still. Pursuing peace with God by any means other than the means of redemption he himself has provided always results in hardening. Only God's plan of redemption creates the Shalom our hearts most deeply desire. Only that plan demonstrates for you and for the world God's deep delight in *you!*

The Good News is that the God of the Bible has done everything necessary to secure for us peace with him and within us. He offers it freely to us as a gift—a free gift of God's grace, a gift that cost God the life of his one only Son. God expects us to receive that gift with realistic self-awareness, brokenness, relief, joy, and a deep gratitude that bears the fruit of righteousness and devotion. Please don't cheapen that gift by proposing to add your own merit to it. Rather, just receive it! Receive it as the free gift God intended it to be.

To help you unpack that gift with deeper appreciation and hope, I have included here an explanation of various key facets. A few pages cannot begin to exhaust the beauty of the plan. Nor can it hope to delve deeply into all the details. But it does explain that plan in broad and biblical strokes. While my words are fallible, the plan itself cannot fail! It is built on the character and promises of God.

Read on to discover the unsurpassed joy of knowing more deeply the infinite, yet intimate God who is at work in you and for you, the God who wants you to receive the spectacular benefits of his redeeming work.

1. Effectual Calling—This is the supernatural work of God's Holy Spirit, by his own sovereign and free will, to convince a person of his sin and misery, enlighten his mind in the knowledge of Christ, and renew, persuade, and enable him to embrace Christ as he is freely offered in the gospel. "This effectual call is of God's free and special grace alone, not from anything at all foreseen in man, who is altogether passive therein, until, being quickened and renewed by the Holy Spirit, he is thereby enabled to answer this call, and to embrace the grace offered and conveyed in it."[51]

2. Regeneration—This work of God is closely, yet mysteriously, linked with his effectual calling so that the two could conceivably be considered one simultaneous work of God. It is distinguished as that act of God's grace whereby he supernaturally implants a new, Christ-aware heart and spiritual life in us so that our internal spiritual governance changes. It "carries with it the operative grace whereby a person called is enabled to answer [God's specific and effectual] call... to embrace Jesus Christ as he is freely offered in the gospel."[52] This supernatural work of the Triune God working separately and in union is frequently illustrated in Scripture as God's gift of a new heart, a heart that is alive and honorably responsive to Biblical truth. It is God's work alone that initially changes the heart, and yet Christians are called to evangelize and make disciples. This apparent contradiction or tension is God's to command and ours to obey, nonetheless.[53]

3. Faith and Repentance—These actions are demonstrated only by those whom God has first effectually called and regenerated. They are interdependent so that faith leads to repentance and repentance requires true faith. Faith, therefore, consists of knowledge, conviction, and trust specifically in Christ as Lord and Savior as he is presented in the gospel.[54] Repentance, most simply, means "to turn." Christian repentance is a specific kind of turning. It happens when we are first made aware of and grieved by our sin and our utter confusion apart from Jesus Christ as Savior and Lord. We then hate the sin and turn away from it to Christ for mercy, forgiveness, and the grace for new obedience—all based upon gratitude and no longer hoping to earn merit of any kind for ourselves.[55]

4. Justification—How can sinful people be just or right with a holy God, and therefore justified before our Judge? This also is a work of God alone and is a gift from him, a gift freely offered to those whom he effectually calls and regenerates. It has to do with how we are made just (legally right, righteous, or "at peace") with the God of the Bible. More specifically, justification is an act of God's free grace which takes place at one specific point in time. It involves his freely pardoning all our sins and declaring us righteous, not based on anything we have done, but solely upon the righteous life and sin-paying death of Jesus Christ.[56]

5. Adoption—"But as many as received him, to them gave he the authority to become children of God, to those who believe in his name" (John 1:12). We become children of God because he bestows that right upon us. He gives this right to all who believe on Jesus' name. God adopts believers in Christ, and we become his own children. This adoption is the embrace of God made possi-

ble by justification. In this joyous movement of God, he receives those he has justified as his own children, puts his name upon them, gives his Spirit to them, and binds them to himself forever for his care and protection.[57]

6. Sanctification—This is a continual work of God's grace that begins at justification and ends at glorification. As the word implies, sanctification involves God's "scrubbing program," carried out by him as he graciously and sovereignly applies the realities of the Gospel and the various Christian disciplines to the hearts of his regenerated, justified, adopted, and faithful people. In so doing, God works to release us from the power of sin and grows us up to be more like Christ, both in our inward thoughts and outward behaviors. In regeneration, God gives us new hearts. In sanctification, he nourishes and strengthens that new heart, sheltering it so that it may grow as a tender vine to full, fruit-bearing Christian maturity.

Christians are called to be willing participants with God in this grand work of sanctification, much like a little child is called to cooperate with his mom who is giving him a bath. Cooperation does not necessarily or ultimately determine whether growth happens. But it does certainly determine the joy and depth of the endeavor to the one sanctified. True Truth, as it has its way in the re-born human heart, sanctifies it. In contrast, when falsehood has its way, it condemns, defiles, desecrates, and disintegrates our hearts.

Ultimately, we are sanctified and made more holy, not for ourselves, but for service. Sanctification sets us apart for serving God by serving those around us—just as Jesus came, not to be served, but to serve. We grow more and more like him as God applies the Gospel to our lives, day by day.[58]

7. Perseverance—Like all that has come before, perseverance has to do with God's work in and for his adopted
children. Many mistakenly pivot perseverance on a new
Christian's dutiful discipline or continued faithfulness.
While these things are essential to our experience of
security in Christ, they do not determine it. Perseverance is a work of God whereby he seals and secures his
adopted children as such to the very end, to glorification. This Christian teaching glorifies God in his kingly
power to keep his children spiritually safe in his arms
for all time. It is upon this platform of divine security
that an adopted child of God joyfully, not fearfully,
nourishes his relationship with Christ and freely, not
full of guilt, serves him.

The lesson of the seed sowed on rocky ground,[59] is
that the seed took root and sprang up, but when the
sun rose, it was scorched (the heat of the battle) and
brought forth no fruit. It did not persevere. Jesus said,
"If you abide in my word, you are truly my disciples, and
you will know the truth, and the truth will set you free"
(John 8:31–32). Everyone who is truly called is called
to persevere. As Paul wrote, "Not that I have already
obtained this or am already perfect, but I press on to
make it my own, because Christ Jesus has made me his
own. Brothers, I do not consider that I have made it my
own. But one thing I do: forgetting what lies behind and
straining forward to what lies ahead, I press on toward
the goal for the prize of the upward call of God in Christ
Jesus" (Philippians 3:12–14).

8. Glorification—If justification is God's freeing his people
from the penalty of sin, and sanctification is his freeing
us from the power of sin, then glorification is his freeing us completely from the presence of sin. Even more,
glorification is God's giving us, his beloved, adopted
children, other indescribable gifts as well:

- Impenetrably holy souls.
- Unfettered and direct access to himself.
- Complete freedom from all sin and misery, and pure and unending pleasures of immeasurable magnitude.

Like justification, this is an instantaneous change that will take place for the whole company of the redeemed in Christ when Christ will come again in glory to judge the living and the dead. He will descend from heaven with a shout as he triumphs over death, the last enemy:

> *Then we'll come to pass this chain that is written, death is swallowed up in victory. Oh death, where is thy victory? Oh death, where is thy sting?"* (1 Corinthians 15:54–55).

"Rejoice", Peter writes, *"insofar as you share Christ's sufferings, that you may also rejoice and be glad when his glory is revealed"* (1 Peter 4:13). Glorification has cosmic proportions:

> *According to his promise we are waiting for new heavens and a new earth in which righteousness dwells (2 Peter 3:13).*

> *Then comes the end, when he delivers the kingdom to God the Father after destroying every rule and every authority and power (1 Corinthians 15:24).*

UNION WITH JESUS CHRIST: THE CONTEXT FOR ALL GOD'S WORK

If anything is clear from the plan of redemption described here, it is that God alone is the Initiator and Actor. He either does the work directly (as in justification), or he makes that work possible (as in faith and repentance). While we have a duty to respond to his actions, what should be equally clear is the absolutely astounding fact that God gives us a new heart and everything that flows from it as free gifts and expects us to receive them with joy and gratitude. He gives them despite the fact that we are so undeserving. In fact, we deserve precisely the opposite!

Still, you may be asking, "Since I am so undeserving, how is it that God offers me these gifts?" Good question! He offers them to you based on something called "union with Christ."

In brief, this is a phrase the Bible uses more than 160 times to describe God's working an "intimate, vital, and spiritual joining together of Christ and his people, in virtue of which he is the source of their life and strength, of their blessedness and salvation."[60] Adopted children of God receive his blessings because Jesus deserved God's blessings. Since God put us in Jesus, we get to enjoy God's blessings, too!

For example, in Jesus by faith, we died with him on Calvary's cross. In Jesus by faith, we rose with Christ when God raised him from the dead. Similarly, all the other blessings that come along with the new birth belong to us, all because the Father has placed us in Christ. Celebrate these astounding provisions of God today![61]

Union with Christ is the central truth in the whole doctrine of salvation. All to which the people of God have been predestined in the eternal election of God, all that has been secured and procured for them in the once and for all accomplishment of redemption, all of which they become the actual partakers in the application of redemption, and all that by God's grace they will become in the state of glorification is embraced within the compass of union and communion with Christ. Not only does the new life of regeneration faith, repentance, justification, and adoption have as its inception being in Christ, it is also continued by virtue of the same relationship to him.

For now, we live in Christ as we go about our everyday activities. It is in Christ that believers are dead to sin and that we are resurrected. When Christ returns, the union will be complete.[62] Glorification with Christ at his second coming will mark the beginning of that consummation as Jesus makes all things new and ushers in the New Heavens and New Earth.

Amen! And Amen.

GOING DEEPER...

All of this delicious doctrine—a delicacy for the heart and delight to the spirit—can be further enjoyed by studying some of Christianity's timeless resources. For example:

- The Westminster Confession of Faith
- The Westminster Shorter Catechism
- The Heidelberg Confession
- The Canons of the Synod of Dordt
- The Nicene Creed
- St. Augustine's *Confessions*
- *The Pilgrim's Progress* by John Bunyan

Interested readers will also enjoy:

Lewis, C.S. The Weight of Glory. New York: HarperCollins. 1949.

Lewis, C.S. Mere Christianity. New York: HarperCollins. 1952.

Lewis, C.S. The Four Loves. Orlando, FL: Harcourt Brace & Co. 1960.

Schaeffer, F.A. True Spirituality. Wheaton, IL: Tyndale House Publishers, Inc. 1971.

Stott, J.R.W. Why I Am A Christian. Downers Grove, IL: InterVarsity Press. 2003.

Sproul, R. C. Essential Truths of the Christian Faith. Wheaton, IL: Tyndale House Publishers, Inc. 1998.

Sproul, R. C. What's In The Bible: The Story Of God Through Time And Eternity. Nashville, TN: Thomas Nelson, Inc. 2001.

Edwards, J. The Religious Affections (The Works of Jonathan Edwards) London, England: Diggory Press, Ltd. 2007.

Guinness, O. Rising to the Call: Discover the Ultimate Purpose of Your Life. Nashville, TN: Thomas Nelson, Inc. 2003.

"THE WEEPING, THE WINDOW, THE WAY" BIBLE CHAPTER-VERSE REFERENCE

References that are inordinately long are not referenced below.

INTRODUCTION

Matthew 5:13—You are the salt of the earth, but if salt has lost its taste, how shall its saltiness be restored? It is no longer good for anything except to be thrown out and trampled under people's feet.

Psalm 30

Psalm 119:71—It is good for me that I was afflicted; that I might learn your statutes.

2 Corinthians 12:5, 9, 10—On behalf of this man I will boast, but on my own behalf I will not boast, except of my weaknesses; But he said to me, "My grace is sufficient for you, for my power is made perfect in weakness." Therefore I will boast all the more gladly of my weaknesses, so that the power of Christ may rest upon me; For the sake of Christ, then, I am content with weaknesses, insults, hardships, persecutions, and calamities. For when I am weak, then I am strong.

Romans 5

Hebrews 1

Proverbs 3:11–12—My son, do not despise the Lord's discipline or be weary of his reproof, for the LORD reproves him whom he loves, as a father the son in whom he delights.

John 17:17—Sanctify them in the truth; your word is truth.

Romans 8:28—And we know that for those who love God all things work together for good, for those who are called according to his purpose.

1 Corinthians 11:32—But when we are judged by the Lord, we are disciplined so that we may not be condemned along with the world.

Hebrews 12:8; 13:12—If you are left without discipline, in which all have participated, then you are illegitimate children and not sons; So Jesus also suffered outside the gate in order to sanctify the people through his own blood.

Proverbs 66:10—Have you not rejected us, O God? You do not go forth, O God, with our armies.

Romans 8:29; 12:2—For those whom he foreknew he also predestined to be conformed to the image of his Son, in order that he might be the firstborn among many brothers; Do not be conformed to this world, but be transformed by the renewal of your mind, that by testing you may discern what is the will of God, what is good and acceptable and perfect.

Hebrews 2:10—For it was fitting that he, for whom and by whom all things exist, in bringing many sons to glory, should make the founder of their salvation perfect through suffering.

Romans 11:33–34—Oh, the depth of the riches and wisdom and knowledge of God! How unsearchable are his judgments and how inscrutable his ways! "For who has known the mind of the Lord, or who has been his counselor?"

James 1

Colossians 1:24—Now I rejoice in my sufferings for your sake, and in my flesh I am filling up what is lacking in Christ's afflictions for the sake of his body, that is, the church.

Psalm 72:12—For he delivers the needy when he calls, the poor and him who has no helper.

2 Corinthians 1:3–7—Blessed be the God and Father of our Lord Jesus Christ, the Father of mercies and God of all comfort, who comforts us in all our affliction, so that we may be able to comfort those who are in any affliction, with the comfort with which we ourselves are comforted by God. For as we share abundantly in Christ's sufferings, so through Christ we share abundantly in comfort too. If we are afflicted, it is for your comfort and salvation; and if we are comforted, it is for your comfort, which you experience when you patiently endure the same sufferings that we suffer. Our hope for you is unshaken, for we know that as you share in our sufferings, you will also share in our comfort.

James 1:27—Religion that is pure and undefiled before God, the Father, is this: to visit orphans and widows in their affliction, and to keep oneself unstained from the world.

Matthew 3:8—Bear fruit in keeping with repentance.

John 12:24—Truly, truly, I say to you, unless a grain of wheat falls into the earth and dies, it remains alone; but if it dies, it bears much fruit.

Galatians 5

Ezekiel 11:18–21—"And when they come there, they will remove from it all its detestable things and all its abominations. And I will give them one heart, and a new spirit I will put within them. I will remove the heart of stone from their flesh and give them a heart of flesh, that they may walk in my statutes and keep my rules and obey them. And they shall be my people, and I will be their God. But as for those whose heart goes after their detestable things and their abominations, I will bring their deeds upon their own heads," declares the Lord GOD.

Luke 24:26—Was it not necessary that the Christ should suffer these things and enter into his glory?"

2 Corinthians 1:5—For as we share abundantly in Christ's sufferings, so through Christ we share abundantly in comfort too.

Philippians 3:8—Indeed, I count everything as loss because of the surpassing worth of knowing Christ Jesus my Lord. For his sake I have suffered the loss of all things and count them as rubbish, in order that I may gain Christ.

1 Peter 5

Psalm 39:6—Surely a man goes about as a shadow! Surely for nothing they are in turmoil; man heaps up wealth and does not know who will gather!

John 2:12—After this he went down to Capernaum, with his mother and his brothers and his disciples, and they stayed there for a few days.

1 Corinthians 7:31—And those who deal with the world as though they had no dealings with it. For the present form of this world is passing away.

2 Corinthians 12:7—So to keep me from becoming conceited because of the surpassing greatness of the revelations, a thorn was given me in the flesh, a messenger of Satan to harass me, to keep me from becoming conceited.

1 Peter 1:24—All flesh is like grass and all its glory like the flower of grass. The grass withers, and the flower falls.

Genesis 48:4—And said to me, "Behold, I will make you fruitful and multiply you, and I will make of you a company of peoples and will give this land to your offspring after you for an everlasting possession."

Hebrews 13

Romans 1:12—That is, that we may be mutually encouraged by each other's faith, both yours and mine.

Colossians 2:2—That their hearts may be encouraged, being knit together in love, to reach all the riches of full assurance of understanding and the knowledge of God's mystery, which is Christ.

Galatians 6:2—Bear one another's burdens, and so fulfill the law of Christ.

Deuteronomy 30:11–30—"For this commandment that I command you today is not too hard for you, neither is it far off. It is not in heaven, that you should say, 'Who will ascend to heaven for us and bring it to us, that we may hear it and do it?' Neither is it beyond the sea, that you should say, 'Who will go over the sea for us and bring it to us, that we may hear it and do it?' But the word is very near you. It is in your mouth and in your heart, so that you can do it. See, I have set before you today life and good, death and evil. If you obey the commandments of the LORD your God that I command you today, by loving the LORD your God, by walking in his ways, and by keeping his commandments and his statutes and his rules, then you shall live and multiply, and the LORD your God will bless you in the land that you are entering to take possession of it. But if your heart turns away, and you will not hear, but are drawn away to worship other gods and serve them, I declare to you today, that you shall surely perish. You shall not live long in the land that you are going over the Jordan to enter and possess. I call heaven and earth to witness against you today, that I have set before you life and death, blessing and curse. Therefore choose life, that you and your offspring may live, loving the LORD your God, obeying his voice and holding fast to him, for he is your life and length of days, that you may dwell in the land that the LORD swore to your fathers, to Abraham, to Isaac, and to Jacob, to give them."

John 4:11; 15:4—The woman said to him, "Sir, you have nothing to draw water with, and the well is deep. Where do you get that living water? Abide in me, and I in you. As the branch cannot bear fruit by itself, unless it abides in the vine, neither can you, unless you abide in me.

Isaiah 55:11—So shall my word be that goes out from my mouth; it shall not return to me empty, but it shall accomplish that which I purpose, and shall succeed in the thing for which I sent it.

2 Timothy 3:16–17—All Scripture is breathed out by God and profitable for teaching, for reproof, for correction, and for training in righteousness, that the man of God may be competent, equipped for every good work.

Genesis 1:26–27—Then God said, "Let us make man in our image, after our likeness. And let them have dominion over the fish of the sea and over the birds of the heavens and over the livestock and over all the earth and over every creeping thing that creeps on the earth." So God created man in his own image, in the image of God he created him; male and female he created them.

Hebrews 12:28–13:9—Therefore let us be grateful for receiving a kingdom that cannot be shaken, and thus let us offer to God acceptable worship, with reverence and awe, 29for our God is a consuming fire. Let brotherly love continue. Do not neglect to show hospitality to strangers, for thereby some have entertained angels unawares. Remember those who are in prison, as though in prison with them, and those who are mistreated, since you also are in the body. Let marriage be held in honor among all, and let the marriage bed be undefiled, for God will judge the sexually immoral and adulterous. Keep your life free from love of money, and be content with what you have, for he has said, "I will never leave you nor forsake you." So we can confidently say, "The Lord is my helper; I will not fear; what can man do to me?"

Remember your leaders, those who spoke to you the word of God. Consider the outcome of their way of life, and imitate their faith. Jesus Christ is the same yesterday and today and forever. Do not be led away by diverse and strange teachings, for it is good for the heart to be strengthened by grace, not by foods, which have not benefited those devoted to them.

CHAPTER 1—THE FREEFALL AND A FIRM FOUNDATION

Genesis 1:1—In the beginning, God created the heavens and the earth.

John 1:1—In the beginning was the Word, and the Word was with God, and the Word was God.

Deuteronomy 31:6—Be strong and courageous. Do not fear or be in dread of them, for it is the LORD your God who goes with you. He will not leave you or forsake you.

CHAPTER 2—FALLEN, FORGIVEN AND FREE

Ezekiel 11; 36

John 3:3—Jesus answered him, "Truly, truly, I say to you, unless one is born again he cannot see the kingdom of God."

2 Corinthians 5:17—Therefore, if anyone is in Christ, he is a new creation. The old has passed away; behold, the new has come.

John 17

Romans 6:5–6—For if we have been united with him in a death like his, we shall certainly be united with him in a resurrection like his. We know that our old self was crucified with him in order that the body of sin might be brought to nothing, so that we would no longer be enslaved to sin.

2 Corinthians 4:7–18—But we have this treasure in jars of clay, to show that the surpassing power belongs to God and not to us. We are afflicted in every way, but not crushed; perplexed, but not driven to despair; persecuted, but not forsaken; struck down, but not destroyed; always carrying in the body the death of Jesus, so that the life of Jesus may also be manifested in our bodies. For we who live are always being given over to death for Jesus' sake, so that the life of Jesus also may be manifested in our mortal flesh. So death is at work in us, but life in you. Since we have the same spirit of faith according to what has been written, "I believed, and so I spoke," we also believe, and so we also speak, knowing that he who raised the Lord Jesus will raise us also with Jesus and bring us with you into his presence. For it is all for your sake, so that as grace extends to more and more people it may increase thanksgiving, to the glory of God. So we do not lose heart. Though our outer self is wasting away, our inner self is being renewed day by day. For this light momentary affliction is preparing for us an eternal weight of glory beyond all comparison, as we look not to the things that are seen but to the things that are unseen. For the things that are seen are transient, but the things that are unseen are eternal.

James 1:1–3—James, a servant of God and of the Lord Jesus Christ, To the twelve tribes in the Dispersion: Greetings. Count it all joy, my brothers, when you meet trials of various kinds, for you know that the testing of your faith produces steadfastness.

Romans 8:13—For if you live according to the flesh you will die, but if by the Spirit you put to death the deeds of the body, you will live.

Philippians 3:10—That I may know him and the power of his resurrection, and may share his sufferings, becoming like him in his death.

CHAPTER 3—REDEEMED TO REDEEM

CHAPTER 4—THE FOUR MIRACULOUS MESSENGERS FROM GOD

Lamentations 3:22–24—The steadfast love of the LORD never ceases; his mercies never come to an end; they are new every morning; great is your faithfulness. "The LORD is my portion," says my soul, "therefore I will hope in him."

Psalm 95:7–8—For he is our God, and we are the people of his pasture, and the sheep of his hand. Today, if you hear his voice, do not harden your hearts, as at Meribah, as on the day at Massah in the wilderness ...

Luke 18:1—And he told them a parable to the effect that they ought always to pray and not lose heart.

Romans 12:12—Rejoice in hope, be patient in tribulation, be constant in prayer.

1 Thessalonians 5:17—pray without ceasing.

CHAPTER 5—REMEMBERING: THE HEART OF THE BIBLE

Genesis 1:1—In the beginning, God created the heavens and the earth.

Genesis 1:26–27—Then God said, "Let us make man in our image, after our likeness. And let them have dominion over the fish of the sea and over the birds of the heavens and over the livestock and over all the earth and over every creeping thing that creeps on the earth." So God created man in his own image,in the image of God he created him; male and female he created them.

Psalm 150—Praise the LORD! Praise God in his sanctuary; praise him in his mighty heavens! Praise him for his mighty deeds; praise him according to his excellent greatness! Praise him with trumpet sound; praise him with lute and harp! Praise him with tambourine and dance; praise him with strings and pipe! Praise him with sounding cymbals; praise him with loud clashing cymbals! Let everything that has breath praise the Lord! Praise the Lord!

Genesis 2:17—but of the tree of the knowledge of good and evil you shall not eat, for in the day that you eat of it you shall surely die.

Romans 1:18–32—For the wrath of God is revealed from heaven against all ungodliness and unrighteousness of men, who by their unrighteousness suppress the truth. For what can be known about God is plain to them, because God has shown it to them. For his invisible attributes, namely, his eternal power and divine nature, have been clearly perceived, ever since the creation of the world, in the things that have been made. So they are without excuse. For although they knew God, they did not honor him as God or give thanks to him, but they became futile in their thinking, and their foolish hearts were darkened. Claiming to be wise, they became fools, and exchanged the glory of the immortal God for images resembling mortal man and birds and animals and creeping things. Therefore God gave them up in the lusts of their hearts to impurity, to the dishonoring of their bodies among themselves, because they exchanged the truth about God for a lie and worshiped and served the creature rather than the Creator, who is blessed forever! Amen. For this reason God gave them up to dishonorable passions. For their women exchanged natural relations for those that are contrary to nature; and the men likewise gave up natural relations with women and were consumed with passion for one another, men committing shameless acts with men and receiving in themselves the due penalty for their error. And since they did not see fit to acknowledge God, God gave them up to a debased mind to do what ought not to be done. They were filled with all manner of unrighteousness, evil, covetousness, malice. They are full of envy, murder, strife, deceit, maliciousness. They are gossips, slanderers, haters of God, insolent, haughty, boastful, inventors of evil, disobedient to parents, foolish, faithless, heartless, ruthless. Though they know God's decree that those who practice such things deserve to die, they not only do them but give approval to those who practice them.

Ephesians 4:19—They have become callous and have given themselves up to sensuality, greedy to practice every kind of impurity.

2 Peter 2:14—They have eyes full of adultery, insatiable for sin. They entice unsteady souls. They have hearts trained in greed. Accursed children!

2 Thessalonians 2:11—Therefore God sends them a strong delusion, so that they may believe what is false.

Leviticus 26:1, 30—You shall not make idols for yourselves or erect an image or pillar, and you shall not set up a figured stone in your land to bow down to it, for I am the LORD your God. And I will destroy your high places and cut down your incense altars and cast your dead bodies upon the dead bodies of your idols, and my soul will abhor you.

Deuteronomy 30:17—But if your heart turns away, and you will not hear, but are drawn away to worship other gods and serve them.

Exodus 20:1–7—And God spoke all these words, saying, "I am the LORD your God, who brought you out of the land of Egypt, out of the house of slavery. You shall have no other gods before me. You shall not make for yourself a carved image, or any likeness of anything that is in heaven above, or that is in the earth beneath, or that is in the water under the earth. You shall not bow down to them or serve them, for I the LORD your God am a jealous God, visiting the iniquity of the fathers on the children to the third and the fourth generation of those who hate me, but showing steadfast love to thousands of those who love me and keep my commandments. You shall not take the name of the LORD your God in vain, for the LORD will not hold him guiltless who takes his name in vain."

Psalm 97:7—All worshipers of images are put to shame, who make their boast in worthless idols; worship him, all you gods!

Ezekiel 11:21—"But as for those whose heart goes after their detestable things and their abominations, I will bring their deeds upon their own heads," declares the Lord GOD.

Luke 16:15—And he said to them, "You are those who justify yourselves before men, but God knows your hearts. For what is exalted among men is an abomination in the sight of God."

2 Thessalonians 3:5—May the Lord direct your hearts to the love of God and to the steadfastness of Christ.

Jeremiah 9:26—Egypt, Judah, Edom, the sons of Ammon, Moab, and all who dwell in the desert who cut the corners of their hair, for all these nations are uncircumcised, and all the house of Israel are uncircumcised in heart.

Ezekiel 44:7—In admitting foreigners, uncircumcised in heart and flesh, to be in my sanctuary, profaning my temple, when you offer to me my food, the fat and the blood. You have broken my covenant, in addition to all your abominations.

Acts 7:51—You stiff-necked people, uncircumcised in heart and ears, you always resist the Holy Spirit. As your fathers did, so do you.

Exodus 4:21—And the LORD said to Moses, "When you go back to Egypt, see that you do before Pharaoh all the miracles that I have put in your power. But I will harden his heart, so that he will not let the people go."

Proverbs 26:23—Like the glaze covering an earthen vessel are fervent lips with an evil heart.

Proverbs 11:20—Those of crooked heart are an abomination to the LORD, but those of blameless ways are his delight.

Job 36:13—"The godless in heart cherish anger; they do not cry for help when he binds them.

Romans 7:15–20—For I do not understand my own actions. For I do not do what I want, but I do the very thing I hate. Now if I do what I do not want, I agree with the law, that it is good. So now it is no longer I who do it, but sin that dwells within me. For I know that nothing good dwells in me, that is, in my flesh. For I have the desire to do what is right, but not the ability to carry it out. For I do not do the good I want, but the evil I do not want is what I keep on doing. Now if I do what I do not want, it is no longer I who do it, but sin that dwells within me.

Psalm 51:5—Behold, I was brought forth in iniquity, and in sin did my mother conceive me.

1 Corinthians 10:14—Therefore, my beloved, flee from idolatry.

Exodus 20:1–7—(Ten Commandments)

1 Samuel 13:13–14—And Samuel said to Saul, "You have done foolishly. You have not kept the command of the LORD your God, with which he commanded you. For then the LORD would have established your kingdom over Israel forever. But now your kingdom shall not continue. The LORD has sought out a man after his own heart, and the LORD has commanded him to be prince over his people, because you have not kept what the LORD commanded you."

James 1:17—Every good gift and every perfect gift is from above, coming down from the Father of lights with whom there is no variation or shadow due to change.

Romans 1:18–32

CHAPTER 6—RECONCILING: THE HEART AND GOD

Deuteronomy 5:6–11, 32:31—I am the LORD your God, who brought you out of the land of Egypt, out of the house of slavery. You shall have no other gods before me. You shall not make for yourself a carved image, or any likeness of anything that is in heaven above, or that is on the earth beneath, or that is in the water under the earth. You shall not bow down to them or serve them; for I the LORD your God am a jealous God, visiting the iniquity of the fathers on the children to the third and fourth generation of those who hate me, but showing steadfast love to thousands of those who love me and keep my commandments. You shall not take the name of the LORD your God in vain, for the LORD will not hold him guiltless who takes his name in vain (5:6–11); For their rock is not as our Rock; our enemies are by themselves. (32:31)

Romans 1:21–22—For although they knew God, they did not honor him as God or give thanks to him, but they became futile in their thinking, and their foolish hearts were darkened. Claiming to be wise, they became fools.

Proverbs 4, 12, 18, 119

John 1:1–5—In the beginning was the Word, and the Word was with God, and the Word was God. He was in the beginning with God. All things were made through him, and without him was not any thing made that was made. In him was life, and the life was the light of men. The light shines in the darkness, and the darkness has not overcome it.

Matthew 2:1—Now after Jesus was born in Bethlehem of Judea in the days of Herod the king, behold, wise men from the east came to Jerusalem.

John 3:3—Jesus answered him, "Truly, truly, I say to you, unless one is born again he cannot see the kingdom of God."

1 John 5:1—Everyone who believes that Jesus is the Christ has been born of God, and everyone who loves the Father loves whoever has been born of him.

John 3:3—Jesus answered him, "Truly, truly, I say to you, unless one is born again he cannot see the kingdom of God."

2 Corinthians 5:17—Therefore, if anyone is in Christ, he is a new creation. The old has passed away; behold, the new has come.

Isaiah 57:11–13—Whom did you dread and fear, so that you lied, and did not remember me, did not lay it to heart? Have I not held my peace, even for a long time, and you do not fear me? I will declare your righteousness and your deeds, but they will not profit you. When you cry out, let your collection of idols deliver you! The wind will carry them off, a breath will take them away. But he who takes refuge in me shall possess the land and shall inherit my holy mountain.

John 1:12–13, 3:3–8—But to all who did receive him, who believed in his name, he gave the right to become children of God, who were born, not of blood nor of the will of the flesh nor of the will of man, but of God (1:12–13); Jesus answered him, "Truly, truly, I say to you, unless one is born again he cannot see the kingdom of God." Nicodemus said to him, "How can a man be born when he is old? Can he enter a second time into his mother's womb and be born?" Jesus answered, "Truly, truly, I say to you, unless one is born of water and the Spirit, he cannot enter the kingdom of God. That which is born of the flesh is flesh, and that which is born of the Spirit is spirit. Do not marvel that I said to you, 'You must be born again.' The wind blows where it wishes, and you hear its sound, but you do not know where it comes from or where it goes. So it is with everyone who is born of the Spirit."

Ephesians 2:9—Not a result of works, so that no one may boast.

1 John 2:29, 3:9, 4:7, 5:1—If you know that he is righteous, you may be sure that everyone who practices righteousness has been born of him (2:29); No one born of God makes a practice of sinning, for God's seed abides in him, and he cannot keep on sinning because he has been born of God (3:9); Beloved, let us love one another, for love is from God, and whoever loves has been born of God and knows God (4:7); Everyone who believes that Jesus is the Christ has been born of God, and everyone who loves the Father loves whoever has been born of him (5:1).

Romans 3:9–18—What then? Are we Jews any better off? No, not at all. For we have already charged that all, both Jews and Greeks, are under sin, as it is written: "None is righteous, no, not one; no one understands; no one seeks for God. All have turned aside; together they have become worthless; no one does good, not even one. Their throat is an open grave; they use their tongues to deceive. The venom of asps is under their lips. Their mouth is full of curses and bitterness. Their feet are swift to shed blood; in their paths are ruin and misery, and the way of peace they have not known." "There is no fear of God before their eyes."

Deuteronomy 30:6—And the LORD your God will circumcise your heart and the heart of your offspring, so that you will love the LORD your God with all your heart and with all your soul, that you may live.

2 Corinthians 3:3—And you show that you are a letter from Christ delivered by us, written not with ink but with the Spirit of the living God, not on tablets of stone but on tablets of human hearts.

Acts 2:36–41—"Let all the house of Israel therefore know for certain that God has made him both Lord and Christ, this Jesus whom you crucified." Now when they heard this they were cut to the heart, and said to Peter and the rest of the apostles, "Brothers, what shall we do?" And Peter said to them, "Repent and be baptized every one of you in the name of Jesus Christ for the forgiveness of your sins, and you will receive the gift of the Holy Spirit. For the promise is for you and for your children and for all who are far off, everyone whom the Lord our God calls to himself." And with many other words he bore witness and continued to exhort them, saying, "Save yourselves from this crooked generation." So those who received his word were baptized, and there were added that day about three thousand souls.

Acts 15:6–11—The apostles and the elders were gathered together to consider this matter. And after there had been much debate, Peter stood up and said to them, "Brothers, you know that in the early days God made a choice among you, that by my mouth the Gentiles should hear the word of the gospel and believe. And God, who knows the heart, bore witness to them, by giving them the Holy Spirit just as he did to us, and he made no distinction between us and them, having cleansed their hearts by faith. Now, therefore, why are you putting God to the test by placing a yoke on the neck of the disciples that neither our fathers nor we have been able to bear? But we believe that we will be saved through the grace of the Lord Jesus, just as they will."

Ephesians 2:1–10—And you were dead in the trespasses and sins in which you once walked, following the course of this world, following the prince of the power of the air, the spirit that is now at work in the sons of disobedience—among whom we all once lived in the passions of our flesh, carrying out the desires of the body and the mind, and were by nature children of wrath, like the rest of mankind. But God, being rich in mercy, because of the great love with which he loved us, even when we were dead in our trespasses, made us alive together with Christ—by grace you have been saved—and raised us up with him and seated us with him in the heavenly places in Christ Jesus, so that in the coming ages he might show the immeasurable riches of his grace in kindness toward us in Christ Jesus. For by grace you have been saved through faith. And this is not your own doing; it is the gift of God, not a result of works, so that no one may boast. For we are his workmanship, created in Christ Jesus for good works, which God prepared beforehand, that we should walk in them.

Romans 6:11—So you also must consider yourselves dead to sin and alive to God in Christ Jesus.

1 Corinthians 15:22—For as in Adam all die, so also in Christ shall all be made alive.

Romans 15:1-2—We who are strong have an obligation to bear with the failings of the weak, and not to please ourselves. Let each of us please his neighbor for his good, to build him up.

Psalm 126:6—He who goes out weeping, bearing the seed for sowing, shall come home with shouts of joy, bringing his sheaves with him.

Romans 8:17—And if children, then heirs—heirs of God and fellow heirs with Christ, provided we suffer with him in order that we may also be glorified with him.

Hebrews 12:3—Consider him who endured from sinners such hostility against himself, so that you may not grow weary or fainthearted.

Matthew 7:13—Enter by the narrow gate. For the gate is wide and the way is easy that leads to destruction, and those who enter by it are many.

Hebrews 3:15—As it is said, "Today, if you hear his voice, do not harden your hearts as in the rebellion."

Acts28:26–28—"'Go to this people, and say, You will indeed hear but never understand, and you will indeed see but never perceive. For this people's heart has grown dull, and with their ears they can barely hear, and their eyes they have closed; lest they should see with their eyes and hear with their ears and understand with their heart and turn, and I would heal them.' Therefore let it be known to you that this salvation of God has been sent to the Gentiles; they will listen."

Revelation 3:18–22—"I counsel you to buy from me gold refined by fire, so that you may be rich, and white garments so that you may clothe yourself and the shame of your nakedness may not be seen, and salve to anoint your eyes, so that you may see. Those whom I love, I reprove and discipline, so be zealous and repent. Behold, I stand at the door and knock. If anyone hears my voice and opens the door, I will come in to him and eat with him, and he with me. The one who conquers, I will grant him to sit with me on my throne, as I also conquered and sat down with my Father on his throne. He who has an ear, let him hear what the Spirit says to the churches."

2 Peter 2:21—For it would have been better for them never to have known the way of righteousness than after knowing it to turn back from the holy commandment delivered to them.

Hebrews 6:4–6—For it is impossible, in the case of those who have once been enlightened, who have tasted the heavenly gift, and have shared in the Holy Spirit, and have tasted the goodness of the word of God and the powers of the age to come, and then have fallen away, to restore them again to repentance, since they are crucifying once again the Son of God to their own harm and holding him up to contempt.

Matthew 12:31–32—Therefore I tell you, every sin and blasphemy will be forgiven people, but the blasphemy against the Spirit will not be forgiven. And whoever speaks a word against the Son of Man will be forgiven, but whoever speaks against the Holy Spirit will not be forgiven, either in this age or in the age to come.

Psalm 18

Mark 11:15—And they came to Jerusalem. And he entered the temple and began to drive out those who sold and those who bought in the temple, and he overturned the tables of the money-changers and the seats of those who sold pigeons.

Ephesians 4:15–16—Rather, speaking the truth in love, we are to grow up in every way into him who is the head, into Christ, from whom the whole body, joined and held together by every joint with which it is equipped, when each part is working properly, makes the body grow so that it builds itself up in love.

Matthew 3:8—Bear fruit in keeping with repentance.

Acts 26:20—But declared first to those in Damascus, then in Jerusalem and throughout all the region of Judea, and also to the Gentiles, that they should repent and turn to God, performing deeds in keeping with their repentance.

2 Corinthians 6:14, 13:14—The grace of the Lord Jesus Christ and the love of God and the fellowship of the Holy Spirit be with you all (6:14); The grace of the Lord Jesus Christ and the love of God and the fellowship of the Holy Spirit be with you all (13:14).

1 John 1:7—But if we walk in the light, as he is in the light, we have fellowship with one another, and the blood of Jesus his Son cleanses us from all sin.

Ezekiel 11, 36

Jeremiah 2

Romans 15:1—We who are strong have an obligation to bear with the failings of the weak, and not to please ourselves.

CHAPTER 7—RECOILING: RECOGNIZING THE IMPLICATIONS OF THE HEART "LIVING IN A CULTURE OF COMFORT"

John 3:16—For God so loved the world that he gave his one and only Son, that whoever believes in him shall not perish but have eternal life.

John 1:12—Yet to all who received him, to those who believed in his name, he gave the right to become children of God.

Romans 1:18–32

Romans 8:1–39

Matthew 5:29–30; 10:34–42—"If your right eye causes you to sin, gouge it out and throw it away. It is better for you to lose one part of your body than for your whole body to be thrown into hell. And if your right hand causes you to sin, cut it off and throw it away. It is better for you to lose one part of your body than for your whole body to go into hell" (5:29–30); "Do not think that I have come to bring peace to the earth. I have not come to bring peace, but a sword. For I have come to set a man against his father, and a daughter against her mother, and a daughter-in-law against her mother-in-law. And a person's enemies will be those of his own household. Whoever loves father or mother more than me is not worthy of me, and whoever loves son or daughter more than me is not worthy of me. And whoever does not take his cross and follow me is not worthy of me. Whoever finds his life will lose it, and whoever loses his life for my sake will find it. Whoever receives you receives me, and whoever receives me receives him who sent me. The one who receives a prophet because he is a prophet will receive a prophet's reward, and the one who receives a righteous person because he is a righteous person will receive a righteous person's reward. And whoever gives one of these little ones even a cup of cold water because he is a disciple, truly, I say to you, he will by no means lose his reward" (10:34–42).

1 John 1:5–10—This is the message we have heard from him and proclaim to you, that God is light, and in him is no darkness at all. If we say we have fellowship with him while we walk in darkness, we lie and do not practice the truth. But if we walk in the light, as he is in the light, we have fellowship with one another, and the blood of Jesus his Son cleanses us from all sin. If we say we have no sin, we deceive ourselves, and the truth is not in us. If we confess our sins, he is faithful and just to forgive us our sins and to cleanse us from all unrighteousness. If we say we have not sinned, we make him a liar, and his word is not in us.

Philippians 4:17—Not that I am looking for a gift, but I am looking for what may be credited to your account.

Hebrews 4:13; 13:17—Nothing in all creation is hidden from God's sight. Everything is uncovered and laid bare before the eyes of him to whom we must give account (4:13); Not that I am looking for a gift, but I am looking for what may be credited to your account (13:17).

1 Peter 4:5—But they will have to give account to him who is ready to judge the living and the dead.

2 Corinthians 5:17—Therefore, if anyone is in Christ, he is a new creation; the old has gone, the new has come!

Galatians 6:15—Neither circumcision nor uncircumcision means anything; what counts is a new creation.

1 Peter 1:3, 23—Praise be to the God and Father of our Lord Jesus Christ! In his great mercy he has given us new birth into a living hope through the resurrection of Jesus Christ from the dead; For you have been born again, not of perishable seed, but of imperishable, through the living and enduring word of God (23).

Philippians 3:10—I want to know Christ and the power of his resurrection and the fellowship of sharing in his sufferings, becoming like him in his death ...

Colossians 1:24—Now I rejoice in what was suffered for you, and I fill up in my flesh what is still lacking in regard to Christ's afflictions, for the sake of his body, which is the church.

James 1

Hebrews 5:8—Although he was a son, he learned obedience from what he suffered.

Galatians 5:16–26—But I say, walk by the Spirit, and you will not gratify the desires of the flesh. For the desires of the flesh are against the Spirit, and the desires of the Spirit are against the flesh, for these are opposed to each other, to keep you from doing the things you want to do. But if you are led by the Spirit, you are not under the law. Now the works of the flesh are evident: sexual immorality, impurity, sensuality, idolatry, sorcery, enmity, strife, jealousy, fits of anger, rivalries, dissensions, divisions, envy, drunkenness, orgies, and things like these. I warn you, as I warned you before, that those who do such things will not inherit the kingdom of God. But the fruit of the Spirit is love, joy, peace, patience, kindness, goodness, faithfulness, gentleness, self-control; against such things there is no law. And those who belong to Christ Jesus have crucified the flesh with its passions and desires. If we live by the Spirit, let us also walk by the Spirit. Let us not become conceited, provoking one another, envying one another.

Psalm 51; 58; 139

1 Peter 4:12—Dear friends, do not be surprised at the painful trial you are suffering, as though something strange were happening to you.

Revelation 2:10—Do not be afraid of what you are about to suffer. I tell you, the devil will put some of you in prison to test you, and you will suffer persecution for ten days. Be faithful, even to the point of death, and I will give you the crown of life.

2 Corinthians 1:3–7—Praise be to the God and Father of our Lord Jesus Christ, the Father of compassion and the God of all comfort, who comforts us in all our troubles, so that we can comfort those in any trouble with the comfort we ourselves have received from God. For just as the sufferings of Christ flow over into our lives, so also through Christ our comfort overflows. If we are distressed, it is for your comfort and salvation; if we are comforted, it is for your comfort, which produces in you patient endurance of the same sufferings we suffer. And our hope for you is firm, because we know that just as you share in our sufferings, so also you share in our comfort.

Philippians 2

2 Timothy 3:16–17—All Scripture is breathed out by God and profitable for teaching, for reproof, for correction, and for training in righteousness, that the man of God may be competent, equipped for every good work.

Psalm 119:24—Your testimonies are my delight; they are my counselors.

Acts 1:2—Until the day when he was taken up, after he had given commands through the Holy Spirit to the apostles whom he had chosen.

John 17

Revelation 3:18—I counsel you to buy from me gold refined by fire, so that you may be rich, and white garments so that you may clothe yourself and the shame of your nakedness may not be seen, and salve to anoint your eyes, so that you may see.

Hebrews 3:8, 15—Do not harden your hearts as in the rebellion, on the day of testing in the wilderness; As it is said, "Today, if you hear his voice, do not harden your hearts as in the rebellion (15)."

Matthew 7:13–14—Enter by the narrow gate. For the gate is wide and the way is easy that leads to destruction, and those who enter by it are many. 14For the gate is narrow and the way is hard that leads to life, and those who find it are few.

Psalm 51:12—Restore to me the joy of your salvation, and uphold me with a willing spirit.

Hebrews 4:13; 13:17—And no creature is hidden from his sight, but all are naked and exposed to the eyes of him to whom we must give account (4:13); Obey your leaders and submit to them, for they are keeping watch over your souls, as those who will have to give an account. Let them do this with joy and not with groaning, for that would be of no advantage to you (13:17).

Romans 14:12—So then each of us will give an account of himself to God.

1 Peter 4:5—But they will give account to him who is ready to judge the living and the dead.

Isaiah 53:3—He was despised and rejected by men; a man of sorrows, and acquainted with grief; and as one from whom men hide their faces he was despised, and we esteemed him not.

Luke 19:21—For I was afraid of you, because you are a severe man. You take what you did not deposit, and reap what you did not sow.

John 11:28—When she had said this, she went and called her sister Mary, saying in private, "The Teacher is here and is calling for you."

Romans 6:14; 10:5–13—For sin will have no dominion over you, since you are not under law but under grace (6:14); For Moses writes about the righteousness that is based on the law, that the person who does the commandments shall live by them. But the righteousness based on faith says, "Do not say in your heart, 'Who will ascend into heaven?'" (that is, to bring

Christ down) or "'Who will descend into the abyss?'" (that is, to bring Christ up from the dead). But what does it say? "The word is near you, in your mouth and in your heart" (that is, the word of faith that we proclaim); because, if you confess with your mouth that Jesus is Lord and believe in your heart that God raised him from the dead, you will be saved. For with the heart one believes and is justified, and with the mouth one confesses and is saved. For the Scripture says, "Everyone who believes in him will not be put to shame." For there is no distinction between Jew and Greek; for the same Lord is Lord of all, bestowing his riches on all who call on him. For "everyone who calls on the name of the Lord will be saved (10:5–13).

Hebrews 1

Ephesians 4:15–16—Rather, speaking the truth in love, we are to grow up in every way into him who is the head, into Christ, from whom the whole body, joined and held together by every joint with which it is equipped, when each part is working properly, makes the body grow so that it builds itself up in love.

1 John 5:4—For everyone born of God overcomes the world. This is the victory that has overcome the world, even our faith.

Matthew 12:25—Jesus knew their thoughts and said to them, "Every kingdom divided against itself will be ruined, and every city or household divided against itself will not stand."

Mark 2:8—Immediately Jesus knew in his spirit that this was what they were thinking in their hearts, and he said to them, "Why are you thinking these things?"

Luke 5:22—Jesus knew what they were thinking and asked, "Why are you thinking these things in your hearts?"

John 2:24—But Jesus would not entrust himself to them, for he knew all men.

Hebrews 5:8—Although he was a son, he learned obedience from what he suffered.

Genesis 3

Psalm 23

Psalm 119:50—My comfort in my suffering is this: Your promise preserves my life.

Romans 8:28—And we know that in all things God works for the good of those who love him, who have been called according to his purpose.

Isaiah 56:1–8

Acts 2:40–47—With many other words he warned them; and he pleaded with them, "Save yourselves from this corrupt generation." Those who accepted his message were baptized, and about three thousand were added to their number that day. They devoted themselves to the apostles' teaching and to the fellowship, to the breaking of bread and to prayer. Everyone was filled with awe, and many wonders and miraculous signs were done by the apostles. All the believers were together and had everything in common. Selling their possessions and goods, they gave to anyone as he had need. Every day they continued to meet together in the temple courts. They broke bread in their homes and ate together with glad and sincere hearts, praising God and enjoying the favor of all the people. And the Lord added to their number daily those who were being saved.

Hebrews 11:13–16; 13:10–16—All these people were still living by faith when they died. They did not receive the things promised; they only saw them and welcomed them from a distance. And they admitted that they were aliens and strangers on earth. People who say such things show that they are looking for a country of their own. If they had been thinking of the country they had left, they would have had

opportunity to return. Instead, they were longing for a better country—a heavenly one. Therefore God is not ashamed
to be called their God, for he has prepared a city for them
(13:16); We have an altar from which those who minister
at the tabernacle have no right to eat. The high priest carries the blood of animals into the Most Holy Place as a
sin offering, but the bodies are burned outside the camp.
And so Jesus also suffered outside the city gate to make the
people holy through his own blood. Let us, then, go to him
outside the camp, bearing the disgrace he bore. For here we
do not have an enduring city, but we are looking for the city
that is to come. Through Jesus, therefore, let us continually
offer to God a sacrifice of praise—the fruit of lips that confess his name. And do not forget to do good and to share
with others, for with such sacrifices God is pleased (10-16).

CHAPTER 8—ALL WEEPING: ALL TEARS, ALL TRIALS, ARE AN OFFER OF INCREASED GOD- AND SELF-AWARENESS AND FIRMING UP FOUNDATIONS.

Psalm 139

Matthew 10

John 6:37—All that the Father gives me will come to me, and
whoever comes to me I will never cast out.

John 14

Philippines 2

2 Corinthians 2:11—So that we would not be outwitted by Satan;
for we are not ignorant of his designs; But I am afraid that as
the serpent deceived Eve by his cunning, your thoughts will
be led astray from a sincere and pure devotion to Christ.

2 Corinthians 11:3—But I am afraid that as the serpent deceived
Eve by his cunning, your thoughts will be led astray from a
sincere and pure devotion to Christ.

Revelation 1:1–22, 21

1 John 1:1–4—That which was from the beginning, which we have heard, which we have seen with our eyes, which we looked upon and have touched with our hands, concerning the word of life—the life was made manifest, and we have seen it, and testify to it and proclaim to you the eternal life, which was with the Father and was made manifest to us—that which we have seen and heard we proclaim also to you, so that you too may have fellowship with us; and indeed our fellowship is with the Father and with his Son Jesus Christ. And we are writing these things so that our joy may be complete.

Deuteronomy 30

John 15

John 14:18, 28; 21:22–23—"I will not leave you as orphans; I will come to you (14:18); You heard me say to you, 'I am going away, and I will come to you.' If you loved me, you would have rejoiced, because I am going to the Father, for the Father is greater than I (14:28); Jesus said to him, "If it is my will that he remain until I come, what is that to you? You follow me!" So the saying spread abroad among the brothers that this disciple was not to die; yet Jesus did not say to him that he was not to die, but, "If it is my will that he remain until I come, what is that to you?" (21:22-23)

2 Peter 3

Revelation 7

Revelation 12:13–17—And when the dragon saw that he had been thrown down to the earth, he pursued the woman who had given birth to the male child. But the woman was given the two wings of the great eagle so that she might fly from the serpent into the wilderness, to the place where she is to be nourished for a time, and times, and half a time. The serpent poured water like a river out of his mouth after the woman, to sweep her away with a flood. But the earth came to the help of the woman, and the earth opened its mouth and swallowed the river that the dragon had poured from his mouth. Then the dragon became furious with the woman and went off to make war on the rest of her offspring, on those who keep the commandments of God and hold to the testimony of Jesus. And he stood on the sand of the sea.

John 19:30—When Jesus had received the sour wine, he said, "It is finished," and he bowed his head and gave up his spirit.

Revelation 12:7–16—Now war arose in heaven, Michael and his angels fighting against the dragon. And the dragon and his angels fought back, but he was defeated, and there was no longer any place for them in heaven. And the great dragon was thrown down, that ancient serpent, who is called the devil and Satan, the deceiver of the whole world—he was thrown down to the earth, and his angels were thrown down with him. And I heard a loud voice in heaven, saying, "Now the salvation and the power and the kingdom of our God and the authority of his Christ have come, for the accuser of our brothers has been thrown down, who accuses them day and night before our God. And they have conquered him by the blood of the Lamb and by the word of their testimony, for they loved not their lives even unto death. Therefore, rejoice, O heavens and you who dwell in them! But woe to you, O earth and sea, for the devil has come down to you in great wrath, because he knows that his time is short!" And when the dragon saw that he had been thrown down to the earth, he pursued the woman who had given birth to the male child. But the woman was given the two wings of the great eagle so that she might fly from the serpent into the wilderness, to the place where she is to be nourished for a time, and times, and half a time. The serpent poured water like a river out of his mouth after the woman, to sweep her away with a flood. But the earth came to the help of the woman, and the earth opened its mouth and swallowed the river that the dragon had poured from his mouth.

Isaiah 25:4–8—For you have been a stronghold to the poor, a stronghold to the needy in his distress, a shelter from the storm and a shade from the heat; for the breath of the ruthless is like a storm against a wall, like heat in a dry place. You subdue the noise of the foreigners; as heat by the shade of a cloud, so the song of the ruthless is put down. On this mountain the LORD of hosts will make for all peoples a feast of rich food, a feast of well-aged wine, of rich food full of marrow, of aged wine well refined. And he will swallow up on this mountain the covering that is cast over all peoples, the veil that is spread over all nations. He will swallow up death forever; and the Lord GOD will wipe away tears from all faces, and the reproach of his people he will take away from all the earth, for the LORD has spoken.

Matthew 11:28–30—Come to me, all who labor and are heavy laden, and I will give you rest. Take my yoke upon you, and learn from me, for I am gentle and lowly in heart, and you will find rest for your souls. For my yoke is easy, and my burden is light.

Revelation 21:1–4—Then I saw a new heaven and a new earth, for the first heaven and the first earth had passed away, and the sea was no more. And I saw the holy city, new Jerusalem, coming down out of heaven from God, prepared as a bride adorned for her husband. And I heard a loud voice from the throne saying, "Behold, the dwelling place of God is with man. He will dwell with them, and they will be his people, and God himself will be with them as their God. He will wipe away every tear from their eyes, and death shall be no more, neither shall there be mourning, nor crying, nor pain anymore, for the former things have passed away."

Romans 5:8

Matthew 22:36–40—"Teacher, which is the great commandment in the Law?" And he said to him, "You shall love the
Lord your God with all your heart and with all your soul
and with all your mind. This is the great and first commandment. And a second is like it: You shall love your neighbor
as yourself. On these two commandments depend all the
Law and the Prophets."

Deuteronomy 30

Romans 10

Romans 8:28—And we know that for those who love God all
things work together for good, for those who are called
according to his purpose.

Hebrews 4:14, 5:7—Since then we have a great high priest who
has passed through the heavens, Jesus, the Son of God, let
us hold fast our confession; 5:7 In the days of his flesh, Jesus
offered up prayers and supplications, with loud cries and
tears, to him who was able to save him from death, and he
was heard because of his reverence.

2 Corinthians 1:3–7—Blessed be the God and Father of our Lord
Jesus Christ, the Father of mercies and God of all comfort,
who comforts us in all our affliction, so that we may be able
to comfort those who are in any affliction, with the comfort
with which we ourselves are comforted by God. For as we
share abundantly in Christ's sufferings, so through Christ
we share abundantly in comfort too. If we are afflicted, it is
for your comfort and salvation; and if we are comforted, it is
for your comfort, which you experience when you patiently
endure the same sufferings that we suffer. Our hope for you
is unshaken, for we know that as you share in our sufferings,
you will also share in our comfort.

CHAPTER 9—YOUR WEEPING: STOPPING THE FREEFALL, RESETTING THE FOUNDATIONS OF THE FAITH—APPLYING GENESIS 1: 1; JOHN 1:1; DEUTERONOMY 31:6

John 3:1–21

Galatians 6:15—For neither circumcision counts for anything, nor uncircumcision, but a new creation.

Revelation 21; 22

2 Peter 3:13—But according to his promise we are waiting for new heavens and a new earth in which righteousness dwells.

Psalm 104:5—He set the earth on its foundations, so that it should never be moved.

Proverbs 30:4—Who has ascended to heaven and come down? Who has gathered the wind in his fists?

Who has wrapped up the waters in a garment? Who has established all the ends of the earth? What is his name, and what is his son's name? Surely you know!

Proverbs 8:24–29—When there were no depths I was brought forth, when there were no springs abounding with water. Before the mountains had been shaped, before the hills, I was brought forth, before he had made the earth with its fields, or the first of the dust of the world. When he established the heavens, I was there; when he drew a circle on the face of the deep, when he made firm the skies above, when he established the fountains of the deep, when he assigned to the sea its limit, so that the waters might not transgress his command, when he marked out the foundations of the earth.

2 Corinthians 5:17—Therefore, if anyone is in Christ, he is a new creation. The old has passed away; behold, the new has come.

Romans 4:15–17—For the law brings wrath, but where there is no law there is no transgression. That is why it depends on faith, in order that the promise may rest on grace and be guaranteed to all his offspring—not only to the adherent of the law but also to the one who shares the faith of Abraham, who is the father of us all, as it is written, "I have made you the father of many nations"—in the presence of the God in whom he believed, who gives life to the dead and calls into existence the things that do not exist.

Romans 3:26—It was to show his righteousness at the present time, so that he might be just and the justifier of the one who has faith in Jesus.

Hebrews 6:13—For when God made a promise to Abraham, since he had no one greater by whom to swear, he swore by himself,

2 Timothy 2:11–13—The saying is trustworthy, for: If we have died with him, we will also live with him; if we endure, we will also reign with him; if we deny him, he also will deny us; if we are faithless, he remains faithful—for he cannot deny himself.

Luke 2

Luke 7:22—And he answered them, "Go and tell John what you have seen and heard: the blind receive their sight, the lame walk, lepers are cleansed, and the deaf hear, the dead are raised up, the poor have good news preached to them."

Isaiah 55:10–11—For as the rain and the snow come down from heaven and do not return there but water the earth, making it bring forth and sprout, giving seed to the sower and bread to the eater, so shall my word be that goes out from my mouth; it shall not return to me empty, but it shall accomplish that which I purpose, and shall succeed in the thing for which I sent it.

CHAPTER 10—ALL WINDOWS: BLOWN OPEN INTO THE HEART BY THE TRIAL TO DISCERN THE TRUTHS FROM THE FALSEHOODS WITHIN THE HEART

James 1

John 14:16, 26; 15:26;—And I will ask the Father, and he will give you another Helper, to be with you forever. But the Helper, the Holy Spirit, whom the Father will send in my name, he will teach you all things and bring to your remembrance all that I have said to you.

15:26—But when the Helper comes, whom I will send to you from the Father, the Spirit of truth, who proceeds from the Father, he will bear witness about me.

John 17:1–26—Read it today: "The High Priestly Prayer".

Romans 1:1—Paul, a servant of Christ Jesus, called to be an apostle, set apart for the gospel of God ...

Hebrews 3

1 Peter 3:15—But in your hearts honor Christ the Lord as holy, always being prepared to make a defense to anyone who asks you for a reason for the hope that is in you; yet do it with gentleness and respect ...

CHAPTER 11—YOUR WINDOWS: FALLEN. FORGIVEN. FREE.—APPLYING ROMANS 1:18, ROMANS 8:1

John 15:1–11

Isaiah 9:6—For to us a child is born, to us a son is given, and the government shall be upon his shoulder, and his name shall be called Wonderful Counselor, Mighty God, Everlasting Father, Prince of Peace.

Romans 8:34—Who is to condemn? Christ Jesus is the one who died—more than that, who was raised—who is at the right hand of God, who indeed is interceding for us.

Psalm 107; 139

Matthew 10:43—(Jesus said) Do not think that I have come to bring peace to the earth. I have not come to bring peace, but a sword.

Psalm 25:18—Consider my affliction and my trouble, and forgive all my sins.

Deuteronomy 6:5; 11:18—You shall love the LORD your God with all your heart and with all your soul and with all your might; 11:18 You shall therefore lay up these words of mine in your heart and in your soul, and you shall bind them as a sign on your hand, and they shall be as frontlets between your eyes.

Mark 12:31—"The second is this: 'You shall love your neighbor as yourself.' There is no other commandment greater than these."

Jeremiah 9:23–24—Thus says the LORD: "Let not the wise man boast in his wisdom, let not the mighty man boast in his might, let not the rich man boast in his riches, but let him who boasts boast in this, that he understands and knows me, that I am the LORD who practices steadfast love, justice, and righteousness in the earth. For in these things I delight, declares the LORD."

John 17:3—And this is eternal life, that they know you the only true God, and Jesus Christ whom you have sent.

Romans 8:18—For I consider that the sufferings of this present time are not worth comparing with the glory that is to be revealed to us.

2 Corinthians 5:15—And he died for all, that those who live might no longer live for themselves but for him who for their sake died and was raised.

Philippians 2

Hebrews 11

Galatians 5:19–24—Now the works of the flesh are evident: sexual immorality, impurity, sensuality, idolatry, sorcery, enmity, strife, jealousy, fits of anger, rivalries, dissensions, divisions, envy, drunkenness, orgies, and things like these. I warn you, as I warned you before, that those who do such things will not inherit the kingdom of God. But the fruit of the Spirit is love, joy, peace, patience, kindness, goodness, faithfulness, gentleness, self-control; against such things there is no law. And those who belong to Christ Jesus have crucified the flesh with its passions and desires.

Romans 1:21–22—For although they knew God, they did not honor him as God or give thanks to him, but they became futile in their thinking, and their foolish hearts were darkened. Claiming to be wise, they became fools.

Romans 1:18—For the wrath of God is revealed from heaven against all ungodliness and unrighteousness of men, who by their unrighteousness suppress the truth.

Romans 8:1—There is therefore now no condemnation for those who are in Christ Jesus.

Romans 5:8—But God shows his love for us in that while we were still sinners, Christ died for us.

1 Samuel 2:3—Talk no more so very proudly, let not arrogance come from your mouth; for the LORD is a God of knowledge, and by him actions are weighed.

Matthew 10:29; 24:36—Are not two sparrows sold for a penny? And not one of them will fall to the ground apart from your Father; 24:36 But concerning that day and hour no one knows, not even the angels of heaven, nor the Son, but the Father only.

Psalm 139:7–12—Where shall I go from your Spirit? Or where shall I flee from your presence? If I ascend to heaven, you are there! If I make my bed in Sheol, you are there! If I take the wings of the morning and dwell in the uttermost parts of the sea, even there your hand shall lead me, and your right hand shall hold me. If I say, "Surely the darkness shall cover me, and the light about me be night," even the darkness is not dark to you; the night is bright as the day, for darkness is as light with you.

Hebrews 4:13—And no creature is hidden from his sight, but all are naked and exposed to the eyes of him to whom we must give account.

Isaiah 40:21–31

Revelation 19:6—Then I heard what seemed to be the voice of a great multitude, like the roar of many waters and like the sound of mighty peals of thunder, crying out, "Hallelujah! For the Lord our God the Almighty reigns."

Psalm 90:2—Before the mountains were brought forth, or ever you had formed the earth and the world, from everlasting to everlasting you are God.

John 1:1–3—In the beginning was the Word, and the Word was with God, and the Word was God. He was in the beginning with God. All things were made through him, and without him was not any thing made that was made.

Colossians 3:1–17

Hebrews 11:1ff—Now faith is the assurance of things hoped for, the conviction of things not seen.

1 John 3:1–24

CHAPTER 12—ALL WAYS: MOVING BACK INTO
THE CHAOS OF THE WORLD...RADICALLY
CHANGED TO BE AN AGENT OF CHANGE

Genesis 3:1—Now the serpent was more crafty than any other beast of the field that the Lord God had made. He said to the woman, "Did God actually say, 'You shall not eat of any tree in the garden?'"

CHAPTER 13—YOUR WAY: BECOMING
COURAGEOUS, COMPELLING, COMPASSIONATE
CO-REDEEMERS—APPLYING EZEKIEL 11:19,
ROMANS 8:28, ROMANS 12:2, JOB 19:25

Ephesians 3

2 Corinthians 1:3–7—Blessed be the God and Father of our Lord
Jesus Christ, the Father of mercies and God of all comfort,
who comforts us in all our affliction, so that we may be able
to comfort those who are in any affliction, with the comfort
with which we ourselves are comforted by God. For as we
share abundantly in Christ's sufferings, so through Christ
we share abundantly in comfort too. If we are afflicted, it is
for your comfort and salvation; and if we are comforted, it is
for your comfort, which you experience when you patiently
endure the same sufferings that we suffer. Our hope for you
is unshaken, for we know that as you share in our sufferings,
you will also share in our comfort.

Philippians 2

Matthew 3:7ff—But when he saw many of the Pharisees and
Sadducees coming to his baptism, he said to them, "You
brood of vipers! Who warned you to flee from the wrath to
come?"

Matthew 23:25—Woe to you, scribes and Pharisees, hypocrites!
For you clean the outside of the cup and the plate, but inside
they are full of greed and self-indulgence.

Romans 15:1–7—We who are strong have an obligation to bear
with the failings of the weak, and not to please ourselves.
Let each of us please his neighbor for his good, to build him
up. For Christ did not please himself, but as it is written,
"The reproaches of those who reproached you fell on me."
For whatever was written in former days was written for our
instruction, that through endurance and through the encour-

agement of the Scriptures we might have hope. May the God of endurance and encouragement grant you to live in such harmony with one another, in accord with Christ Jesus, that together you may with one voice glorify the God and Father of our Lord Jesus Christ. Therefore welcome one another as Christ has welcomed you, for the glory of God.

1 Corinthians 13

Colossians 1:11—May you be strengthened with all power, according to his glorious might, for all endurance and patience with joy.

Ephesians 5:2—And walk in love, as Christ loved us and gave himself up for us, a fragrant offering and sacrifice to God.

Philippians 2:5–11—Have this mind among yourselves, which is yours in Christ Jesus, who, though he was in the form of God, did not count equality with God a thing to be grasped, but made himself nothing, taking the form of a servant, being born in the likeness of men. And being found in human form, he humbled himself by becoming obedient to the point of death, even death on a cross. Therefore God has highly exalted him and bestowed on him the name that is above every name, so that at the name of Jesus every knee should bow, in heaven and on earth and under the earth, and every tongue confess that Jesus Christ is Lord, to the glory of God the Father.

2 Timothy 1:7—For God gave us a spirit not of fear but of power and love and self-control.

2 Timothy 2:1–2—You then, my child, be strengthened by the grace that is in Christ Jesus, and what you have heard from me in the presence of many witnesses entrust to faithful men who will be able to teach others also.

Revelations 21

1 Peter 1:16—since it is written, "You shall be holy, for I am holy."

Matthew 16:26—For what will it profit a man if he gains the whole world and forfeits his soul? Or what shall a man give in return for his soul?

John 1:10—He was in the world, and the world was made through him, yet the world did not know him.

John 17

Colossians 2:8—See to it that no one takes you captive by philosophy and empty deceit, according to human tradition, according to the elemental spirits of the world, and not according to Christ.

Romans 11:26—And in this way all Israel will be saved, as it is written, "The Deliverer will come from Zion, he will banish ungodliness from Jacob."

Galatians 6:16—And as for all who walk by this rule, peace and mercy be upon them, and upon the Israel of God.

Exodus 16

John 6:43, 61—Jesus answered them, "Do not grumble among yourselves. But Jesus, knowing in himself that his disciples were grumbling about this, said to them, "Do you take offense at this?"

1 Peter 4:9—Show hospitality to one another without grumbling.

Luke 10:27—And he answered, "You shall love the Lord your God with all your heart and with all your soul and with all your strength and with all your mind, and your neighbor as yourself."

Galatians 5:16–26—But I say, walk by the Spirit, and you will not gratify the desires of the flesh. For the desires of the flesh are against the Spirit, and the desires of the Spirit are against the flesh, for these are opposed to each other, to keep you from doing the things you want to do. But if you are led by the Spirit, you are not under the law. Now the works of the flesh are evident: sexual immorality, impurity, sensuality, idolatry, sorcery, enmity, strife, jealousy, fits of anger, rivalries, dissensions, divisions, envy, drunkenness, orgies, and things like these. I warn you, as I warned you before, that those who do such things will not inherit the kingdom of God. But the fruit of the Spirit is love, joy, peace, patience, kindness, goodness, faithfulness, gentleness, self-control; against such things there is no law. And those who belong to Christ Jesus have crucified the flesh with its passions and desires. If we live by the Spirit, let us also walk by the Spirit. Let us not become conceited, provoking one another, envying one another.

APPENDIX A

John 17:15–17—I do not ask that you take them out of the world, but that you keep them from the evil one. They are not of the world, just as I am not of the world. Sanctify them in the truth; your word is truth.

ENDNOTES

INTRODUCTION

1   Psychologists call this kind of egocentric vacuum within the heart, narcissism. As I have learned from intense counseling and through long-term, in-depth personal study in the years since, I have come to believe my mom's condition, her deep deprivation in heart and spirit and her resultant neediness, was *pathological narcissism*. One definition of this disorder is, *"A pattern of traits and behaviors which signify infatuation and obsession with one's self to the exclusion of all others and the egotistic and ruthless pursuit of one's gratification, dominance and ambition. Narcissistic Personality Disorder is a pernicious, vile and tortuous disease, which affects not only the Narcissist. It infects and forever changes people who are in daily contact with the Narcissist. In other words: it is contagious. It is my contention that Narcissism is the mental epidemic of the twentieth century, a plague to be fought by all means."* (*Malignant Self Love - Narcissism Revisited*, by Dr. Sam Vaknin, Ph.D.) The nurture and care a child's heart receives in childhood makes a life-long difference. We cannot address this disorder and the ways in which it affects a child's heart at this point, but readers may want to not only consider the ways in which they are proactively and intentionally nurturing the young hearts now in their care but know that, in Christ, "retroactive care of the heart" is available as well.

2   See: Appendix B–Remember the big picture of God's Redemptive Plan.

3   This book will describe that process in detail. For now, you might explore Ezekiel 11 and 36.

4   In Simonson, H. P. (1974). *Jonathan Edwards, Theologian of the Heart.* Grand Rapids: W.B. Eerdmans Pub. Jonathan Edwards served God has a pastor, preacher, teacher, and friend in early 18th century New England. His passion for God and for the hearts of the people he so devotedly shepherded has secured him a place among the most influential people in church history. A focus like his on the heart's true and false affections might inspire a Great Awakening in our day. It might spur an *awakening* even in individual hearts, hearts like yours, like mine. At least, that is the contention this chapter will make.

5   Nouwen, Henri. Life of the Beloved: Spiritual Living in a Secular World. Page 28. New York: The Crossroad Publishing Company, 1998.

CHAPTER 4

6   Lewis, C. S. The Problem of Pain. New York: HarperOne, 2001.

7   Lewis, C. S. The Last Battle—Book Seven Chronicles of Narnia. Collector's Edition. New York: HarperCollins. 2002.

8   I truly believe Dad was saved on Christmas night, though I won't know for sure until I enter eternity myself. I base that belief on what the counterintuitive nature of God is like throughout history and what the "four messengers" from this chapter told me. In any case, I completely trust the fact that God is in charge and that His will has been done with Dad. Those who wonder about the issue of suicide from a Christian perspective may find this website helpful: http://

www.desiringgod.org/ResourceLibrary/TopicIndex/118_
Suicide/1686_Funeral_Meditation_for_a_Christian_Who_
Committed_Suicide_1988/

9   McArthur, J. Alone With God. Colorado Springs, CO.
David C. Cook Publishing. 2006.

CHAPTER 5

10 In Simonson, H. P. (1974). *Jonathan Edwards, theologian of*
the heart. Grand Rapids: W.B. Eerdmans Pub. Jonathan
Edwards served God has a pastor, preacher, teacher, and
friend in early 18th century New England. His passion for
God and for the hearts of the people he so devotedly shepherded has secured him a place among the most influential
people in church History. A focus like His on the heart's
true and false affections might inspire a Great Awakening
in our day. It might spur an *awakening* even in individual
hearts, hearts like yours, like mine. At least, that is the contention this chapter will make.

11 The dictionary defines "split personality" as "a relatively rare
dissociative disorder in which the usual integrity of the personality breaks down and two or more independent person-
alities emerge." In Romans 7:15–20, Paul plainly describes
the old and new man vying for power. This is not a psychi-
atric disorder, but the human condition "by nature" since
the Fall.

12 "Peter Kreft.com: What Is God's Answer to Suffering?".
Making Sense Out of Suffering. Ignatius Press. <http://
www.peterkreeft.com/topics/suffering.htm>

CHAPTER 6

13 See: Appendix B–God's Redemptive Plan—and where
sanctification fits into the big picture.

14 Granted, speaking these Biblical truths into the hearts of many who have abandoned the supernatural in favor of only what can be seen requires that we slow down and re-think our unconscious and conscious presuppositions. When you minister in situations like that, take the time it requires and don't do it alone. As Jesus warns us:

"Truly, truly, I say to you, unless one is born of water and the Spirit, he cannot enter the kingdom of God" (John 3:5).

"If you love me, you will keep my commandments. And I will ask the Father, and he will give you another Helper, to be with you forever, even the Spirit of truth, whom the world cannot receive, because it neither sees him nor knows him. You know him, for he dwells with you and will be in you" (John 14: 15–17, 25–26).

15 See also John 14:6.

16 Lewis, C. S. The Problem of Pain. New York: HarperOne, 2001.

CHAPTER 7

17 No culture becomes "a culture of comfort" overnight. Rather, innumerable influences established over a long period of time are in play. The downward spiral in western culture has been at work for many years. Ideas have consequences. Documenting it lies beyond the scope of this book. Readers interested in exploring its origins may be interested in reading about the impact of the likes of Descartes, Locke, Kant, Marx, Kierkegaard, Nietzsche, Sartre, Darwin and Freud. Those in the church who have warned us, and continue to warn us, of the implications include Jonathan Edwards, Charles Spurgeon, Martin Lloyd-Jones, Martin Luther King, Jr., G.K. Chesterton, Francis Schaeffer, J.R.R. Tolkien, Os Guinness, C.S. Lewis, R.C. Sproul,

Tim Keller, Harold Bloom, Dan Allender, John McArthur, John Piper, Stephen Covey, George Barna, Ravi Zacharias, Brian Chappell, Scotty Smith, and many more.

18   See also John 17:15–24; 1 Corinthians 7:31; Ephesians 2:2–10; Colossians 2:20–23; and Galatians 4:3–7.

19   Today, the majority of children in our culture live with the heartbreak and emotional despair of fatherlessness. See: *Fathers for Life*, http://fathersforlife.org/; D. Blankenhorn. Fatherless America. (New York: BasicBooks, 1995); Effects of Fatherlessness on Children–Social Consequences, http://www.ancpr.org/affects_of_fatherlessness_on_chi.htm;_

20   Abortions Worldwide: approx. 46 million in the U.S. since Roe vs. Wade in 1973. Source: Center for Bio-Ethical Reform, The Alan Guttmacher Institute and Planned Parenthood's *Family Planning Perspectives.*

21   This is a very complex and sensitive subject area. I do not, by any means, intend to trivialize, generalize, or downplay the importance and helpfulness of medications prescribed for physical dysfunction and/or chemical imbalances in the brain. There is still much research to do on the vitally important issue of cause and effect regarding many mental illnesses. But in a culture of comfort, healthcare providers— few of whom take into account the whole person—can be easily persuaded to over-prescribe mood-altering drugs to mask the discomfort by which God intends to bring the light of the Gospel to bear in our heart. Such drugs may make it possible for an individual to postpone or completely avoid the heart-work needed to resolve key spiritual issues. We are made by a Spirit-God; most every root causes can be boiled down to spiritual issues. Individuals living in a culture of comfort may well turn first to medication rather than turning first to the Great Physician, Jesus Christ, and at His direction confronting heart issues that seem too shameful or

painful, as well as those that are culturally taboo. I believe that especially in a culture that is increasingly secularized, pluralized, and privatized, it is essential to avoid over-prescribing drugs or other "treatments" that will only postpone real, and holistic healing. The heart's estrangement from God will always spur on the creation of industries designed to help us deny, adopt distractions, and/or in some other way disconnect ourselves from the pain of losing a personal relationship with our heart's Maker, the one who is himself love, the one who gives life and who gives life meaning.

22 See Titus 2:11–15.

23 See: Appendix B–God's Redemptive Plan.

24 Don't forget that we almost always underestimate the time, the cost and the help needed in any renovation!

25 I am using the term "depression" in its common, everyday sense to mean malaise, general sadness, dejection, feeling disheartened and the like, rather than in the clinical, medical sense of the term. Readers diagnosed with clinical depression and those whose symptoms indicate they may be clinically depressed should with peace and a clear conscience seek competent medical care. Such care comes to us as our Creator's good gift in a world broken by sin, a world in which brain chemistry and other physical, bodily processes sometimes go awry.

26 Or not. Many Christians find suffering (consciously or unconsciously) repelling and run from it. These believers choose isolation over community. Overtime, Christ's ministering spirit of *compassion* cannot grow in a heart left fallow for so many seasons. We will probe this behavior and its consequences more deeply in a later chapter.

CHAPTER 9

27 Tada, Joni Eareckson. When God Weeps. Grand Rapids, MI: Zondervan Publishing House. 2000.

28 Lewis, C.S. The Four Loves. Orlando, FL: Harcourt Brace & Co. 1960.

29 Whether the freefall stops or continues forever solely depends on the validity of our faith, the doctrines, and True Truths on which we attempt to rest secure. Do you believe it? Please don't be fooled into thinking I'm simply advising we become "people of faith." *Everyone has faith in something.* Some people have already had their faith put to the test in ways that revealed its validity, reliability, and foundational merit. Those who as yet remain untested will one day experience this. It's not a question of "if," but rather one of "when." There are many people who have no faith in God and have suffered a great deal. But if you could spend some time with people like that, you would discover an extremely complex superstructure of coping and control mechanisms at work beneath the person's *apparent* ability to sustain the battering of the heart. At some point, that superstructure will come down, and come down hard. Pray that God will send you or someone else to be there for that person when it does. This is central to your calling as a wounded healer, as the very hand of Christ in a broken world. Do not underestimate your high calling and priestly mission!

30 In John 14:6, Jesus claimed to be "The Way, The Truth and The Life." Simple logic, then, implies that those who exist apart from Christ do not know the way, are living a lie, and experience spiritual death, even while they walk through the 30, 70, or 100 years God grants them on this planet. If you haven't already done so, dear friends, stop the freefall in your own heart right now! Choose LIFE (Deuteronomy 30:19)!

31 Scholars usually reference five major covenants between God and His people. An in-depth look at these lies beyond the scope of this book. I urge you to study them carefully for further insight God may give you through them in your own time of weeping and growth in God's foundational assurances:

The covenant between God and Noah (Genesis 9; Hebrew 11:7).

The covenant between God and Abraham and Abraham's descendents (Genesis 12; 13; 15; 17; 22; Acts 7:1–8; Galatians 3:6–29; Hebrews 11).

The covenant between God and Moses (Exodus 2:24; 20; 32:12; Jeremiah 31:31–34; Acts 15; Romans 10).

The covenant between God and David (2 Samuel 7:12–13; Matthew 1:1; Acts 2:29–36).

The covenant God made with himself in Jesus Christ (Genesis 3; John 1; 2 Corinthians 3:7, 9; Matthew 26:28; Galatians 4:24–26; Hebrews 8:13).

CHAPTER 10

32 Resolution # 24 from *The Resolutions of Jonathan Edwards*, (1722–1723).

33 In *The Problem of Pain*, C.S. Lewis asserted: "The doors of Hell are locked from the inside." We experience some of that hellishness right here on earth when we lock our hearts up tight, refusing the Holy Spirit's or an agent of God in human form to offer of counsel, comfort, and consolation in our times of weeping.

CHAPTER 11

34 "Sermon Index.Net". A. W. Pink. An Honest Heart.http://sermonindex.net/modules/ articles/index php?view=article&aid=1115

35 See 1 Corinthians 15, especially verses 17–19.

36 For further reading, see *"Identifying Idols,"* Harbor Presbyterian Church, by permission Redeemer Presbyterian Church; *"Restoring Broken Things,"* Pastor Scotty Smith; *"Breaking the Idols of Your Heart: How to Navigate the Temptations of Life,"* Dan Allender; *"A Grace Disguised,"* Gerald Lawson Sittser; *"Idols of the Heart and Vanity Fair,"* Powlison

CHAPTER 12

37 Resolution # 67 from *The Resolutions of Jonathan Edwards,* (1722–1723).

38 Please don't misinterpret my words as coming from a heart filled with spiritual arrogance. Rather, they spring from the experience of my own brokenness and a heart-felt love and compassion for human hearts—for your heart. We are both on this earthly journey. I would never have loved the Savior as I do, had I not seen the darkness and damage in my own heart, the depth of my own guilt, the near-laughable fact that God would choose me, my own enormous need for the salvation, the forgiveness, and freedom Jesus Christ has earned for me!

39 As you examine the examples here, you may also want to study these accounts from the Old Testament: Hezekiah (2 *Kings* 20:5); Job (*Job* 16:20); King David (*Psalms* 6:6, 39:12, 42: 3, 56:8, 116:8, 126:5–6); the Preacher (*Ecclesiastes* 4:1); Isaiah (*Isaiah* 16:9); Jeremiah (*Jeremiah* 9:1; *Lamentations* 2:18); Ezekiel (*Ezekiel* 24:16); ancient Israel (*Malachi* 2:13–16). From the New Testament, the following texts will be helpful: the Prostitute (*Luke* 7:38); St. Paul's anguish for the lost in Rome and Corinth (*Romans* 9:1–4; 2 *Corinthians* 2:4).

CHAPTER 13

40 Lewis, C. S. The Problem of Pain. New York: HarperOne, 2001.

41 Readers often misinterpret 1 Corinthians 13, "the love and marriage passages" as a compliment to the church in Corinth for the love they have displayed. It is not. Rather, in this chapter Paul admonishes the recipients for withholding love, and he catalogs the specific ways in which they have done so. See the earlier chapters (e.g., 5–8) of this letter which detail the Corinthians' abuse of their new found "freedoms"—now turned to bondage as they have turned grace into a license for gratifying the flesh. Consider also their decision to withhold the Gospel from others because of their worldly, selfish, and hardened hearts.

42 *Mercy always precedes the law.* Not one thing we could ever do, but only the mercy of God, re-gathers His people, we who have been scattered by our obstinate hearts and distrust of God. It's only His promised compassion and forgiveness that makes our return to him remotely possible.

43 *Idol work proceeds from a foundation of mercy.* The desire and ability to examine the idols that reside in our hearts come only when we realize God's unconditional acceptance of us in Christ. His acceptance makes it possible for us to hear and heed Jesus' call upon our heart and lives. It makes it possible to exchange the falsehoods we cherish for the True Truth that will supernaturally transform our hearts from stone to flesh.

44 *Repentant, humble obedience* follows God's forgiveness and our realization that God no longer condemns us. We are redeemed to redeem. Forgiven much, we love much. We love enough to humbly, yet boldly, pass along warnings and encouragement as stern as necessary to those who would ignore the mercy of God.

45 A character I imagined myself as for a long time during my childhood was "Johnny Appleseed". Today, I'm even more passionate about the call and great blessing we are given to sow seeds of True Truth into the hearts of any who God places in our midst. Other than maintaining relationships of spiritual friendship and direction, which is no small order, the germinating and fruitfulness of those seeds sown into the soil of the heart are not our responsibility—the Holy Spirit works to flourish the seeds we joyfully sow each and every day. Sow on, beloved!

46 From the Latin cōnfōrmāre, *to shape after.*

47 See Exodus 20:3; Deuteronomy 5:7; 6:13; Matthew 4:10; Luke 4:8; Acts 10:26; 14:15; Galatians 5; Colossians 2:18; and Revelation 19:10; 22:8. Many other passages could be cited in defense of this proposition.

48 See Proverbs 4:23; Ephesians 4:23; Philippians 2:5; and 1 Peter 4:1. Again, many other passages stress this truth.

49 See Psalm 89:26 in which Jesus is called "The Rock of our salvation."

APPENDIX B

50 Lewis, C. S. The Problem of Pain. New York: HarperOne, 2001.

51 Westminster Confession of Faith; see also Matthew 22:14; John 6:37; Romans 8:7–9; 30; 9:11; 1 Corinthians 1:9; Ephesians 2:8–9; 2 Timothy 1:9; and 1 John 3:1; 3:9; 5:1.

52 Berkhoff, *Systematic Theology*

53 See Ezekiel 11:19; 36:26–26; John 1:13; 3:8; 6:44–45; 1 Corinthians 2:5,12, 14; 2 Corinthians 3:3, 6; 1 John 2:29, 3:9, 4:7, 5:1, 4, 18; James 1:18; and 2 Thessalonians 2:13–14.

54 See Isaiah 45:21–22; Ezekiel 33:11, 18:23, 32; Romans 19:17; and Ephesians 2:8.

55 See Thessalonians 1:9–10; Luke 24:46–47; Acts 2:37–38, 5:3; Romans 6:2, 6; and Hebrews 6:1.

56 See Deuteronomy 25:1; Psalm 89:15–16; Proverbs 17:15; Romans 3:14, 20, 4:2, 10:3, 8:33–34; Galatians 2:16, 3:11, 5:4; and Philippians 3:9.

57 See Matthew 6:9; Romans 8:15–16; 1 Corinthians 2: 9–10, and Galatians 4:6.

58 See Matthew 5:48; Romans 7:22; 1 Corinthians 2:14–15; 1 Corinthians 15:54; Phil 3:21; 1 John 2:16, 3:3, 4:4, Deuteronomy 30:1–10; John 14; and the Book of Titus.

59 Mark 4: 5–6, 16–17

UNION WITH JESUS CHRIST: THE CONTEXT FOR ALL GOD'S WORK

60 Berkhoff, *Systematic Theology*

61 See Romans. 6:23, 8:1, 39; 1 Corinthians 1:2, 15:18; Ephesians 1–2; Colossians 1–2; and 1 Peter 5:10.

62 See Romans 6: 4; 1 Corinthians1:4, 5; and 1 Corinthians 6:15–17.

Made in the USA
San Bernardino, CA
07 December 2015